Lecture Notes in Computer Science 13839

The series Lecture Notes in Computer Science (LNCS), including its subseries Lecture Notes in Artificial Intelligence (LNAI) and Lecture Notes in Bioinformatics (LNBI), has established itself as a medium for the publication of new developments in computer science and information technology research, teaching, and education.

LNCS enjoys close cooperation with the computer science R & D community, the series counts many renowned academics among its volume editors and paper authors, and collaborates with prestigious societies. Its mission is to serve this international community by providing an invaluable service, mainly focused on the publication of conference and workshop proceedings and postproceedings. LNCS commenced publication in 1973.

Jean-Christophe Deneuville
Editor

Code-Based Cryptography

10th International Workshop, CBCrypto 2022
Trondheim, Norway, May 29–30, 2022
Revised Selected Papers

Springer

Editor
Jean-Christophe Deneuville
ENAC - University of Toulouse
Toulouse, France

ISSN 0302-9743 ISSN 1611-3349 (electronic)
Lecture Notes in Computer Science
ISBN 978-3-031-29688-8 ISBN 978-3-031-29689-5 (eBook)
https://doi.org/10.1007/978-3-031-29689-5

This Springer imprint is published by the registered company Springer Nature Switzerland AG
The registered company address is: Gewerbestrasse 11, 6330 Cham, Switzerland

Preface

Post-quantum cryptography has known tremendous interest these past few years, especially since the call for standardization of quantum-safe primitives by the US National Institute of Standards and Technology (NIST) back in 2017. Earlier this summer, NIST announced the first algorithms to be standardized, including proposals based on lattices and hash functions, as well as the beginning of the fourth and last round. To date, the latter only features proposals relying on coding theory assumptions, making the field of code-based cryptography of utmost importance. Originally named the "Code-Based Cryptography (CBC) Workshop", the series was initiated in 2009 as an informal forum with the goal of bringing together researchers active in the analysis and development of code-based encryption and authentication schemes. Over the years, the workshop has grown from a Europe-based, regional event to become a worldwide venue for the code-based cryptography community. The workshop was renamed "CBCrypto" in 2020, its organization was co-located with the flagship conference Eurocrypt, and extended to include the publication of revised selected manuscripts in the form of a post-conference proceedings volume. The 2022 edition of CBCrypto was held in Trondheim, Norway in a hybrid mode due to the COVID-19 pandemic. With more than 70 registrations for physical attendance and 150 for online participation, this edition was a great success. Featuring 8 sessions and 1 invited talk, there were 19 contributed talks over 2 days, presenting recent research and works in progress. This book collects the 8 contributions that were selected for publication by the Program Committee through a careful peer review process. These contributions span all aspects of code-based cryptography, from design to implementation, including studies of security, new systems, and improved decoding algorithms. As such, the works presented in this book provide a synthesized yet significant overview of the state-of-the-art of code-based cryptography, laying out the groundwork for future developments. We wish to thank the Program Committee members and the external reviewers for their hard and timely work, as well as Edoardo Persichetti for the local organization, and Marco Baldi for administrative support.

December 2022 Jean-Christophe Deneuville

Organization

General Chair

Jean-Christophe Deneuville	ENAC, University of Toulouse, France

Local Organization

Edoardo Persichetti	Florida Atlantic University, USA

Program Committee

Carlos Aguilar	SandBoxAQ, France
Marco Baldi	Università Politecnica delle Marche, Italy
Gustavo Banegas	Inria and École polytechnique, France
Alessandro Barenghi	Politecnico di Milano, Italy
Hannes Bartz	German Aerospace Center (DLR), Germany
Emanuele Bellini	Technology Innovation Institute, UAE
Pierre-Louis Cayrel	Laboratoire Hubert Curien, France
Franco Chiaraluce	Università Politecnica delle Marche, Italy
Jean-Christophe Deneuville	École Nationale de l'Aviation Civile, France
Taraneh Eghlidos	Sharif University of Technology, Iran
Jérôme Lacan	ISAE-SUPAERO, France
Gianluigi Liva	German Aerospace Center (DLR), Germany
Pierre Loidreau	Celar and Irmar, Université de Rennes 1, France
Chiara Marcolla	Technology Innovation Institute, UAE
Giacomo Micheli	University of South Florida, USA
Kirill Morozov	University of North Texas, USA
Ayoub Otmani	University of Rouen, France
Gerardo Pelosi	Politecnico di Milano, Italy
Edoardo Persichetti	Florida Atlantic University, USA
Joachim Rosenthal	University of Zurich, Switzerland
Simona Samardjiska	Radboud University, The Netherlands
Paolo Santini	Università Politecnica delle Marche, Italy
Antonia Wachter-Zeh	Technical University of Munich, Germany
Øyvind Ytrehus	University of Bergen, Norway

External Reviewers

Luca Bastioni
Austin Dukes
Lukas Kölsch
Vincenzo Pallozzi Lavorante

Contents

Contents

Distinguishing and Recovering Generalized Linearized Reed–Solomon Codes

Felicitas Hörmann[1,2(✉)], Hannes Bartz[1], and Anna-Lena Horlemann[2]

[1] Institute of Communications and Navigation, German Aerospace Center (DLR), Oberpfaffenhofen-Wessling, Germany
{felicitas.hoermann,hannes.bartz}@dlr.de

[2] School of Computer Science, University of St. Gallen, St. Gallen, Switzerland
anna-lena.horlemann@unisg.ch

Abstract. We study the distinguishability of linearized Reed–Solomon (LRS) codes by defining and analyzing analogs of the square-code and the Overbeck distinguisher for classical Reed–Solomon and Gabidulin codes, respectively. Our main results show that the square-code distinguisher works for generalized linearized Reed–Solomon (GLRS) codes defined with the trivial automorphism, whereas the Overbeck-type distinguisher can handle LRS codes in the general setting. We further show how to recover defining code parameters from any generator matrix of such codes in the zero-derivation case. For other choices of automorphisms and derivations simulations indicate that these distinguishers and recovery algorithms do not work. The corresponding LRS and GLRS codes might hence be of interest for code-based cryptography.

1 Introduction

Researchers have made tremendous progress in the design and realization of quantum computers in the last decades. As it was shown that quantum comput-ers are capable of solving both the prime-factorization and the discrete-logarithm problem in polynomial time, attackers can break most of today's public-key cryp-osystems (as e.g. RSA and ECC) if they have a powerful quantum computer t hand. The urgent need for quantum-safe cryptography is obvious, especially ince *store now, harvest later* attacks allow to save encrypted data now and lecrypt it as soon as the resources are available. This is reflected in the stan-ardization process that NIST started for post-quantum cryptography in 2016. he first key-encapsulation mechanisms (KEMs) were standardized in July 2022 fter three rounds of the competition and some of the submissions were for-arded to a fourth round for further investigation [1]. Three out of the four maining KEM candidates in round four are code-based. Moreover, the fourth ie (namely, SIKE) was recently broken [7]. This explains why the community s high hopes and trust in coding-related primitives even though no code-based ndidate has been chosen for standardization so far.

C. Deneuville (Ed.): CBCrypto 2022, LNCS 13839, pp. 1–20, 2023.
ps://doi.org/10.1007/978-3-031-29689-5_1

Code-based cryptography mostly relies on McEliece-like schemes that are inspired by the seminal paper [17]. The main idea is to choose a generator matrix of a secret code and disguise its algebraic structure by applying some, in most cases isometric or near-isometric, transformations such that an adversary cannot derive the known (or any other) efficient decoder from the mere knowledge of the scrambled matrix.

McEliece-like instances based on a variety of code families and disguising functions in the Hamming and the rank metric were proposed over time. For example, the works [4,25] are based on Reed–Solomon (RS) codes in the Hamming metric and the GPT system and its variants (see e.g. [8,9,23]) use Gabidulin codes in the rank metric. But in both cases, polynomial-time attacks were proposed and broke several of the systems: RS codes can be distinguished from random codes by using the square-code approach introduced in [25,28] and Overbeck-like strategies [10,11,19–21] yield a distinguisher for Gabidulin codes. The works also explain the recovery of an equivalent secret key which enables the attacker to decrypt with respect to the public code.

The sum-rank metric was first established in 2005 [13, Sect. III] and generalizes both the Hamming and the rank metric. It is thus natural to investigate if McEliece-like cryptosystems based on sum-rank-metric codes can ensure secure communication. The work [22] considers generic decoding of sum-rank-metric codes and hence gives guidance for the security-level estimation of sum-rank-based cryptography. Martínez-Peñas [14] introduced linearized Reed–Solomon (LRS) codes which are the sum-rank analogs of RS and Gabidulin codes and thus could be a first naive choice for secret codes in McEliece-like systems.

We focus on the task of distinguishing LRS codes from random codes and present two distinguishers that are inspired by the square-code idea and by Overbeck's approach, respectively. Our results can be applied to distinguish generalized linearized Reed–Solomon (GLRS) codes which we define as LRS codes with nonzero block multipliers. As this more general code family is closed under semilinear equivalence, the methods also apply to GLRS codes with isometric disguising. We finally focus on the zero-derivation case and show how an efficient decoding algorithm can be recovered from a GLRS generator matrix that was disguised by means of semilinear isometries.

2 Preliminaries

Let us first gather some notions and results that we will use later on. In particular, let q be a prime power and denote the finite field of order q by $\mathbb{F}_q$. For $m \geq 1$, we further consider the extension field $\mathbb{F}_{q^m} \supseteq \mathbb{F}_q$ of order q^m. For a matrix $\boldsymbol{M} \in \mathbb{F}_{q^m}^{k \times n}$, let $\langle \boldsymbol{M} \rangle$ denote the $\mathbb{F}_{q^m}$-linear vector space spanned by the rows of $\boldsymbol{M}$.

2.1 The Sum-Rank Metric

An *(integer) composition* of $n \in \mathbb{N}^*$ into $\ell \in \mathbb{N}^*$ parts (or *ℓ-composition* for short) is a vector $\boldsymbol{n} = (n_1, \ldots, n_\ell) \in \mathbb{N}^\ell$ with $n_i > 0$ for all $1 \leq i \leq \ell$ that satisfies $n = \sum_{i=1}^{\ell} n_i$. If $\boldsymbol{n}$ contains k distinct elements $\tilde{n}_1, \ldots, \tilde{n}_k$, let λ_j denote the number of occurrences of $\tilde{n}_j$ in $\boldsymbol{n}$ for each $j = 1, \ldots, k$ and write $\lambda(\boldsymbol{n}) := (\lambda_1, \ldots, \lambda_k) \in \mathbb{N}^k$.

Throughout the paper, $n \in \mathbb{N}^*$ usually refers to the length of the considered codes and we will stick to one particular ℓ-composition $\boldsymbol{n} = (n_1, \ldots, n_\ell)$ of n. We often divide vectors $\boldsymbol{x} \in \mathbb{F}_{q^m}^n$ or matrices $\boldsymbol{M} \in \mathbb{F}_{q^m}^{k \times n}$ with $k \in \mathbb{N}^*$ into blocks with respect to $\boldsymbol{n}$. Namely, we write $\boldsymbol{x} = (\boldsymbol{x}^{(1)} \mid \cdots \mid \boldsymbol{x}^{(\ell)})$ with $\boldsymbol{x}^{(i)} \in \mathbb{F}_{q^m}^{n_i}$ for all $1 \leq i \leq \ell$ and $\boldsymbol{M} = (\boldsymbol{M}^{(1)} \mid \cdots \mid \boldsymbol{M}^{(\ell)})$ with $\boldsymbol{M}^{(i)} \in \mathbb{F}_{q^m}^{k \times n_i}$ for all $1 \leq i \leq \ell$, respectively.

The *sum-rank weight* of a vector $\boldsymbol{x} \in \mathbb{F}_{q^m}^n$ (with respect to $\boldsymbol{n}$) is defined as $\mathrm{wt}_{\Sigma R}^{\boldsymbol{n}}(\boldsymbol{x}) = \sum_{i=1}^{\ell} \mathrm{rk}_q(\boldsymbol{x}^{(i)})$, where $\mathrm{rk}_q(\boldsymbol{x}^{(i)})$ is the maximum number of $\mathbb{F}_q$-linearly independent entries of $\boldsymbol{x}^{(i)}$ for $i = 1, \ldots, \ell$. The hereby induced *sum-rank metric* is given by $d_{\Sigma R}^{\boldsymbol{n}}(\boldsymbol{x}, \boldsymbol{y}) = \mathrm{wt}_{\Sigma R}^{\boldsymbol{n}}(\boldsymbol{x} - \boldsymbol{y})$ for $\boldsymbol{x}, \boldsymbol{y} \in \mathbb{F}_{q^m}^n$. Since we always consider the same ℓ-composition $\boldsymbol{n}$, we write $\mathrm{wt}_{\Sigma R}$ and $d_{\Sigma R}$ for simplicity.

An $\mathbb{F}_{q^m}$*-linear sum-rank-metric code* $\mathcal{C}$ is an $\mathbb{F}_{q^m}$-subspace of $\mathbb{F}_{q^m}^n$. Its length is n and its dimension $k := \dim(\mathcal{C})$. We further define its *minimum (sum-rank) distance* as

$$d(\mathcal{C}) := \{d_{\Sigma R}(\boldsymbol{c}_1, \boldsymbol{c}_2) : \boldsymbol{c}_1, \boldsymbol{c}_2 \in \mathcal{C}, \boldsymbol{c}_1 \neq \boldsymbol{c}_2\} = \{\mathrm{wt}_{\Sigma R}(\boldsymbol{c}) : \boldsymbol{c} \in \mathcal{C}, \boldsymbol{c} \neq \boldsymbol{0}\},$$

where the last equality follows from the linearity of the code. A matrix $\boldsymbol{G} \in \mathbb{F}_{q^m}^{k \times n}$ is a *generator matrix* of $\mathcal{C}$ if $\mathcal{C} = \langle \boldsymbol{G} \rangle$. If $\mathcal{C}$ is the kernel of a matrix $\boldsymbol{H} \in \mathbb{F}_{q^m}^{(n-k) \times n}$, $\boldsymbol{H}$ is called a *parity-check matrix* of $\mathcal{C}$. The code generated by any parity-check matrix $\boldsymbol{H}$ of $\mathcal{C}$ is the *dual code* of $\mathcal{C}$ and denoted by $\mathcal{C}^\perp$.

2.2 Automorphisms, Derivations, and Conjugacy

An *automorphism* θ on $\mathbb{F}_{q^m}$ is a mapping $\theta : \mathbb{F}_{q^m} \to \mathbb{F}_{q^m}$ with the properties $\theta(a+b) = \theta(a) + \theta(b)$ and $\theta(a \cdot b) = \theta(a) \cdot \theta(b)$ for all $a, b \in \mathbb{F}_{q^m}$. We denote the group of all $\mathbb{F}_{q^m}$-automorphisms by $\mathrm{Aut}(\mathbb{F}_{q^m})$. Note that every automorphism fixes a subfield of $\mathbb{F}_{q^m}$ pointwise. The cyclic subgroup of $\mathrm{Aut}(\mathbb{F}_{q^m})$, whose elements fix (at least) $\mathbb{F}_q$ pointwise, is called the *Galois group* of the field extension $\mathbb{F}_{q^m}/\mathbb{F}_q$ and we denote it by $\mathrm{Gal}(\mathbb{F}_{q^m}/\mathbb{F}_q)$. Every $\sigma \in \mathrm{Gal}(\mathbb{F}_{q^m}/\mathbb{F}_q)$ is a power of the *Frobenius automorphism* (with respect to q) that is defined as

$$\varphi : \mathbb{F}_{q^m} \to \mathbb{F}_{q^m}, \quad a \mapsto a^q.$$

Namely, $\sigma \in \{\varphi^0, \ldots, \varphi^{m-1}\}$. The fixed field of $\sigma = \varphi^l$ with $l \in \{0, \ldots, m-1\}$ is $\mathbb{F}_{q^{\gcd(l,m)}}$. For simplicity, assume in the following that $\sigma = \varphi^l$ with $\gcd(l, m) = 1$, i.e., let the fixed field of σ be $\mathbb{F}_q$.

A *σ-derivation* is a map $\delta : \mathbb{F}_{q^m} \to \mathbb{F}_{q^m}$ that satisfies both $\delta(a + b) = \delta(a) + \delta(b)$ and $\delta(a \cdot b) = \delta(a) \cdot b + \sigma(a) \cdot \delta(b)$ for all $a, b \in \mathbb{F}_{q^m}$. In our finite-field setting, every σ-derivation is an inner derivation, that is $\delta = \gamma(\mathrm{Id} - \sigma)$ for a $\gamma \in \mathbb{F}_{q^m}$ and the identity Id on $\mathbb{F}_{q^m}$. When the automorphism σ is clear from the context, we often write δ_γ to refer to the derivation corresponding to $\gamma \in \mathbb{F}_{q^m}$.

For a fixed pair (σ, δ), we can group the elements of $\mathbb{F}_{q^m}$ with respect to an equivalence relation called (σ, δ)-conjugacy:

Definition 1. *Two elements $a, b \in \mathbb{F}_{q^m}$ are called* (σ, δ)-conjugate *if there is a $c \in \mathbb{F}_{q^m}^*$ with*

$$a^c := \sigma(c)ac^{-1} + \delta(c)c^{-1} = b.$$

All conjugates of $a \in \mathbb{F}_{q^m}$ are collected in the respective conjugacy class

$$\mathcal{K}(a) := \{a^c : c \in \mathbb{F}_{q^m}^*\} \subseteq \mathbb{F}_{q^m}.$$

For $\delta = \delta_\gamma$ with $\gamma \in \mathbb{F}_{q^m}$, the class $\mathcal{K}(\gamma)$ is called trivial conjugacy class.

2.3 Isometries in the Sum-Rank Metric

As most code-based cryptosystems use isometric disguising, we quickly recall the characterization of sum-rank isometries. Note that we have to differentiate between $\mathbb{F}_q$-linear and $\mathbb{F}_{q^m}$-linear isometries. The former were studied in [18, Prop. 4.26], whereas the latter were considered in [2,15]. Precisely, the special case of equal block lengths (i.e., $\boldsymbol{n} = (\frac{n}{\ell}, \dots, \frac{n}{\ell})$) was treated in [15, Thm. 2] and the generalization to arbitrary block lengths and the extension to semilinear isometries is due to [2, Sect. 3.3]. We focus on $\mathbb{F}_{q^m}$-(semi)linear isometries because of our motivation from code-based cryptography. Namely, we consider the following:

Definition 2. *A bijective map $\iota : \mathbb{F}_{q^m}^n \to \mathbb{F}_{q^m}^n$ is a* (sum-rank) isometry *on $\mathbb{F}_{q^m}^n$ if it is sum-rank preserving, that is if $d_{\Sigma R}(\boldsymbol{x}) = d_{\Sigma R}(\iota(\boldsymbol{x}))$ holds for all $\boldsymbol{x} \in \mathbb{F}_{q^m}^n$. We call an isometry* linear *when it is $\mathbb{F}_{q^m}$-linear. A* semilinear *isometry ι is additive and there exists an $\mathbb{F}_{q^m}$-automorphism θ such that ι fulfills $\iota(a\boldsymbol{x}) = \theta(a)\iota(\boldsymbol{x})$ for all $a \in \mathbb{F}_{q^m}$ and all $\boldsymbol{x} \in \mathbb{F}_{q^m}^n$.*

Recall that the *general linear group* $\mathrm{GL}(n, \mathbb{F}_q)$ contains all full-rank matrices of size $n \times n$ over $\mathbb{F}_q$ and that the *symmetric group* Sym_n consists of all permutations of n elements. We introduce the notations

$$\begin{aligned} \mathrm{GL}(\boldsymbol{n}, \mathbb{F}_q) &:= \mathrm{GL}(n_1, \mathbb{F}_q) \times \dots \times \mathrm{GL}(n_\ell, \mathbb{F}_q) \\ \text{and} \quad \mathrm{Sym}_{\lambda(\boldsymbol{n})} &:= \mathrm{Sym}_{\lambda_1} \times \dots \times \mathrm{Sym}_{\lambda_k}, \end{aligned}$$

where $\lambda(\boldsymbol{n})$ counts the occurrences of distinct entries of $\boldsymbol{n}$ (see Subsect. 2.1). Note that $\mathrm{Sym}_{\lambda(\boldsymbol{n})}$ is a subgroup of $\mathrm{Sym}_{\sum_j \lambda_j} = \mathrm{Sym}_\ell$.

Theorem 1 (Sum-Rank Isometries [2,15]**).** *The group of $\mathbb{F}_{q^m}$-linear isometries on $\mathbb{F}_{q^m}^n$ is*

$$\mathrm{LI}(\mathbb{F}_{q^m}^n) := \left((\mathbb{F}_{q^m}^*)^\ell \times \mathrm{GL}(\boldsymbol{n}, \mathbb{F}_q)\right) \rtimes \mathrm{Sym}_{\lambda(\boldsymbol{n})}.$$

Its action $\mathrm{act}_{\mathrm{LI}} : \mathrm{LI}(\mathbb{F}_{q^m}^n) \times \mathbb{F}_{q^m}^n \to \mathbb{F}_{q^m}^n$ *is defined as*

$$\mathrm{act}_{\mathrm{LI}}(\iota, \boldsymbol{x}) := \left(c_1 \boldsymbol{x}^{(\pi^{-1}(1))} \boldsymbol{M}_1 \mid \dots \mid c_\ell \boldsymbol{x}^{(\pi^{-1}(\ell))} \boldsymbol{M}_\ell\right)$$

for $\iota = ((c_1, \ldots, c_\ell), (\boldsymbol{M}_1, \ldots, \boldsymbol{M}_\ell), \pi)$ *and* $\boldsymbol{x} \in \mathbb{F}_{q^m}^n$. *Similarly, the group of* $\mathbb{F}_{q^m}$*-semilinear isometries on* $\mathbb{F}_{q^m}^n$ *is*

$$\mathrm{SI}(\mathbb{F}_{q^m}^n) := \mathrm{LI}(\mathbb{F}_{q^m}^n) \rtimes \mathrm{Aut}(\mathbb{F}_{q^m})$$

and its action $\mathrm{act}_{\mathrm{SI}} : \mathrm{SI}(\mathbb{F}_{q^m}^n) \times \mathbb{F}_{q^m}^n \to \mathbb{F}_{q^m}^n$ *is given by*

$$\mathrm{act}_{\mathrm{SI}}((\iota, \theta), \boldsymbol{x}) := \theta(\mathrm{act}_{\mathrm{LI}}(\iota, \boldsymbol{x}))$$

for $(\iota, \theta) \in \mathrm{SI}(\mathbb{F}_{q^m}^n)$ *and* $\boldsymbol{x} \in \mathbb{F}_{q^m}^n$.

Since MacWilliams' extension theorem does not hold in this general setting (see [3, Ex. 2.9 (a)] for a counterexample in the rank-metric case), code equivalence in the sum-rank metric is defined by means of isometries of the whole space (cp. [2, Def. 3.9]).

Definition 3. *Two sum-rank-metric codes* $\mathcal{C}, \mathcal{D} \subseteq \mathbb{F}_{q^m}^n$ *are called* linearly equivalent *if there is a linear isometry* $\iota \in \mathrm{LI}(\mathbb{F}_{q^m}^n)$ *such that*

$$\mathrm{act}_{\mathrm{LI}}(\iota, \mathcal{C}) := \{\mathrm{act}_{\mathrm{LI}}(\iota, \boldsymbol{c}) : \boldsymbol{c} \in \mathcal{C}\} = \mathcal{D}.$$

They are semilinearly equivalent *if there is* $(\iota, \theta) \in \mathrm{SI}(\mathbb{F}_{q^m}^n)$ *such that*

$$\mathrm{act}_{\mathrm{SI}}((\iota, \theta), \mathcal{C}) := \{\mathrm{act}_{\mathrm{SI}}((\iota, \theta), \boldsymbol{c}) : \boldsymbol{c} \in \mathcal{C}\} = \mathcal{D}.$$

2.4 Skew Polynomials

The *skew-polynomial ring* $\mathbb{F}_{q^m}[x; \sigma, \delta]$ is defined as the set of polynomials $f(x) = \sum_i f_i x^i$ with finitely many nonzero coefficients $f_i \in \mathbb{F}_{q^m}$. It is equipped with conventional polynomial addition but the multiplication is determined by the rule $xa = \sigma(a)x + \delta(a)$. Similar to conventional polynomial rings, we define the *degree* of a nonzero skew polynomial $f(x) = \sum_i f_i x^i \in \mathbb{F}_{q^m}[x; \sigma, \delta]$ as $\deg(f) := \max\{i : f_i \neq 0\}$ and set the degree of the zero polynomial to $-\infty$.

Note that despite lots of similarities to $\mathbb{F}_{q^m}[x]$, the same evaluation strategy (i.e., $f(c) = \sum_i f_i c^i$ for $c \in \mathbb{F}_{q^m}$) does not work in this setting. Instead, the literature provides two different ways to adequately evaluate skew polynomials: remainder evaluation and generalized operator evaluation. We will focus on the latter in this work.

For $a, b \in \mathbb{F}_{q^m}$, define the operator

$$\mathcal{D}_a(b) := \sigma(b)a + \delta(b)$$

and its powers $\mathcal{D}_a^i(b) := \mathcal{D}_a(\mathcal{D}_a^{i-1}(b))$ for $i \geq 0$ (with $\mathcal{D}_a^0(b) = b$ and $\mathcal{D}_a^1(b) = \mathcal{D}_a(b)$). For $\boldsymbol{a} = (a_1, \ldots, a_\ell) \in \mathbb{F}_{q^m}^\ell$, and $\boldsymbol{B} \in \mathbb{F}_{q^m}^{k \times n}$, we write $\mathcal{D}_{\boldsymbol{a}}(\boldsymbol{B}) := (\mathcal{D}_{a_1}(\boldsymbol{B}^{(1)}) \mid \cdots \mid \mathcal{D}_{a_\ell}(\boldsymbol{B}^{(\ell)}))$, where $\mathcal{D}_{a_i}(\boldsymbol{B}^{(i)})$ stands for the elementwise application of $\mathcal{D}_{a_i}(\cdot)$ to the entries of $\boldsymbol{B}^{(i)}$ for $1 \leq i \leq \ell$. This notation also applies to vectors $\boldsymbol{b} \in \mathbb{F}_{q^m}^n$ and can be extended to powers of the operator.

In the zero-derivation case, the i-fold application of the above defined operator can be expressed as

$$\mathcal{D}_a^i(b) = \sigma^i(b) \cdot \mathcal{N}_i(a)$$

for any $a, b \in \mathbb{F}_{q^m}$ and $i \in \mathbb{N}^*$. Here, $\mathcal{N}_i(a) := \prod_{j=0}^{i-1} \sigma^j(a) = \sigma^{i-1}(a) \dots \sigma(a) \cdot a$ denotes the *generalized power function.*

Lemma 1. *The equality* $\mathcal{D}_a(bc) = \sigma(b)\mathcal{D}_a(c) + \delta(b)c$ *holds for any* $a, b, c \in \mathbb{F}_{q^m}$.

Proof. The definition of $\mathcal{D}_a(\cdot)$ and the product rule for derivations yield

$$\begin{aligned}\mathcal{D}_a(bc) &= \sigma(bc)a + \delta(bc) = \sigma(bc)a + \delta(b)c + \sigma(b)\delta(c) \\ &= \sigma(b)(\sigma(c)a + \delta(c)) + \delta(b)c = \sigma(b)\mathcal{D}_a(c) + \delta(b)c.\end{aligned}$$

□

Let us now define the generalized operator evaluation of skew polynomials:

Definition 4. *The* generalized operator evaluation *of a skew polynomial* $f(x) = \sum_i f_i x^i \in \mathbb{F}_{q^m}[x; \sigma, \delta]$ *at a point* $b \in \mathbb{F}_{q^m}$ *with respect to an evaluation parameter* $a \in \mathbb{F}_{q^m}$ *is given by*

$$f(b)_a := \sum_i f_i \mathcal{D}_a^i(b).$$

For a vector $\boldsymbol{x} \in \mathbb{F}_{q^m}^n$, a vector $\boldsymbol{a} = (a_1, \dots, a_\ell) \in \mathbb{F}_{q^m}^\ell$, and a parameter $d \in \mathbb{N}^*$, the *generalized Moore matrix* $\mathfrak{M}_d(\boldsymbol{x})_{\boldsymbol{a}}$ is defined as

$$\mathfrak{M}_d(\boldsymbol{x})_{\boldsymbol{a}} := \left(\boldsymbol{V}_d(\boldsymbol{x}^{(1)})_{a_1}, \dots, \boldsymbol{V}_d(\boldsymbol{x}^{(\ell)})_{a_\ell}\right) \in \mathbb{F}_{q^m}^{d \times n},$$

$$\text{where } \boldsymbol{V}_d(\boldsymbol{x}^{(i)})_{a_i} := \begin{pmatrix} x_1^{(i)} & \cdots & x_{n_i}^{(i)} \\ \mathcal{D}_{a_i}(x_1^{(i)}) & \cdots & \mathcal{D}_{a_i}(x_{n_i}^{(i)}) \\ \vdots & \ddots & \vdots \\ \mathcal{D}_{a_i}^{d-1}(x_1^{(i)}) & \cdots & \mathcal{D}_{a_i}^{d-1}(x_{n_i}^{(i)}) \end{pmatrix} \quad \text{for } 1 \leq i \leq \ell.$$

If $\boldsymbol{a}$ contains representatives of pairwise distinct nontrivial conjugacy classes of $\mathbb{F}_{q^m}$ and $\mathrm{rk}_q\left(\boldsymbol{x}^{(i)}\right) = n_i$ for all $1 \leq i \leq \ell$, we have by [14, Thm. 2] and [12, Thm. 4.5] that $\mathrm{rk}_{q^m}\left(\mathfrak{M}_d(\boldsymbol{x})_{\boldsymbol{a}}\right) = \min(d, n)$.

2.5 (Generalized) Linearized Reed–Solomon Codes

Let us recall the definition of LRS codes that generalize both RS and Gabidulin codes. LRS codes are evaluation codes with respect to skew polynomials, which specialize to conventional and linearized polynomials in the Hamming- and the rank-metric setting, respectively.

Definition 5 (Linearized Reed–Solomon Codes [14, Def. 31]). *Let $\boldsymbol{a} = (a_1, \ldots, a_\ell) \in \mathbb{F}_{q^m}^\ell$ consist of representatives of distinct nontrivial conjugacy classes of $\mathbb{F}_{q^m}$. Choose a vector $\boldsymbol{\beta} \in \mathbb{F}_{q^m}^n$ whose blocks $\boldsymbol{\beta}^{(i)} = \left(\beta_1^{(i)}, \ldots, \beta_{n_i}^{(i)}\right)$ contain $\mathbb{F}_q$-linearly independent elements for all $i = 1, \ldots, \ell$. Then, a* linearized Reed-Solomon (LRS) code *of length n and dimension k is defined as*

$$\mathrm{LRS}[\boldsymbol{\beta}, \boldsymbol{a}; \boldsymbol{n}, k] := \left\{ \left(\boldsymbol{c}^{(1)}(f) \mid \cdots \mid \boldsymbol{c}^{(\ell)}(f) \right) : f \in \mathbb{F}_{q^m}[x; \sigma, \delta]_{<k} \right\} \subseteq \mathbb{F}_{q^m}^n$$

where $\boldsymbol{c}^{(i)}(f) := \left(f(\beta_1^{(i)})_{a_i}, \ldots, f(\beta_{n_i}^{(i)})_{a_i} \right)$.

Note that LRS codes reach the Singleton-like bound $d \leq n - k + 1$ from [14, Prop. 34] with equality, where d denotes the minimum sum-rank distance of the code. They are thus *maximum sum-rank distance (MSRD)* codes.

The generalized Moore matrix $\mathfrak{M}_k(\boldsymbol{\beta})_{\boldsymbol{a}}$ is a generator matrix of the code $\mathrm{LRS}[\boldsymbol{\beta}, \boldsymbol{a}; \boldsymbol{n}, k]$. Since a generator matrix of this form is desirable as it e.g. gives rise to known efficient decoding algorithms, we call it a *canonical* generator matrix of $\mathrm{LRS}[\boldsymbol{\beta}, \boldsymbol{a}; \boldsymbol{n}, k]$. Note that the parameters $\boldsymbol{\beta}$ and $\boldsymbol{a}$ of a canonical generator matrix are in general not uniquely determined, and not even fixing a particular $\boldsymbol{a}$ ensures the uniqueness of $\boldsymbol{\beta}$.

In the zero-derivation case, the dual of an LRS code can be described as

$$\mathrm{LRS}[\boldsymbol{\beta}, \boldsymbol{a}; \boldsymbol{n}, k]^\perp = \mathrm{LRS}[\boldsymbol{\alpha}, \sigma^{-1}(\boldsymbol{a}); \boldsymbol{n}, n-k]_{\sigma^{-1}}, \tag{1}$$

where the index σ^{-1} on the right-hand side stands for the fact that it is an LRS code with respect to the inverse automorphism σ^{-1} (see [5,6]). The vector $\boldsymbol{\alpha} = (\boldsymbol{\alpha}^{(1)} \mid \cdots \mid \boldsymbol{\alpha}^{(\ell)}) \in \mathbb{F}_{q^m}^n$ satisfies

$$\sum_{i=1}^{\ell} \sum_{j=1}^{n_i} \alpha_j^{(i)} \mathcal{D}_{a_i}^{h-1}(\beta_j^{(i)}) = 0 \quad \text{for all } h = 1, \ldots, n-1 \tag{2}$$

and has sum-rank weight $\mathrm{wt}_{\Sigma R}(\boldsymbol{\alpha}) = n$ according to [16, Thm. 4]. In particular, the dual of a zero-derivation LRS code is again an LRS code. When nonzero derivations are allowed, the duals of LRS codes are linearized Goppa codes which are (noncanonically) isomorphic to LRS codes [5,6].

As the proof of Theorem 2 shows, codes that are (semi)linearly equivalent to LRS codes are not necessarily LRS codes themselves. However, this is true for a more general code family that is obtained by allowing nonzero block multipliers. We define GLRS codes as follows:

Definition 6 (Generalized Linearized Reed–Solomon Codes). *Let $\mathcal{C} := \mathrm{LRS}[\boldsymbol{\beta}, \boldsymbol{a}; \boldsymbol{n}, k]$ be an LRS code as in Definition 5. Further, let $\boldsymbol{v} = (v_1, \ldots, v_\ell) \in \mathbb{F}_{q^m}^\ell$ be a vector of nonzero $\mathbb{F}_{q^m}$-elements. We define the* generalized linearized Reed–Solomon code $\mathrm{GLRS}[\boldsymbol{\beta}, \boldsymbol{a}, \boldsymbol{v}; \boldsymbol{n}, k]$ *as*

$$\mathrm{GLRS}[\boldsymbol{\beta}, \boldsymbol{a}, \boldsymbol{v}; \boldsymbol{n}, k] := \left\{ \left(v_1 \boldsymbol{c}^{(1)} \mid \cdots \mid v_\ell \boldsymbol{c}^{(\ell)} \right) : \boldsymbol{c} \in \mathcal{C} \right\} \subseteq \mathbb{F}_{q^m}^n.$$

Remark that we recover LRS codes from GLRS codes for $\boldsymbol{v}$ being the all-one vector. Since multiplying blocks with different nonzero $\mathbb{F}_{q^m}$-elements is a sum-rank isometry according to Theorem 1, we obtain the following corollary:

Corollary 1. *The minimum sum-rank distance of the code* $\mathrm{GLRS}[\boldsymbol{\beta}, \boldsymbol{a}, \boldsymbol{v}; \boldsymbol{n}, k]$ *is* $d = n - k + 1$. *Therefore, GLRS codes are MSRD.*

The code $\mathrm{GLRS}[\boldsymbol{\beta}, \boldsymbol{a}, \boldsymbol{v}; \boldsymbol{n}, k]$ has a generator matrix of the form

$$\boldsymbol{G} = \left(v_1 \boldsymbol{V}_k(\boldsymbol{\beta}^{(1)})_{a_1} \mid \cdots \mid v_\ell \boldsymbol{V}_k(\boldsymbol{\beta}^{(\ell)})_{a_\ell} \right).$$

Similar to the LRS case, we call any generator matrix of this form a *canonical* generator matrix of $\mathrm{GLRS}[\boldsymbol{\beta}, \boldsymbol{a}, \boldsymbol{v}; \boldsymbol{n}, k]$. Note that a canonical generator matrix of a GLRS code depends not only on the parameters $\boldsymbol{\beta}$ and $\boldsymbol{a}$ but also on the block multipliers $\boldsymbol{v}$.

3 Problem Statement

The main problem we want to solve is distinguishing GLRS codes, that were disguised by means of $\mathbb{F}_{q^m}$-semilinear isometries, from random sum-rank-metric codes of the same length and dimension. Formally, we state this task as follows:

Problem 1 (Distinguishing GLRS Codes up to Semilinear Equivalence). Given a full-rank matrix $\boldsymbol{M} \in \mathbb{F}_{q^m}^{k \times n}$, decide if there are parameters $\boldsymbol{\beta} \in \mathbb{F}_{q^m}^{n}$, $\boldsymbol{a} \in \mathbb{F}_{q^m}^{\ell}$, $\boldsymbol{v} \in \mathbb{F}_{q^m}^{\ell}$, $\sigma \in \mathrm{Gal}(\mathbb{F}_{q^m}/\mathbb{F}_q)$, and δ being a σ-derivation, such that $\langle \boldsymbol{M} \rangle$ is semilinearly equivalent to $\mathrm{GLRS}[\boldsymbol{\beta}, \boldsymbol{a}, \boldsymbol{v}; \boldsymbol{n}, k]$.

We now investigate how $\mathbb{F}_{q^m}$-semilinear transformations affect GLRS codes to get a better understanding of the problem. Theorem 2 shows that every semilinear isometry (cp. Theorem 1) transforms a GLRS code into another GLRS code with possibly different parameters:

Theorem 2. *Let* $\mathcal{C} = \mathrm{GLRS}[\boldsymbol{\beta}, \boldsymbol{a}, \boldsymbol{v}; \boldsymbol{n}, k]$ *be a GLRS code with respect to* σ *and* $\delta := \delta_\gamma$. *Let further* $\iota \in \mathrm{LI}(\mathbb{F}_{q^m}^n)$ *denote an* $\mathbb{F}_{q^m}$*-linear isometry with* $\iota = ((c_1, \dots, c_\ell), (\boldsymbol{M}_1, \dots, \boldsymbol{M}_\ell), \pi)$. *Then, the linearly equivalent code* $\hat{\mathcal{C}} := \mathrm{act}_{\mathrm{LI}}(\iota, \mathcal{C})$ *is also a GLRS code with respect to* σ *and* δ. *Namely,* $\hat{\mathcal{C}} = \mathrm{GLRS}[\hat{\boldsymbol{\beta}}, \hat{\boldsymbol{a}}, \hat{\boldsymbol{v}}; \boldsymbol{n}, k]$ *with* $\hat{\boldsymbol{\beta}} = (\boldsymbol{\beta}^{(\pi^{-1}(1))}\boldsymbol{M}_1 \mid \cdots \mid \boldsymbol{\beta}^{(\pi^{-1}(\ell))}\boldsymbol{M}_\ell)$, $\hat{\boldsymbol{a}} = (a_{\pi^{-1}(1)}, \dots, a_{\pi^{-1}(\ell)})$, *and* $\hat{\boldsymbol{v}} = (c_1 v_{\pi^{-1}(1)}, \dots, c_\ell v_{\pi^{-1}(\ell)})$.

For a semilinear isometry $(\iota, \theta) \in \mathrm{SI}(\mathbb{F}_{q^m}^n)$ *with* ι *as above and* $\theta \in \mathrm{Aut}(\mathbb{F}_{q^m})$, *the code* $\mathrm{act}_{\mathrm{SI}}((\iota, \theta), \mathcal{C})$ *is a GLRS code with respect to the automorphism* σ *and the possibly different derivation* $\delta_{\theta(\gamma)} := \theta(\gamma)(\mathrm{Id} - \sigma)$. *Its parameters are* $\theta(\hat{\boldsymbol{\beta}})$, $\theta(\hat{\boldsymbol{a}})$, *and* $\theta(\hat{\boldsymbol{v}})$, *where* θ *is applied elementwise to the vectors.*

Proof. Let us use the shorthand notations $v_{\pi_i} := v_{\pi^{-1}(i)}$, $a_{\pi_i} := a_{\pi^{-1}(i)}$, and $\boldsymbol{\beta}^{(\pi_i)} := \boldsymbol{\beta}^{(\pi^{-1}(i))}$ throughout this proof. $\mathcal{C}$ has a generator matrix of the form

$\boldsymbol{G} := \left(v_1 \boldsymbol{V}_k(\boldsymbol{\beta}^{(1)})_{a_1}, \ldots, v_\ell \boldsymbol{V}_k(\boldsymbol{\beta}^{(\ell)})_{a_\ell}\right)$. If ι acts on the j-th row of $\boldsymbol{G}$ for $j \in \{1, \ldots, k\}$, we obtain

$$\left(c_1 v_{\pi_1} \mathcal{D}_{a_{\pi_1}}^{j-1}(\boldsymbol{\beta}^{(\pi_1)}) \boldsymbol{M}_1 \mid \cdots \mid c_\ell v_{\pi_\ell} \mathcal{D}_{a_{\pi_\ell}}^{j-1}(\boldsymbol{\beta}^{(\pi_\ell)}) \boldsymbol{M}_\ell\right). \tag{3}$$

Since generalized operator evaluation is $\mathbb{F}_q$-linear, we get $\mathcal{D}_{a_{\pi_i}}^{j-1}(\boldsymbol{\beta}^{(\pi_i)})\boldsymbol{M}_i = \mathcal{D}_{a_{\pi_i}}^{j-1}(\boldsymbol{\beta}^{(\pi_i)}\boldsymbol{M}_i)$ for all $i = 1, \ldots, \ell$ and thus, (3) is exactly the j-th row of

$$\hat{\boldsymbol{G}} := \left(c_1 v_{\pi_1} \boldsymbol{V}_k(\boldsymbol{\beta}^{(\pi_1)} \boldsymbol{M}_1)_{a_{\pi_1}}, \ldots, c_\ell v_{\pi_\ell} \boldsymbol{V}_k(\boldsymbol{\beta}^{(\pi_\ell)} \boldsymbol{M}_\ell)_{a_{\pi_\ell}}\right).$$

As $\hat{\boldsymbol{G}}$ generates $\hat{\mathcal{C}}$, this proves the first part of the theorem. The second one follows from the observation

$$\theta(v\mathcal{D}_a^{j-1}(\beta)) = \theta(v)\left(\mathcal{D}_{\theta(a)}^{\sigma,\delta_{\theta(\gamma)}}\right)^{j-1}(\theta(\beta)) \tag{4}$$

for any $v, a, \beta \in \mathbb{F}_{q^m}^*$ and $j \in \mathbb{N}^*$ with $\mathcal{D}^{\sigma,\delta_{\theta(\gamma)}}(\cdot)$ denoting the generalized operator evaluation with respect to the automorphism σ and the derivation $\delta_{\theta(\gamma)} := \theta(\gamma)(\mathrm{Id} - \sigma)$. (4) can be verified by induction over j. □

In fact, this shows that GLRS codes with respect to a fixed automorphism and a fixed derivation are closed under linear equivalence. If we allow different derivations for a fixed automorphism, GLRS codes are even closed under semilinear equivalence. This means, intuitively speaking, that Problem 1 boils down to distinguishing GLRS codes. We hence formulate and focus on Problem 2:

Problem 2 (Distinguishing GLRS Codes). Given a full-rank matrix $\boldsymbol{M} \in \mathbb{F}_{q^m}^{k \times n}$, decide if there are parameters $\boldsymbol{\beta} \in \mathbb{F}_{q^m}^n$, $\boldsymbol{a} \in \mathbb{F}_{q^m}^\ell$, $\boldsymbol{v} \in \mathbb{F}_{q^m}^\ell$, $\sigma \in \mathrm{Gal}(\mathbb{F}_{q^m}/\mathbb{F}_q)$, and δ being a σ-derivation, such that $\langle \boldsymbol{M} \rangle = \mathrm{GLRS}[\boldsymbol{\beta}, \boldsymbol{a}, \boldsymbol{v}; \boldsymbol{n}, k]$.

Let us describe more precisely how the two above-defined problems are related in case we assume the knowledge of the automorphism σ and the derivation $\delta := \delta_\gamma$. If we restrict ourselves to linear equivalence, Problem 1 is equivalent to Problem 2 since every code that is linearly equivalent to a GLRS code with respect to σ and δ is a GLRS code with respect to the same automorphism and derivation. In the more general, semilinear setting, we can solve Problem 1 by solving multiple instances of Problem 2. Namely, we have to consider Problem 2 for all derivations $\delta_{\theta(\gamma)} := \theta(\gamma)(\mathrm{Id} - \sigma)$ with $\theta \in \mathrm{Aut}(\mathbb{F}_{q^m})$ according to Theorem . As $|\mathrm{Aut}(\mathbb{F}_{q^m})| = sm$ for s being the extension degree of $\mathbb{F}_q$ over its prime field, we obtain that Problem 1 is equivalent to sm instances of Problem 2.

We present two polynomial-time distinguishers that partly solve Problem when σ and δ are known in Sect. 4. However, the pure knowledge whether a matrix generates a GLRS code or not does not yet break a hypothetical McEliece-like cryptosystem based on GLRS codes. We rather wish to recover an efficient decoding algorithm for the publicly known code by e.g. finding a canonical generator matrix. Therefore, the following problem is of great interest:

Problem 3 (Recovering a Canonical GLRS Generator Matrix). Given an arbitrary generator matrix $\boldsymbol{G} \in \mathbb{F}_{q^m}^{k \times n}$ of a GLRS code $\mathcal{C}$, find parameters $\boldsymbol{\beta} \in \mathbb{F}_{q^m}^n$, $\boldsymbol{a} \in \mathbb{F}_{q^m}^\ell$, $\boldsymbol{v} \in \mathbb{F}_{q^m}^\ell$, $\sigma \in \mathrm{Gal}(\mathbb{F}_{q^m}/\mathbb{F}_q)$, and δ being a σ-derivation, such that $(v_1 \boldsymbol{V}_k(\boldsymbol{\beta}^{(1)})_{a_1} \mid \cdots \mid v_\ell \boldsymbol{V}_k(\boldsymbol{\beta}^{(\ell)})_{a_\ell})$ is a canonical generator matrix of $\mathcal{C}$.

We study Problem 3 in Sect. 5 and show two techniques to partially solve it for GLRS codes in the zero-derivation case with known automorphism σ.

4 Distinguishers for GLRS Codes

This section contains two approaches that solve Problem 2, that is the task of distinguishing GLRS codes from random codes, for many instances. In both cases, we assume the knowledge of the automorphism σ and the derivation δ with respect to which the code should be distinguished.

In Subsect. 4.1, we focus on a square-code distinguisher that is inspired by an RS-code distinguisher. It works for GLRS codes constructed by means of the identity automorphism and zero derivation.

Afterwards, we present an Overbeck-like distinguisher inspired by the rank-metric case in Subsect. 4.2. This approach can handle any valid combination of automorphism and derivation but requires the knowledge of the evaluation-parameter vector $\boldsymbol{a}$. Moreover, the Overbeck-type distinguisher cannot deal with block multipliers and is thus applicable to LRS codes only. However, GLRS codes can still be handled by applying the distinguisher at most $(q^m - 1)^\ell$ times (see Subsect. 4.2 for more details).

We experimentally verified all results presented in this section for different parameter sets with an implementation in SageMath [26].

4.1 A Square-Code Distinguisher

The first polynomial-time attack on a McEliece/Niederreiter variant based on generalized Reed–Solomon (GRS) codes was proposed by Sidelnikov and Shestakov in [25]. The attack was later on refined by Wieschebrink to attack the improved Berger–Loidreau cryptosystem [27], which is based on GRS subcodes. The approach from [27] was further improved in [28] to work with smaller subcodes and thus to break the cryptosystem for most practical parameters. The attack in [28] is based on the properties of the elementwise product (or *Schur-square*) of a code. For any vectors $\boldsymbol{x}, \boldsymbol{y} \in \mathbb{F}_{q^m}^n$ we define the *elementwise product* (also referred to as *Schur* or *star* product) of $\boldsymbol{x}$ and $\boldsymbol{y}$ as

$$\boldsymbol{x} \star \boldsymbol{y} := (x_1 y_1, x_2 y_2 \ldots, x_n y_n).$$

The *square-code* of an $\mathbb{F}_{q^m}$-linear code $\mathcal{C} \subseteq \mathbb{F}_{q^m}^n$ is defined as

$$\mathcal{C} \star \mathcal{C} := \{\boldsymbol{c}_1 \star \boldsymbol{c}_2 : \boldsymbol{c}_1, \boldsymbol{c}_2 \in \mathcal{C}\}.$$

The main observation for distinguishing a random linear code in $\mathbb{F}_{q^m}^n$ from a GRS code $\mathcal{C}$ is that the squared GRS code has dimension $\dim(\mathcal{C} \star \mathcal{C}) =$

$\min(n, 2k-1)$, which is small compared to the expected dimension of a squared random linear code. Note that a similar technique was used for the power decoding of RS codes beyond the unique-decoding radius (see [24, Lemma 1]).

We will now derive a similar distinguisher for GLRS codes constructed from skew-polynomial rings with identity automorphism $\sigma = \mathrm{Id}$. Observe that in this case the only possible derivation is the zero derivation. Lemma 2 provides some basic results required for deriving a square-code distinguisher for GLRS codes:

Lemma 2. *For $\sigma = \mathrm{Id}$, let $\mathcal{C} = \mathrm{GLRS}[\boldsymbol{\beta}, \boldsymbol{a}, \boldsymbol{v}; \boldsymbol{n}, k]$ be a GLRS code constructed by polynomials from $\mathbb{F}_{q^m}[x;\sigma]_{<k} = \mathbb{F}_{q^m}[x]_{<k}$. Then we have that*

$$\mathcal{C} = \{(f(a_1), \ldots, f(a_1) \mid \cdots \mid f(a_\ell), \ldots, f(a_\ell)) \cdot \mathrm{diag}((v_1\boldsymbol{\beta}^{(1)} \mid \cdots \mid v_\ell \boldsymbol{\beta}^{(\ell)})) \\ : f \in \mathbb{F}_{q^m}[x]_{<k}\},$$

where $f(\cdot)$ denotes ordinary polynomial evaluation.

Proof. Since σ is the identity automorphism, the generalized operator evaluation of $f \in \mathbb{F}_{q^m}[x;\sigma]$ at an element $\beta_j^{(i)} \in \mathbb{F}_{q^m}$ with respect to the evaluation parameter $a_i \in \mathbb{F}_{q^m}$ is

$$f(\beta_j^{(i)})_{a_i} = \sum_{l=0}^{k-1} f_l \mathcal{D}_{a_i}^l(\beta_j^{(i)}) = \sum_{l=0}^{k-1} f_l \sigma^l(\beta_j^{(i)}) \mathcal{N}_l(a_i) = \beta_j^{(i)} \sum_{l=0}^{k-1} f_l a_i^l = \beta_j^{(i)} f(a_i),$$

where $f(\cdot)$ denotes the ordinary polynomial evaluation. Hence, any $\boldsymbol{c} \in \mathcal{C}$ can be written as

$$\begin{aligned}\boldsymbol{c} &= (v_1 f(\beta_1^{(1)})_{a_1}, \ldots, v_1 f(\beta_{n_1}^{(1)})_{a_1} \mid \cdots \mid v_\ell f(\beta_1^{(\ell)})_{a_\ell}, \ldots, v_\ell f(\beta_{n_\ell}^{(\ell)})_{a_\ell}) \\ &= (v_1 \beta_1^{(1)} f(a_1), \ldots, v_1 \beta_{n_1}^{(1)} f(a_1) \mid \cdots \mid v_\ell \beta_1^{(\ell)} f(a_\ell), \ldots, v_\ell \beta_{n_\ell}^{(\ell)} f(a_\ell)).\end{aligned}$$

□

This allows the derivation of Lemma 3 which is a result about the dimension of the square code of GLRS codes and, in contrast, of random linear codes.

Lemma 3. *1. Let $\mathcal{C} \subseteq \mathbb{F}_{q^m}^n$ be a GLRS code of dimension k with respect to $\sigma = \mathrm{Id}$. Then*

$$\dim(\mathcal{C} \star \mathcal{C}) = \min(\ell, 2k-1).$$

2. Let $\mathcal{C} \subseteq \mathbb{F}_{q^m}^n$ be a linear code of dimension k that was chosen uniformly at random. Then

$$\Pr\left(\dim(\mathcal{C} \star \mathcal{C}) < \min\left(n, \frac{k(k+1)}{2}\right)\right) \xrightarrow{k \to \infty} 0,$$

where $\Pr(\cdot)$ denotes the probability of the event in parentheses.

Proof. 1. Let $\mathbf{c}, \mathbf{c}'$ be two codewords from $\mathcal{C} \star \mathcal{C}$ constructed by the evaluation of the polynomials $f, g \in \mathbb{F}_{q^m}[x;\sigma]$ having the maximal degree $\deg(f) = \deg(g) = k-1$. Then, by Lemma 2, we have that $\mathbf{c} \star \mathbf{c}'$ has the form

$$\mathbf{c} \star \mathbf{c}' = ((f \cdot g)(a_1), \ldots, (f \cdot g)(a_1) \mid \cdots \mid (f \cdot g)(a_\ell), \ldots, (f \cdot g)(a_\ell)) \\ \cdot \operatorname{diag}\left(\left(v_1^2 \left(\boldsymbol{\beta}^{(1)}\right)^2 \mid \cdots \mid v_\ell^2 \left(\boldsymbol{\beta}^{(\ell)}\right)^2\right)\right),$$

where the squaring of the blocks $\boldsymbol{\beta}^{(i)}$ for $i = 1, \ldots, \ell$ is understood elementwise. Since $\boldsymbol{a}$ contains representatives of different conjugacy classes of $\mathbb{F}_{q^m}$, the elements in $\boldsymbol{a}$ are pairwise distinct. Since $\boldsymbol{\beta}$ contains block-wise $\mathbb{F}_q$-linearly independent elements, all entries in $\boldsymbol{\beta}$ are nonzero. Together with the fact that $\boldsymbol{v}$ contains only nonzero elements this implies that the diagonal matrix has full rank n. Hence, by considering only the first column of each block, we get a GRS code of length ℓ and dimension $\deg(f \cdot g) + 1 = 2k - 1$. The size of the corresponding generator matrix is $(2k-1) \times \ell$, which yields the statement.
2. This follows directly from [27].

□

Theorem 3 summarizes the results for the Wieschebrink-like square-code distinguisher for GLRS codes in the identity-automorphism case.

Theorem 3 (Square-Code Distinguisher). *Let $2 < k \leq \frac{n}{2}$ and let σ be the identity automorphism. Given a generator matrix of a k-dimensional code in $\mathbb{F}_{q^m}^n$, we can distinguish a GLRS code from a random code with high probability*[1] *in $\mathcal{O}(n^5)$ operations in $\mathbb{F}_{q^m}$.*

Proof. Using Lemma 3 we can distinguish a GLRS code with high probability from a random linear code by considering the dimension of the square code. The complexity, which is in the order of

$$\mathcal{O}(k^4 n + k^2 n + k^2 (n-k)^2 n) \subseteq \mathcal{O}(n^5)$$

operations in $\mathbb{F}_{q^m}$, follows from [28]. □

4.2 An Overbeck-Like Distinguisher

Overbeck proposed a distinguisher for Gabidulin codes in [19–21]. The main idea is to repeatedly apply the Frobenius automorphism to the public generator matrix and stack the results vertically. Since there is a generator matrix of a Gabidulin code whose i-th row is the $(i-1)$-fold application of the Frobenius automorphism to a generating vector, the rank of the stacked matrix will only increase by one for each new matrix block. But random full-rank matrices behave differently and the stacked matrix has much higher rank in general.

[1] In fact, the distinguisher recognizes a GLRS code with probability one. But, with a small probability, it might wrongly declare a non-GLRS code to be a GLRS code.

Horlemann-Trautmann, Marshall, and Rosenthal [11] used a slightly different approach, which we will call *HMR approach* for short, to recover the secret parameters of a Gabidulin code. We mention their technique because it gives rise to a distinguisher and it is similar to Overbeck's approach, as it also makes use of the repeated application of the Frobenius automorphism to the public generator matrix. But instead of considering the sum of the corresponding codes, the HMR approach focuses on the intersection of the codes and shows that its dimension only decreases by one for each iteration step. Again, random codes show a different behavior under this operation.

We now present a generalization of Overbeck's approach to LRS codes in the sum-rank metric. In contrast to the square-code distinguisher, the Overbeck-like distinguisher works for the general setting with an arbitrary automorphism σ and any valid σ-derivation δ. Since it does not support block multipliers, i.e., GLRS codes, let us quickly describe how we can apply distinguishers for LRS codes to GLRS codes in general. Recall therefore that a GLRS code $\mathrm{GLRS}[\boldsymbol{\beta}, \boldsymbol{a}, \boldsymbol{v}; \boldsymbol{n}, k]$ has a generator matrix of the form $(v_1\boldsymbol{G}^{(1)} \mid \cdots \mid v_\ell \boldsymbol{G}^{(\ell)})$, where $\boldsymbol{G} \in \mathbb{F}_{q^m}^{k\times n}$ is a generator matrix of $\mathrm{LRS}[\boldsymbol{\beta}, \boldsymbol{a}; \boldsymbol{n}, k]$. But this implies that the Overbeck-like distinguisher will (at least) succeed if we apply it to the matrix $(v_1^{-1}\boldsymbol{M}^{(1)} \mid \cdots \mid v_\ell^{-1}\boldsymbol{M}^{(\ell)})$, where $\boldsymbol{M} \in \mathbb{F}_{q^m}^{k\times n}$ denotes the public generator matrix of the GLRS code. We can thus run the Overbeck-like distinguisher for different choices of $\boldsymbol{v}^{-1} \in \mathbb{F}_{q^m}^{\ell}$ until it either succeeds or all possible $(q^m-1)^\ell$ (inverse) block multipliers were checked in the worst case.

Lemma 4. *Choose $k < n$, let the entries of $\boldsymbol{a} \in \mathbb{F}_{q^m}^{\ell}$ belong to distinct nontrivial conjugacy classes of $\mathbb{F}_{q^m}$ and let $\boldsymbol{x} \in \mathbb{F}_{q^m}^{n}$ be a vector with $\mathrm{wt}_{\Sigma R}(\boldsymbol{x}) = n$. Then the following holds for the generalized Moore matrix $\mathfrak{M}_k(\boldsymbol{x})_{\boldsymbol{a}}$:*

1. *The addition code $\mathcal{A} := \langle \mathfrak{M}_k(\boldsymbol{x})_{\boldsymbol{a}}\rangle + \langle \mathcal{D}_{\boldsymbol{a}}(\mathfrak{M}_k(\boldsymbol{x})_{\boldsymbol{a}})\rangle$ equals $\langle \mathfrak{M}_{k+1}(\boldsymbol{x})_{\boldsymbol{a}}\rangle$ and thus $\dim(\mathcal{A}) = k+1$.*
2. *The intersection code $\mathcal{I} := \langle \mathfrak{M}_k(\boldsymbol{x})_{\boldsymbol{a}}\rangle \cap \langle \mathcal{D}_{\boldsymbol{a}}(\mathfrak{M}_k(\boldsymbol{x})_{\boldsymbol{a}})\rangle$ is generated by the matrix $\mathfrak{M}_{k-1}(\mathcal{D}_{\boldsymbol{a}}(\boldsymbol{x}))_{\boldsymbol{a}}$ and hence $\dim(\mathcal{I}) = k-1$.*

Proof. 1. Let $\boldsymbol{A} \in \mathbb{F}_{q^m}^{2k\times n}$ denote the matrix that is obtained by vertically stacking $\mathfrak{M}_k(\boldsymbol{x})_{\boldsymbol{a}}$ and $\mathcal{D}_{\boldsymbol{a}}(\mathfrak{M}_k(\boldsymbol{x})_{\boldsymbol{a}})$. Since the first $k-1$ lines of $\mathcal{D}_{\boldsymbol{a}}(\mathfrak{M}_k(\boldsymbol{x})_{\boldsymbol{a}})$ coincide with the last $k-1$ rows of $\mathfrak{M}_k(\boldsymbol{x})_{\boldsymbol{a}}$ due to the Moore-matrix structure, we obtain

$$\mathcal{A} = \langle \boldsymbol{A}\rangle = \left\langle \begin{pmatrix} \mathfrak{M}_k(\boldsymbol{x})_{\boldsymbol{a}} \\ \mathcal{D}_{\boldsymbol{a}}^k(\boldsymbol{x}) \end{pmatrix} \right\rangle = \langle \mathfrak{M}_{k+1}(\boldsymbol{x})_{\boldsymbol{a}}\rangle.$$

As further $k+1 \leq n$ holds and the necessary conditions on $\boldsymbol{a}$ and $\boldsymbol{x}$ apply, we get $\dim(\mathcal{A}) = \mathrm{rk}_{q^m}(\mathfrak{M}_{k+1}(\boldsymbol{x})_{\boldsymbol{a}}) = \min(k+1, n) = k+1$.

2. As the last $k-1$ lines of $\mathfrak{M}_k(\boldsymbol{x})_{\boldsymbol{a}}$ and the first $k-1$ lines of $\mathcal{D}_{\boldsymbol{a}}(\mathfrak{M}_k(\boldsymbol{x})_{\boldsymbol{a}})$ coincide, their span $\langle \mathfrak{M}_{k-1}(\mathcal{D}_{\boldsymbol{a}}(\boldsymbol{x}))_{\boldsymbol{a}}\rangle$ is certainly contained in $\mathcal{I}$. Note that, because of the $\mathbb{F}_q$-linearity of $\mathcal{D}_{\boldsymbol{a}}(\cdot)$, $\mathrm{wt}_{\Sigma R}(\mathcal{D}_{\boldsymbol{a}}(\boldsymbol{x})) = \mathrm{wt}_{\Sigma R}(\boldsymbol{x}) = n$ holds, which implies $\mathrm{rk}_{q^m}(\mathfrak{M}_{k-1}(\mathcal{D}_{\boldsymbol{a}}(\boldsymbol{x}))_{\boldsymbol{a}}) = k-1$. Thus,

$$\begin{aligned}\dim(\mathcal{I}) &= \mathrm{rk}_{q^m}(\mathfrak{M}_k(\boldsymbol{x})_{\boldsymbol{a}}) + \mathrm{rk}_{q^m}(\mathcal{D}_{\boldsymbol{a}}(\mathfrak{M}_k(\boldsymbol{x})_{\boldsymbol{a}})) - \dim(\mathcal{A}) \\ &= 2k - k - 1 = k-1\end{aligned}$$

and $\mathcal{I} = \langle \mathfrak{M}_{k-1}(\mathcal{D}_{\boldsymbol{a}}(\boldsymbol{x}))_{\boldsymbol{a}} \rangle$ follows from the dimension equality. □

Define the operator

$$\Gamma_{\boldsymbol{a}}^{j}: \quad \mathbb{F}_{q^m}^{k\times n} \to \mathbb{F}_{q^m}^{(j+1)k\times n}, \qquad \boldsymbol{M} \mapsto \begin{pmatrix} \boldsymbol{M} \\ \mathcal{D}_{\boldsymbol{a}}(\boldsymbol{M}) \\ \vdots \\ \mathcal{D}_{\boldsymbol{a}}^{j}(\boldsymbol{M}) \end{pmatrix}$$

for a fixed vector $\boldsymbol{a} \in \mathbb{F}_{q^m}^{\ell}$ of evaluation parameters and a natural number $j \in \mathbb{N}$.

Corollary 2. *Let* $\boldsymbol{G}$ *be an arbitrary generator matrix of the code* $\mathrm{LRS}[\boldsymbol{\beta}, \boldsymbol{a}; \boldsymbol{n}, k]$. *Then,* $\Gamma_{\boldsymbol{a}}^{j}(\boldsymbol{G})$ *generates the code* $\mathrm{LRS}[\boldsymbol{\beta}, \boldsymbol{a}; \boldsymbol{n}, k+j]$ *and* $\mathrm{rk}_{q^m}(\Gamma_{\boldsymbol{a}}^{j}(\boldsymbol{G})) = k + j$ *holds for all* $0 \leq j \leq n - k$.

Proof. If $\boldsymbol{G} = \mathfrak{M}_k(\boldsymbol{\beta})_{\boldsymbol{a}}$, the statements follow from an iterative application of Lemma 4. In any other case, there is a matrix $\boldsymbol{S} = (S_{i,j})_{i,j} \in \mathrm{GL}_k(\mathbb{F}_{q^m})$ such that $\boldsymbol{G} = \boldsymbol{S} \cdot \mathfrak{M}_k(\boldsymbol{\beta})_{\boldsymbol{a}}$.

Let us first focus on the smallest nontrivial choice for j, namely $j = 1$. The l-th row of $\mathcal{D}_{\boldsymbol{a}}(\boldsymbol{G}) = \mathcal{D}_{\boldsymbol{a}}(\boldsymbol{S} \cdot \mathfrak{M}_k(\boldsymbol{\beta})_{\boldsymbol{a}})$ is

$$\begin{aligned} \mathcal{D}_{\boldsymbol{a}}\Big(\sum_{i=1}^{k} S_{l,i}\mathcal{D}_{\boldsymbol{a}}^{i-1}(\boldsymbol{\beta})\Big) &= \sum_{i=1}^{k} \mathcal{D}_{\boldsymbol{a}}(S_{l,i}\mathcal{D}_{\boldsymbol{a}}^{i-1}(\boldsymbol{\beta})) \\ &\overset{(*)}{=} \sum_{i=1}^{k} \sigma(S_{l,i})\mathcal{D}_{\boldsymbol{a}}^{i}(\boldsymbol{\beta}) + \delta(S_{l,i})\mathcal{D}_{\boldsymbol{a}}^{i-1}(\boldsymbol{\beta}), \end{aligned} \tag{5}$$

where $(*)$ follows from Lemma 1. But this is a $\mathbb{F}_{q^m}$-linear combination of the elements $\boldsymbol{\beta}, \mathcal{D}_{\boldsymbol{a}}(\boldsymbol{\beta}), \ldots, \mathcal{D}_{\boldsymbol{a}}^{k}(\boldsymbol{\beta})$, i.e., of a basis of $\mathrm{LRS}[\boldsymbol{\beta}, \boldsymbol{a}; \boldsymbol{n}, k{+}1]$. Hence, the inclusion $\langle \mathcal{D}_{\boldsymbol{a}}(\boldsymbol{G}) \rangle \subseteq \mathrm{LRS}[\boldsymbol{\beta}, \boldsymbol{a}; \boldsymbol{n}, k+1]$ applies. Since $\boldsymbol{G}$ generates $\mathrm{LRS}[\boldsymbol{\beta}, \boldsymbol{a}; \boldsymbol{n}, k] \subseteq \mathrm{LRS}[\boldsymbol{\beta}, \boldsymbol{a}; \boldsymbol{n}, k+1]$, it follows further that $\langle \Gamma_{\boldsymbol{a}}(\boldsymbol{G}) \rangle \subseteq \mathrm{LRS}[\boldsymbol{\beta}, \boldsymbol{a}; \boldsymbol{n}, k+1]$.

Let us show the other inclusion $\langle \Gamma_{\boldsymbol{a}}(\boldsymbol{G}) \rangle \supseteq \mathrm{LRS}[\boldsymbol{\beta}, \boldsymbol{a}; \boldsymbol{n}, k+1]$. First realize that $\langle \Gamma_{\boldsymbol{a}}(\boldsymbol{G}) \rangle \supseteq \langle \boldsymbol{G} \rangle = \mathrm{LRS}[\boldsymbol{\beta}, \boldsymbol{a}; \boldsymbol{n}, k]$ and $\mathrm{LRS}[\boldsymbol{\beta}, \boldsymbol{a}; \boldsymbol{n}, k{+}1] = \mathrm{LRS}[\boldsymbol{\beta}, \boldsymbol{a}; \boldsymbol{n}, k] + \langle \mathcal{D}_{\boldsymbol{a}}^{k}(\boldsymbol{\beta}) \rangle$ hold. It is thus enough to show that there is an element of $\langle \Gamma_{\boldsymbol{a}}(\boldsymbol{G}) \rangle$ whose $\mathbb{F}_{q^m}$-linear combination contains a nonzero multiple of $\mathcal{D}_{\boldsymbol{a}}^{k}(\boldsymbol{\beta})$. But since $\boldsymbol{S}$ has full rank, there is a nonzero entry in its k-th column, say $S_{l^*,k}$. Now (5) shows that the l^*-th row of $\mathcal{D}_{\boldsymbol{a}}(\boldsymbol{G})$ has the form

$$\sigma(S_{l^*,k})\mathcal{D}_{\boldsymbol{a}}^{k}(\boldsymbol{\beta}) + \sum_{i=1}^{k-1} \sigma(S_{l,i})\mathcal{D}_{\boldsymbol{a}}^{i}(\boldsymbol{\beta}) + \delta(S_{l,i})\mathcal{D}_{\boldsymbol{a}}^{i-1}(\boldsymbol{\beta}),$$

where the right-hand side is clearly contained in $\mathrm{LRS}[\boldsymbol{\beta}, \boldsymbol{a}; \boldsymbol{n}, k]$. As $\sigma(S_{l^*,k})$ is nonzero if and only if $S_{l^*,k} \neq 0$, this shows $\langle \mathcal{D}_{\boldsymbol{a}}(\boldsymbol{G}) \rangle \supseteq \langle \mathcal{D}_{\boldsymbol{a}}^{k}(\boldsymbol{\beta}) \rangle$ and hence $\langle \Gamma_{\boldsymbol{a}}(\boldsymbol{G}) \rangle \supseteq \mathrm{LRS}[\boldsymbol{\beta}, \boldsymbol{a}; \boldsymbol{n}, k+1]$.

Summing up, we obtain $\langle \Gamma_{\boldsymbol{a}}(\boldsymbol{G}) \rangle = \mathrm{LRS}[\boldsymbol{\beta}, \boldsymbol{a}; \boldsymbol{n}, k{+}1]$, which directly implies $\mathrm{rk}_{q^m}(\Gamma_{\boldsymbol{a}}(\boldsymbol{G})) = k + 1$.

For $j > 1$, the results follow inductively from the fact that

$$\langle \Gamma_{a}^{j}(G) \rangle = \left\langle \begin{pmatrix} \Gamma_{a}^{j-1}(G) \\ \mathcal{D}_{a}^{j}(G) \end{pmatrix} \right\rangle \overset{(\circ)}{=} \langle \Gamma_{a}(\Gamma_{a}^{j-1}(G)) \rangle,$$

since all rows that are added in step ($\circ$) are already contained in the row space of $\Gamma_{a}^{j-1}(G)$. The statements $\langle \Gamma_{a}^{j}(G) \rangle = \mathrm{LRS}[\boldsymbol{\beta}, \boldsymbol{a}; \boldsymbol{n}, k+j]$ and hence $\mathrm{rk}_{q^m}(\Gamma_{a}^{j}(G)) = k+j$ follow with the knowledge of $\Gamma_{a}^{j-1}(G) = \mathrm{LRS}[\boldsymbol{\beta}, \boldsymbol{a}; \boldsymbol{n}, k+j-1]$ and the proof for $j = 1$. □

In contrast, randomly chosen full-rank matrices over $\mathbb{F}_{q^m}$ tend to behave quite differently when Γ_a is applied. This is analogous to [20, Assumption 2].

Conjecture 1. Let $M \in \mathbb{F}_{q^m}^{k \times n}$ be a randomly chosen matrix with full $\mathbb{F}_{q^m}$-rank and such that each block $M^{(i)}$ for $i = 1, \dots, \ell$ has full column rank over $\mathbb{F}_q$. Assume that $\boldsymbol{a} \in \mathbb{F}_{q^m}^{\ell}$ consists of randomly chosen representatives of distinct nontrivial conjugacy classes of $\mathbb{F}_{q^m}$ and fix a parameter $j \in \{1, \dots, n-k\}$. Then, $\mathrm{rk}_{q^m}(\Gamma_{a}^{j}(M)) = \min((j+1)k, n)$ holds with high probability.

With these results, we can solve Problem 2 for LRS codes in polynomial time if σ, δ, and $\boldsymbol{a}$ are known. We summarize it in Theorem 4:

Theorem 4 (Overbeck-like Distinguisher). *Let $M \in \mathbb{F}_{q^m}^{k \times n}$ be an arbitrary full-rank matrix. We can decide with high probability*[2] *if M generates an LRS code with respect to σ, δ, and $\boldsymbol{a}$ in $\mathcal{O}(n^5)$ operations in $\mathbb{F}_{q^m}$.*

Proof. First, choose a $0 \le j \le n-k$ for which $k+j < \min((j+1)k, n)$ holds. We set up the matrix $\Gamma_{a}^{j}(M) \in \mathbb{F}_{q^m}^{(j+1)k \times n}$ in $\mathcal{O}(jkn) \subseteq \mathcal{O}(n^3)$ operations in $\mathbb{F}_{q^m}$. Next, we compute its rank in $\mathcal{O}(n^5)$ $\mathbb{F}_{q^m}$-operations. By Corollary 2 and Conjecture 1, we know with high probability that M generates an LRS code with respect to the given parameters if $\mathrm{rk}_{q^m}(\Gamma_{a}^{j}(M)) = k+j$ holds. If however $\mathrm{rk}_{q^m}(\Gamma_{a}^{j}(M)) > k+j$, we know for sure that M is no generator matrix of an LRS code with respect to the given parameters. □

Remark 1. We empirically verified by simulations that the distinguisher can in most cases *not* recognize an LRS code if it is executed with respect to a different set of evaluation parameters. This is the case even if the conjugacy classes of the evaluation parameters $\boldsymbol{a} = (a_1, \dots, a_\ell)$ are known and only other representatives $:= (a_1{}^{c_1}, \dots, a_\ell{}^{c_\ell})$ with $c_1, \dots, c_\ell \in \mathbb{F}_{q^m}^*$ are used for the distinguisher.

This means that not even side information about the chosen conjugacy classes helps the distinguishing process but knowledge of the exact evaluation parameters is needed. If we do not have access to this information, we have to try exponentially many possibilities in the worst case.

[2] In fact, the distinguisher recognizes a GLRS code with probability one. But, with a small probability, it might wrongly declare a non-GLRS code to be a GLRS code.

We use the remainder of this section to give a short outline of how the distinguisher using the HMR approach can be generalized to the LRS case. If a full-rank matrix $\boldsymbol{M} \in \mathbb{F}_{q^m}^{k \times n}$ and parameters σ, δ, and $\boldsymbol{a}$ are given, we focus on the intersection code instead of considering the addition code as we indicated earlier. Similar to Corollary 2, we can derive Corollary 3 whose proof we omit for brevity.

Corollary 3. *Let $\boldsymbol{G}$ be an arbitrary generator matrix of the code* $\mathrm{LRS}[\boldsymbol{\beta}, \boldsymbol{a}; \boldsymbol{n}, k]$*. Then, the j-fold intersection code $\bigcap_{i=0}^{j} \langle \mathcal{D}_{\boldsymbol{a}}^{i}(\boldsymbol{M}) \rangle$ equals* $\mathrm{LRS}[\mathcal{D}_{\boldsymbol{a}}^{j}(\boldsymbol{\beta}), \boldsymbol{a}; \boldsymbol{n}, k-j]$ *and has thus $\mathbb{F}_{q^m}$-dimension $k-j$ for all $0 \leq j \leq k-1$.*

Heuristically speaking, the application of $\mathcal{D}_{\boldsymbol{a}}(\cdot)$ to a random full-rank matrix produces another essentially random code. For small dimension k, it is hence reasonable to assume that the j-fold intersection code from Corollary 3 has a much lower dimension. This illustrates why Corollary 3 can serve as a distinguisher for LRS codes that can, of course, also be applied to GLRS codes as explained in the beginning of this section.

5 Recovery of a Canonical Generator Matrix

If only a scrambled and possibly further disguised generator matrix of a GLRS code is known, it is a crucial task to recover a canonical generator matrix of the same code. The secret code structure, that is revealed by a canonical generator matrix, is (up to now) directly linked to the knowledge of efficient decoding algorithms. We partly tackle Problem 3 in this section and show how the recovery can be done in the case of GLRS codes with zero derivation for which the automorphism σ is given. As for the distinguishers, the following results were also implemented in SageMath and checked for several parameter sets.

The first approach requires the identity automorphism and finds suitable evaluation parameters $\boldsymbol{a}$ and block multipliers $\boldsymbol{v}$, whereas the second one assumes the knowledge of $\boldsymbol{a}$ and allows to recover $\boldsymbol{\beta}$ for an arbitrary but known automorphism. If GLRS codes with respect to the identity automorphism are considered, we can thus combine the two distinguishers to recover first $\boldsymbol{a}$ and $\boldsymbol{v}$, and then $\boldsymbol{\beta}$.

5.1 Square-Code Approach

For this approach, we focus on the identity automorphism which allows zero derivation only. The recovery strategy is based on the fact that we can extract a GRS code from an arbitrary generator matrix of a GLRS code as described in Subsect. 4.1. We then recover the parameters of the GRS code and afterwards the ones of the GLRS code.

Theorem 5. *Let $\boldsymbol{G} \in \mathbb{F}_{q^m}^{k \times n}$ denote a generator matrix of a GLRS code $\mathcal{C}$ with respect to the identity automorphism and zero derivation. We can recover parameters $\boldsymbol{a}, \boldsymbol{v} \in \mathbb{F}_{q^m}^{\ell}$ for which a canonical generator matrix of $\mathcal{C}$ exists in $\mathcal{O}(k^2 n)$ operations in $\mathbb{F}_{q^m}$.*

Proof. Recall from Lemma 3 that the matrix consisting of one column of each block $\boldsymbol{G}^{(i)}$ of the generator matrix $\boldsymbol{G}$ generates a GRS code of length ℓ and dimension k. If $\ell > k$ this is a nontrivial GRS code, whereas for $\ell \leq k$ the code is the whole space $\mathbb{F}_{q^m}^{\ell}$. For the description of the recovery process we will differentiate between these two cases:

1. In the case where $\ell \geq k$ holds we can simply choose the evaluation points to be $\boldsymbol{a} = (1, \alpha, \alpha^2, \dots, \alpha^{\ell})$ for a primitive element $\alpha \in \mathbb{F}_{q^m}$. Clearly, the Vandermonde matrix with these parameters is full-rank and hence spans the whole space, i.e., it is a generator matrix of the trivial RS code. Furthermore, $1, \alpha, \alpha^2, \dots, \alpha^{\ell}$ represent distinct conjugacy classes (since we consider zero derivation) and are hence a valid choice for the LRS code. Note that we do not need to consider column multipliers in this setting, i.e., we can assume $\boldsymbol{v}$ to be the all-one vector.
2. In the other case, i.e., where $\ell < k$, the resulting GRS code and its dual code are nontrivial, i.e., they both have minimum distance greater than one. We can now use the Sidelnikov–Shestakov algorithm from [25] on the parity-check matrix of our GRS code to find suitable $\boldsymbol{a}$ and $\boldsymbol{v} \in \mathbb{F}_{q^m}^{\ell}$. This requires $\mathcal{O}(k^2 n)$ operations in $\mathbb{F}_{q^m}$. □

Depending on how the code is disguised in a potential cryptosystem, an attacker can use the fact about the square-code dimension from Lemma 3 to find suitable subcodes of the public code. Then, the parameter-recovery algorithm from Theorem 5 can be applied to the obtained subcodes.

5.2 Overbeck-Like Approach

In the literature, there are three different approaches for recovering the secret parameters of Gabidulin codes based on ideas similar to Overbeck's distinguisher:

1. Overbeck [20] considers the sum of the codes obtained by repeated application of the Frobenius automorphism until a code of codimension one is obtained. The secret parameters are then recovered from a generator of the one-dimensional dual code.
2. Horlemann-Trautmann, Marshall, and Rosenthal [11] compute the intersection of the codes that arise from repeated application of the Frobenius automorphism until the result is a one-dimensional code. A generator of the latter yields the secret parameters of the code.
3. Another approach by Horlemann-Trautmann, Marshall, and Rosenthal [10] maps the task to the problem of finding rank-one codewords in the code generated by the public matrix and a corrupted codeword.

We present the first two approaches for LRS codes in the zero-derivation gime where the automorphism σ and the evaluation parameters $\boldsymbol{a} \in \mathbb{F}_{q^m}^{\ell}$ are ıown. Note that the third technique is also applicable to our setting but omitted r brevity. Moreover, the recovery methods extend to GLRS codes by executing em after guessing the block multipliers, similar to the distinguishing strategy plained in Subsect. 4.2.

Theorem 6. *Let $\boldsymbol{G} \in \mathbb{F}_{q^m}^{k \times n}$ denote a generator matrix of an LRS code $\mathcal{C} :=$ LRS$[\boldsymbol{\beta}, \boldsymbol{a}; \boldsymbol{n}, k]$ with respect to a known automorphism σ and zero derivation. If the evaluation parameters $\boldsymbol{a} \in \mathbb{F}_{q^m}^{\ell}$ are known, we can recover code locators $\tilde{\boldsymbol{\beta}} \in \mathbb{F}_{q^m}^{n}$ such that $\mathfrak{M}_k(\tilde{\boldsymbol{\beta}})_{\boldsymbol{a}}$ generates $\mathcal{C}$ in $\mathcal{O}(n^5)$ operations in $\mathbb{F}_{q^m}$.*

Proof. First note that any $\mathbb{F}_{q^m}^*$-multiple $\tilde{\boldsymbol{\beta}}$ of $\boldsymbol{\beta}$ is sufficient because

$$\mathfrak{M}_k(\tilde{\boldsymbol{\beta}})_{\boldsymbol{a}} = \operatorname{diag}\left((c, \sigma(c), \ldots, \sigma^{k-1}(c))\right) \cdot \mathfrak{M}_k(\boldsymbol{\beta})_{\boldsymbol{a}}$$

holds for $\tilde{\boldsymbol{\beta}} := c \cdot \boldsymbol{\beta}$ with $c \in \mathbb{F}_{q^m}^*$. Since the diagonal matrix has full rank, the row spaces of $\mathfrak{M}_k(\tilde{\boldsymbol{\beta}})_{\boldsymbol{a}}$ and $\mathfrak{M}_k(\boldsymbol{\beta})_{\boldsymbol{a}}$ both equal $\mathcal{C}$. We show how to recover such a $\tilde{\boldsymbol{\beta}} \in \mathbb{F}_{q^m}^n$ with the first two of the three approaches mentioned above:

1. From Corollary 2, we obtain the equality $\langle \Gamma_{\boldsymbol{a}}^{n-k-1}(\boldsymbol{G}) \rangle = \mathrm{LRS}[\boldsymbol{\beta}, \boldsymbol{a}; \boldsymbol{n}, n-1]$ and the dual $\mathcal{D}$ of this code has dimension one. The solution $\boldsymbol{H} \in \mathbb{F}_{q^m}^n$ of the system $\Gamma_{\boldsymbol{a}}^{n-k-1}(\boldsymbol{G}) \cdot \boldsymbol{H}^\top = \boldsymbol{0}$ is a generator matrix (or rather a generator vector) of $\mathcal{D}$. Since we are in the zero-derivation case, we can use the result (1) about duals of LRS codes and recover a suitable $\tilde{\boldsymbol{\beta}}$ from $\boldsymbol{H}$ via (2).
2. We first compute the intersection space $\bigcap_{i=0}^{k-1} \langle \mathcal{D}_{\boldsymbol{a}}^i(\boldsymbol{G}) \rangle$ which is equal to $\mathrm{LRS}[\mathcal{D}_{\boldsymbol{a}}^{k-1}(\boldsymbol{\beta}), \boldsymbol{a}; \boldsymbol{n}, 1]$ according to Corollary 3. Therefore, every generator $\boldsymbol{g} \in \mathbb{F}_{q^m}^n$ of this space (and in particular the one that we computed) has the form $c \cdot \mathcal{D}_{\boldsymbol{a}}^{k-1}(\boldsymbol{\beta})$ for a $c \in \mathbb{F}_{q^m}^*$. Note that, in the zero-derivation case, the inverse of the operator $\mathcal{D}_a^i(\cdot)$ for fixed $a \in \mathbb{F}_{q^m}$ and $i \geq 0$ is

$$\left(\mathcal{D}_a^i\right)^{-1}(b) := \sigma^{-i}\left(\frac{b}{\mathcal{N}_i(a)}\right) \quad \text{for all } b \in \mathbb{F}_{q^m}.$$

   We use this fact to derive the following equation from $\boldsymbol{g} = c \cdot \mathcal{D}_{\boldsymbol{a}}^{k-1}(\boldsymbol{\beta})$:

$$\sigma^{-k+1}\left(\left(\frac{\boldsymbol{g}^{(1)}}{\mathcal{N}_{k-1}(a_1)} \mid \cdots \mid \frac{\boldsymbol{g}^{(\ell)}}{\mathcal{N}_{k-1}(a_\ell)}\right)\right) = \sigma^{-k+1}(c) \cdot \boldsymbol{\beta}.$$

   Solving the obtained system of linear equations lets us recover a suitable $\tilde{\boldsymbol{\beta}}$.

The complexity is in both cases dominated by computing the reduced row-echelon form of $\Gamma_{\boldsymbol{a}}^{n-k-1}(\boldsymbol{G})$ and $\Gamma_{\boldsymbol{a}}^{k-1}(\boldsymbol{G})$, respectively. This can be achieved in $\mathcal{O}(n^5)$ operations in $\mathbb{F}_{q^m}$. □

6 Conclusion

We introduced GLRS codes as LRS codes with nonzero block multipliers and proposed two distinguishers for this code family that are inspired by similar techniques in the Hamming and the rank metric. The square-code distinguisher works for the identity automorphism and zero derivation, whereas the Overbeck-like distinguisher can handle arbitrary automorphisms and derivations. Both have polynomial runtime when the automorphism σ, the derivation δ, and in the latter case additionally the evaluation parameters $\boldsymbol{a}$ and the block multipliers $\boldsymbol{v}$ are known.

Since many McEliece-like cryptosystems use isometric disguising, we further studied codes that are semilinearly equivalent to GLRS codes. We showed that GLRS codes are closed under semilinear equivalence for a fixed automorphism and some possible choices for the derivation.

Finally, we partially solved the problem of recovering a canonical generator matrix (and thus finding an efficient decoder) from an arbitrary generator matrix of a GLRS code in the zero-derivation case. The complexity is again polynomial if either $\sigma = \mathrm{Id}$ or σ, $\boldsymbol{v}$ and $\boldsymbol{a}$ are known. More precisely, we showed that the square-code code approach allows to recover suitable evaluation parameters $\boldsymbol{a}$ and block multipliers $\boldsymbol{v}$ of a GLRS code in the identity-automorphism setting, and that an Overbeck-like strategy can recover suitable code locators $\boldsymbol{\beta}$ of a GLRS code for arbitrary automorphisms and zero derivations if $\boldsymbol{a}$ and $\boldsymbol{v}$ are known.

This work is a first step towards building quantum-secure cryptosystems in the sum-rank metric. Naturally, many other research questions arise in this field: As simulations show, the Overbeck-like distinguisher seems not to work when the wrong evaluation parameters are used. This is the case even when the parameters are chosen from the correct conjugacy classes, what makes it interesting to study. Another idea is to find a new operation with respect to which the square-code distinguisher works also for arbitrary automorphisms.

We further want to investigate more distinguishing methods as e.g. augmenting the generator matrix or applying near-isometries and see also how GLRS codes and their distinguishers carry over to the skew metric.

References

1. Alagic, G., et al.: Status report on the third round of the NIST post-quantum cryptography standardization process (2022)
2. Alfarano, G.N., Lobillo, F.J., Neri, A., Wachter-Zeh, A.: Sum-rank product codes and bounds on the minimum distance. Finite Fields Appl. **80**, 102013 (2022)
3. Barra, A., Gluesing-Luerssen, H.: MacWilliams extension theorems and the local-global property for codes over Frobenius rings. J. Pure Appl. Algebra **219**(4), 703–728 (2015)
4. Berger, T.P., Loidreau, P.: How to mask the structure of codes for a cryptographic use. Des. Codes Crypt. **35**(1), 63–79 (2005). https://doi.org/10.1007/s10623-003-6151-2
5. Caruso, X.: Residues of skew rational functions and linearized Goppa codes. arXiv preprint arXiv:1908.08430v1 (2019)
6. Caruso, X., Durand, A.: Duals of linearized Reed-Solomon codes. Des. Codes Crypt. **91**, 241–271 (2022). https://doi.org/10.1007/s10623-022-01102-7
7. Castryck, W., Decru, T.: An efficient key recovery attack on SIDH (preliminary version). Cryptology ePrint Archive ia.cr/2022/975 (2022)
8. Gabidulin, E.M., Paramonov, A.V., Tretjakov, O.V.: Ideals over a non-commutative ring and their application in cryptology. In: Davies, D.W. (ed.) EUROCRYPT 1991. LNCS, vol. 547, pp. 482–489. Springer, Heidelberg (1991). https://doi.org/10.1007/3-540-46416-6_41

9. Gabidulin, E.M.: Attacks and counter-attacks on the GPT public key cryptosystem. Des. Codes Crypt. **48**(2), 171–177 (2008). https://doi.org/10.1007/s10623-007-9160-8
10. Horlemann-Trautmann, A.L., Marshall, K., Rosenthal, J.: Considerations for rank-based cryptosystems. In: 2016 IEEE International Symposium on Information Theory, pp. 2544–2548 (2016)
11. Horlemann-Trautmann, A.L., Marshall, K., Rosenthal, J.: Extension of Overbeck's attack for Gabidulin-based cryptosystems. Des. Codes Crypt. **86**(2), 319–340 (2018). https://doi.org/10.1007/s10623-017-0343-7
12. Lam, T.Y., Leroy, A.: Vandermonde and Wronskian matrices over division rings. J. Algebra **119**(2), 308–336 (1988)
13. Lu, H.f., Kumar, P.V.: A unified construction of space-time codes with optimal rate-diversity tradeoff. IEEE Trans. Inf. Theor. **51**(5), 1709–1730 (2005)
14. Martínez-Peñas, U.: Skew and linearized Reed-Solomon codes and maximum sum rank distance codes over any division ring. J. Algebra **504**, 587–612 (2018)
15. Martínez-Peñas, U.: Hamming and simplex codes for the sum-rank metric. Des. Codes Crypt. **88**(8), 1521–1539 (2020). https://doi.org/10.1007/s10623-020-00772-5
16. Martínez-Peñas, U., Kschischang, F.R.: Reliable and secure multishot network coding using linearized Reed-Solomon codes. IEEE Trans. Inf. Theor. **65**(8), 4785–4803 (2019)
17. McEliece, R.J.: A public-key cryptosystem based on algebraic coding theory. The Deep Space Network Progress Report, vol. 42–44, pp. 114–116 (1978)
18. Neri, A.: Twisted linearized Reed-Solomon codes: a skew polynomial framework. J. Algebra **609**, 792–839 (2022)
19. Overbeck, R.: Structural attacks for public key cryptosystems based on Gabidulin codes. J. Cryptol. **21**(2), 280–301 (2007). https://doi.org/10.1007/s00145-007-9003-9
20. Overbeck, R.: A new structural attack for GPT and variants. In: Dawson, E., Vaudenay, S. (eds.) Mycrypt 2005. LNCS, vol. 3715, pp. 50–63. Springer, Heidelberg (2005). https://doi.org/10.1007/11554868_5
21. Overbeck, R.: Public key cryptography based on coding theory. Ph.D. thesis, Technical University of Darmstadt (2007)
22. Puchinger, S., Renner, J., Rosenkilde, J.: Generic decoding in the sum-rank metric. In: 2020 IEEE International Symposium on Information Theory, pp. 54–59 (2020)
23. Rashwan, H., Gabidulin, E.M., Honary, B.: A smart approach for GPT cryptosystem based on rank codes. In: 2010 IEEE International Symposium on Information Theory, pp. 2463–2467 (2010)
24. Schmidt, G., Sidorenko, V., Bossert, M.: Decoding Reed-Solomon codes beyond half the minimum distance using shift-register synthesis. In: 2006 IEEE International Symposium on Information Theory, pp. 459–463 (2006)
25. Sidelnikov, V.M., Shestakov, S.O.: On insecurity of cryptosystems based on generalized Reed-Solomon codes. Discrete Math. Appl. **2**(4), 439–444 (1992)
26. Stein, W.A., et al.: Sage mathematics software (version 9.7). The Sage Development Team (2022). http://www.sagemath.org
27. Wieschebrink, C.: An attack on a modified Niederreiter encryption scheme. In: Yung, M., Dodis, Y., Kiayias, A., Malkin, T. (eds.) PKC 2006. LNCS, vol. 3958 pp. 14–26. Springer, Heidelberg (2006). https://doi.org/10.1007/11745853_2
28. Wieschebrink, C.: Cryptanalysis of the Niederreiter public-key scheme based on GRS subcodes. In: International Workshop on Post-quantum Cryptography, pp 61–72 (2010)

Verifying Classic McEliece: Examining the Role of Formal Methods in Post-Quantum Cryptography Standardisation

Martin Brain[3], Carlos Cid[2,4], Rachel Player[1], and Wrenna Robson[1](✉)

[1] Royal Holloway University of London, Egham, UK
Wrenna.Robson.2019@live.rhul.ac.uk
[2] Simula UiB, Bergen, Norway
[3] City, University of London, Northampton Square, London, UK
[4] Okinawa Institute of Science and Technology Graduate University, Okinawa, Japan

Abstract. Developers of computer-aided cryptographic tools are optimistic that formal methods will become a vital part of developing new cryptographic systems. We study the use of such tools to specify and verify the implementation of Classic McEliece, one of the code-based cryptography candidates in the fourth round of the NIST Post-Quantum standardisation Process. From our case study we draw conclusions about the practical applicability of these methods to the development of novel cryptography.

1 Introduction

Computer-aided cryptography [10] is the field of study which "develops and applies formal, machine-checkable approaches to the design, analysis, and implementation of cryptography". This can be categorised into three strands:

- Establishing security guarantees at the design level, using symbolic and computational approaches.
- Verifying that implementations (new or pre-existing) are both efficient and functionally correct, by showing they conform to the design about which security guarantees have been established.
- Establishing security guarantees at the implementation level, such as constant-time execution and secret-data-independent memory accesses, both of which indicate resistance to timing attacks.

Panelists in a recent roundtable [29] on computer-aided cryptography xpressed broad optimism on the future of the field, citing the success of tools ıd projects like HACL* [32], Fiat Cryptography [24], and Cryptoline [26]. One ırticipant expressed the view that, within a few years, "the state of the art program proofs will have advanced enough that verifying primitives will be nsidered mundane and a strong requirement for any new proposed algorithm".

C. Deneuville (Ed.): CBCrypto 2022, LNCS 13839, pp. 21–36, 2023.
ps://doi.org/10.1007/978-3-031-29689-5_2

Despite this optimism, most submissions to the NIST Post-Quantum Cryptography standardisation Process [5] made no documented use of computer-aided cryptography in their development. Indeed, only two submissions—NTRU Prime [15] and Classic McEliece [8]—made mention of any potential use of formal methods in improving their designs. The NTRU Prime supporting documentation stated [15] that the design choices of the scheme enabled easier formal verification of its security properties, and that the authors had begun work on verifying the optimised NTRU Prime implementation against the reference implementation [14]. The Classic McEliece specification suggested a need for formally verified proofs of quantum security, and also mentioned the potential of formal verification of defences against timing attacks. Moreover, there has not been much use of computer-aided formal techniques in the evaluation of any of the schemes proposed for standardisation thus far.

Recently, NIST concluded the third round of their standardisation process. After round three, none of the remaining code-based candidates were selected for standardisation, but all of them were moved forward to the fourth round [1]. The isogeny-based scheme SIKE was also advanced to the fourth round, but has subsequently seen a successful attack on its underlying hard problem [21]. If any fourth-round candidates for KEM are selected for standardisation, they are thus likely to be a code-based, which motivates further scrutiny of these candidates.

The security of the remaining code-based candidates is reasonably well-understood, especially Classic McEliece, which has been long studied. Therefore, other criteria will play an important role in evaluating and distinguishing these schemes. We argue that applying the tools of computer-aided cryptography to study these schemes is vital at this stage. Firstly, the amenability of each scheme to being scrutinised and verified using these tools could be a criterion for their evaluation. Secondly, demonstrating that the design or an implementation of a scheme has been verified gives further confidence in this scheme.

In this work, we focus on applying computer-aided cryptography techniques for developing efficient verified implementations to the Classic McEliece scheme. Our main focus is an application of the SAW/Cryptol toolchain [20,25] to the Classic McEliece reference implementation. We also report on our recent efforts using the interactive theorem prover Lean in the verification of the mathematics underlying aspects of the Classic McEliece design.

1.1 Related Work

Verification of Code-Based Cryptography. To the best of our knowledge, there are only two other works [3,4] whose goal, as in this work, is to create a formal specification of Classic McEliece. The first is a partial specification [4] written in Cryptol, which, as far as we are aware, has not been used for the verification of an implementation. The specification is comparable in size to the one we produced in this work, but is incomplete in different ways. Moreover it does not seem to correspond to a named version of the Classic McEliece implementation, and targets a different parameter set that the one we aimed at Thus, we did not derive our own specification from it.

The second is a specification [3] written in Lean 4, that was made public only after this work was concluded. As with our work, the goal of that work was to investigate the use of Lean 4 for cryptographic specification. The specification [3] compiled to an implementation of the Round 3 version of Classic McEliece which passes the Known Answer Tests, and some of its functions have proven properties.

Considering the formalisation of code-based cryptography more broadly, the HOL Light theorem prover was used in [13] to formally verify an algorithm to calculate the "control-bits" of a permutation. The implementation of this algorithm is a key component of Classic McEliece. We also note that there are formalisations in Coq of linear error-correcting codes [7], but they are not orientated towards cryptography.

Applications of the SAW/Cryptol Toolchain. While our application of the SAW/Cryptol toolchain to Classic McEliece is novel, we draw inspiration from prior work applying this toolchain to other cryptographic schemes. The primary work we build on is a work from Galois and Amazon [19]. The paper takes two highly-optimised, trusted implementations of two current primitives, AES-256-GCM and SHA-384, and describes the process of proof engineering and tool development that led to high-level functional correctness proofs for these primitives. It demonstrates some of the current capabilities and limits of the toolchain; as we will discuss, our own work demonstrates different limits.

Developing Verified Implementations. While our work focuses on verifying an existing implementation, another approach [9,18] is to generate verified code directly from the specification. For example, a framework for building verified cryptographic implementations is provided in [9]; delivering assembly code that is provably functionally correct, protected against side-channels, and as efficient as hand-written assembly. The framework is illustrated in [9] by an application to the ChaCha20-Poly1305 cipher suite.

1.2 Our Contributions Towards Classic McEliece Implementation Verification

In our work, our primary goal is explore to what extent the Classic McEliece reference implementation submitted to the NIST standardisation process can be formally specified and verified using the SAW/Cryptol toolchain. Our secondary goal is to see if it is possible to find improvements on the implementation that make it easier to specify and verify, while not impacting performance or its security properties.

To this end, we offer in this paper:

- Formal specifications and verification proofs for large parts of the Classic McEliece reference implementation as of the Round 3 submission, available at [31].
- A revised implementation for one of the core encryption routines in Classic McEliece which both runs faster and admits a verification proof.

- A set of recommendations for designers and those setting standardisation criteria for engaging with computer-aided cryptography.

As an additional contribution, we also report on recent efforts to apply the interactive theorem prover Lean [27,30] to produce verified proofs of certain mathematical constructions used in the design of Classic McEliece.

Our attack model assumes that an attacker has full access to the implementation source code, and is acting as a man-in-the-middle between a client and server attempting to perform key agreement using this KEM. Bugs in the implementation are relevant only when they cause the implementation to deviate from the theoretical design sufficiently that the IND-CCA2 security guaranteed by the design is violated. Deviations between the specification and implementation that do not cause a weakening of security in practice are less relevant. Our verification target, therefore, was the equivalence of parts of the Classic McEliece implementation with equivalent parts of the design.

2 Our Toolchain and Its Target

The SAW/Cryptol toolchain consists of Cryptol [25], a domain-specific language for specifying cryptographic algorithms, and the Software Access Workbench (SAW) [20], a tool for verifying compiled bytecode against specifications defined using Cryptol. They have both been developed, and are maintained, by Galois Inc. Cryptol is a size-polymorphic and strongly typed functional programming language, and a Cryptol specification of an algorithm can resemble its mathematical specification more closely than an implementation in a general purpose language. The SAW/Cryptol toolchain is suitable for verifying pre-existing code against a specification. Thus, it could be applied to code that is highly trusted and so cannot be changed. The SAW/Cryptol toolchain could also form part of a continuous integration framework, where changes to the underlying program are run against tests that include SAW proof scripts.

The Classic McEliece key-establishment scheme is derived from the code-based public-key cryptosystem introduced in 1978 by McEliece [28]. The public key in the McEliece cryptosystem specifies a random binary Goppa code—a linear binary code with certain useful mathematical properties. The private key contains information necessary to perform efficient decoding from an input that is within a bounded error of a codeword. It is the claim of the designers that Classic McEliece is not "new" in any sense: it aims to be a conservative implementation of an established scheme. Where there are relatively novel elements, such as the storage of permutations in the form of control bits, they are not core to the PKE encryption and decryption operations.

Our target system for verification was the reference implementation for the version of Classic McEliece submitted in Round 3 of the NIST process [8], using the `mceliece348864` parameter set (the smallest parameter set). This reference implementation was created by the Classic McEliece team to be the definitive reference for their scheme's operation. It formed a key part of their submission to the NIST process, and has been available for manual public review since it initial release. Its operation and the rationale for its design have been fairly well-documented in the literature by its creators [16] [22], as have the operation of the optimised implementations released alongside it. Our decision to target the reference implementation was partly based on its status as a "golden reference" for the scheme, and partly because as a reference implementation we hoped to avoid verifying too much low-level optimisation, which can be extremely challenging [19].

We aimed to create a specification for this system in Cryptol, using SAW to create proofs of equivalency between the abstract Cryptol specification and the compiled bytecode of key functions used in the implementation. It should be noted that SAW and Cryptol were not originally designed for specifying and verifying asymmetric cryptography, but rather block ciphers, hash functions, and other forms of symmetric cryptography. As such, Cryptol is not a very expressive language for describing complex algebraic constructions, and specifying a scheme in this way can lead to unusably slow performance. On the other hand, expressing asymmetric ciphers in terms of bitwise operations as might suit Cryptol better could obscure the rich mathematical structures that often underlie them. This issue is not specific to Cryptol and reflects a general pattern in the computer-aided cryptography literature: it is a lot easier to find verifications of symmetric cryptographic schemes and implementations. We therefore expected that the task of applying the SAW/Cryptol toolchain to Classic McEliece to be very challenging, and this is why our primary goal was to test the capability limits of SAW/Cryptol in this task.

We emphasise that our SAW/Cryptol work sits in the 'second strand' of research in computer-aided cryptography (see Sect. 1). It does not cover aspects in the 'first strand' (such as formal verification of the Classic McEliece security proofs) or the 'third strand' (such as verifying that the implementations possess the claimed resistance to constant-time attacks).

3 Verifying Classic McEliece with SAW/Cryptol

We begin with an overview of what was successfully verified and what was not.)iscounting those functions that are part of the RNG or that call the external 1ash function used in Classic McEliece, there are 41 different functions that make 1p the `mceliece348864` reference implementation. Of these, 18 were completely pecified and verified; a further five were partially verified. All verifications were erformed within WSL2 on a Windows 10 PC with 16 GB of RAM and an Intel 5-8400 2.8 Ghz processor. The limit on performance was generally memory: it conceivable that, in a few cases, with a higher-specification machine it would ave been possible for some additional proofs to complete, but this would require ırther testing to verify. This work represents around 5.5 months of person-time.

In general, the lower-level "utility" functions were easily verifiable. The most ıbstantial successes on cryptographically-relevant functions were in verifying e implementation of the finite field operations, both against a mathematically-fined specification and a literal translation of the C source, which we could prove were equivalent under relevant preconditions. The PKE encryption and decryption functions were where we found partial success, with full verification of the key calculation loops. We found little success with the KEM wrapper, which needed functions that Cryptol could not implement efficiently, and so it was impractical to test them.

Of the five functions that we partially verified, these can be split into three categories. Firstly, there were two functions for which it was possible to verify the core loop used in the function but not the function's effect across all loops. Secondly, there were two functions for which we found errors in the original code. These were the two sorting functions, which contain small but vital bugs in their comparators. Our discovery of these issues—which do not impact Classic McEliece directly but are nevertheless real bugs in these functions—demonstrates that verification can find problems that current methods of scrutiny might miss. Finally, there was one function that we found we could rewrite into a form that appears both slightly higher in performance and possible to verify. This function is especially interesting as it demonstrates that it is possible to write implementations that are "more verifiable", and this does not have to come at the cost of performance (in this case, quite the opposite) or, indeed, security.

The above information is summarised in Fig. 1, which shows the call graph of functions in the implementation, with functions and their groupings colour-coded to signify the level of verification achieved. Green denotes that the contents of that box have been fully specified and verified, orange that the contents have been partially verified, red that the contents have been verified and a bug found, purple that a refactored version of the contents has been verified, and blue that the contents have not been specified or verified. A standalone version of this diagram is available at https://github.com/linesthatinterlace/verifying-cmce/blob/main/docs/graph.pdf.

It should also be noted that all functions for which it was possible to symbolically execute them using SAW—which include all verified functions but also some that could not be fully verified—are thus guaranteed to be memory-safe and free of undefined behaviour, simply by virtue of having been executed through SAW's internal model.

3.1 Verification Details

In the following, we highlight certain representative examples to demonstrate the different classes of function we considered. These are chosen in order to illustrate the strengths and weaknesses of the tools we used. Details of the specifications and proof scripts are omitted here but are available in a public repository [6].

Transposition. The function `transpose_64x64` transposes a 64×64 matrix over the binary field $\mathbb{F}_2$, represented as a sequence of 64 64-bit unsigned integers taken as little-endian bitstrings. In the reference implementation, this is 33 lines of-code, with the method of its operation being non-obvious, using masks to avoid any branching. We produced a two-line specification for this. This specification

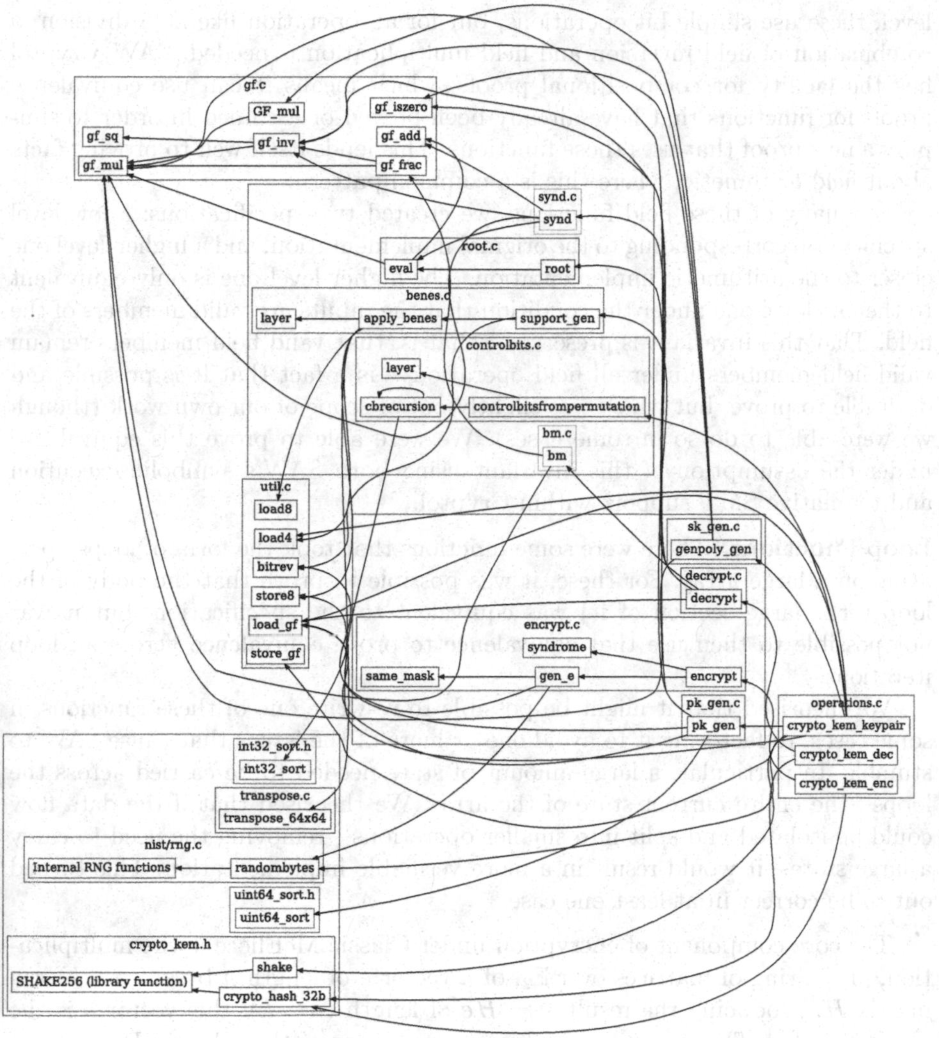

Fig. 1. The call graph of the Classic McEliece implementation with verification status ıighlighted.

xactly captures the mathematical definition of `transpose_64x64`, adjusting ɔr Cryptol's big-endian representation of 64-bit integers. There were multiple ınctions with simple definitions that had complex implementations (often to void branching for constant-time reasons), and these often admitted simple pecifications against which they could be easily verified. The SAW/Cryptol oolchain excels at handling situations like these.

ield Operations. There is a set of low-level functions for performing operaɔns over a finite field of prime order and one of its extensions. At the lowest level, these use simple bit operations, but for an operation like field division, a combination of field inversion and field multiplication is needed. SAW/Cryptol has the facility for compositional proofs, which means it can use equivalence proofs for functions that have already been proved or assumed in order to simplify a new proof that uses those functions. This lends itself well to proving facts about field arithmetic, where this is a common pattern.

For many of these field functions, we created two specifications: a low-level specification corresponding to the original implementation, and a higher-level one closer to the arithmetic implementation. The higher-level one is only equivalent to the low-level one under the condition that the inputs are valid members of the field. That this invariant is preserved—that is, that valid field members remain valid field members under all field operations—is a fact that it is possible and desirable to prove, but which was slightly out of scope of our own work (though we were able to do so in some cases). We were able to prove this equivalence under the assumption of this invariant using both SAW's symbolic execution and the native SMT support within Cryptol.

Loop Functions. There were some functions that took the form of loops operating on a large array. For these, it was possible to prove that the body of the loop (or a large section of it) was equivalent to the specification, but it was not possible to then use that equivalence to prove equivalence across all loop iterations.

We theorised that it might be possible to re-write one of these functions in some cases, re-factoring it to avoid one or more of the issues that cause SAW to stumble. In particular, a large amount of state needed to be carried across the loops—the entire current state of the array. We theorised that if the data flow could be isolated and split into smaller operations—removing the need to carry a large state—it would result in a more verifiable implementation. This turned out to be correct in at least one case.

The core component of encryption under Classic McEliece is the multiplication, in the ring of matrices over $\mathbb{F}_2$, of a vector e of length n by an $(n-k) \times n$ matrix H, producing the result $s := He$ of length $(n-k)$; this vector s is the *syndrome* of e. The values n and k are parameters of the scheme. For a given parameter set, n is the code length and k the code dimension of the underlying permuted Goppa code, the linear code on which Classic McEliece is based. H has the form $(I_{n-k} \mid T)$, where I_{n-k} is the identity matrix of dimension $(n-k)$, and T, the public key, is a $(n-k) \times k$ matrix.

For all parameter sets, n and k divide by 8, and thus so too does $n-k$. The data for e, T, and s are stored in the implementation as byte arrays, treating bytes as little-endian as with `transpose_64x64`. These byte arrays have length $\frac{n}{8}$, $(n-k) \times \frac{k}{8}$, and $\frac{(n-k)}{8}$ respectively.

The implementation version of the function `syndrome` takes the byte array storing T and e and the pointer of the byte array that will store s, reconstructs H, and loops over its $(n-k)$ rows. Each iteration of the loop sets a bit in s performing the appropriate row multiplication of H for the current index with e. This is done using bit-manipulation to avoid branching.

```
void syndrome(unsigned char *s, const unsigned char *pk,
  unsigned char *e)
{ unsigned char b, row[SYS_N/8];
  const unsigned char *pk_ptr = pk;

  int i, j;

  for (i = 0; i < SYND_BYTES; i++)
    s[i] = 0;

  for (i = 0; i < PK_NROWS; i++)
  { for (j = 0; j < SYS_N/8; j++)
      row[j] = 0;

    for (j = 0; j < PK_ROW_BYTES; j++)
      row[ SYS_N/8 - PK_ROW_BYTES + j ] = pk_ptr[j];

    row[i/8] |= 1 << (i%8);

    b = 0;
    for (j = 0; j < SYS_N/8; j++)
      b ^= row[j] & e[j];

    b ^= b >> 4;
    b ^= b >> 2;
    b ^= b >> 1;
    b &= 1;

    s[ i/8 ] |= (b << (i%8));

    pk_ptr += PK_ROW_BYTES; } }
```

Listing 1. Original syndrome implementation.

The issue for verification is that this means each loop stores the entire state of s. We found that while we could verify that one loop correctly modified s per the specification, the symbolic execution of all of syndrome could not complete when we applied the compositional override. As each loop sets the appropriate bit of s by performing an accumulative OR on the appropriate byte with a suitably shifted weight-1 byte, every iteration was storing more and more accumulative information about the byte array s that SAW had to keep track of in the execution. We suspect that the loop became too large for SAW to support.

However, we were able to rewrite `syndrome` to avoid this issue. The key insight was the following one: each eight rows, a byte in s is completely determined, and thereafter plays no role in what follows. This is easy to see as a human reader, but is not information that SAW can derive. This is possibly because the index of the byte set each loop is calculated each time as $\frac{i}{8}$, where in our loop function we simply model the row index i as a 16-bit integer. It is possible that SAW, internally, cannot conclude that this implies that as i is incremented by one each time, after eight values of i a byte in s is fixed. Our idea was to implement not only a row-multiplication function, but also a function to take a block of eight rows and perform the corresponding multiplications across all of them, producing the resultant byte.

In addition, we noted that because e is multiplied by the identity matrix, it can be split into $(e_{id}, e_{pk}) := e$, where e_{id} and e_{pk} are stored as byte arrays of length $\frac{n-k}{8}$ and $\frac{k}{8}$ respectively. This means that $s = e_{id} + Te_{pk}$, and so we can focus on performing Te_{pk}, with no need to reconstruct H. We can calculate Te_{pk} a byte at a time, exclusive-or this byte to the corresponding byte of e_{id}, and this gives the corresponding byte of s.

This means that we are performing $\frac{n-k}{8}$ loops rather than $(n-k)$, but at each loop we perform eight row multiplications instead of one, albeit also on a smaller matrix. The crucial part is that then each loop sets a byte of s without reference to the current state of s. This is unlike the original implementation, which modifies s each loop by performing an OR operation on one of its bytes.

Not only does this implementation of `syndrome` actually allow efficient symbolic execution and a verification proof, but our re-implementation appears to result in a modest performance improvement over the original. In testing on random data, we found it ran in an average of 1.4 ms as opposed to an average of 1.5 ms for the original implementation. We should note that this implementation is also used in the scheme's optimised implementation, though not the additionally optimised implementation that uses assembly-level code. In addition, we believe we have maintained the side-channel resistance properties of the original – in testing, there did not appear to be an appreciable difference in performance with different random inputs, and there is no branching or memory accesses indexed with secret data.

In summary, we were able to produce an implementation of `syndrome` that was faster, as secure, and, crucially, more verifiable than the original. This is evidence for the following claim: it is meaningful to consider one implementation being more verifiable than another, and there are properties a function can have that make it inherently easier to find a more verifiable implementation. If it was not the case that the data flow for `syndrome` could be separated as we did here, then the above approach would not have worked. Thus, at the design stage, such "separability" could be considered as a desirable attribute that can make an implementation more verifiable (for some chosen definition of verifiability).

```
unsigned char bytes_bit_dotprod(const unsigned char *u,
  const unsigned char *v, size_t n)
{ unsigned char b;
  int i;
  b = 0;
  for (i = 0; i < n; i++)
    b ^= u[i] & v[i];

  return b_func(b); }

unsigned char bytes_bit_mul_block(const unsigned char *u
  , const unsigned char *v, size_t n)
{ const unsigned char *u_ptr = u;
  unsigned char b;
  int i;
  b = 0;
  for (i = 0; i < 8; i++)
  {
    b += (bytes_bit_dotprod(u_ptr, v, n) << i);
    u_ptr += n;
  }
  return b; }

void syndrome_bytewise(unsigned char *s, const unsigned
  char *pk, unsigned char *e)
{ const unsigned char *pk_ptr = pk;
  const unsigned char *eid = e;
  const unsigned char *epk = e + SYND_BYTES;
  int i;
  for (i = 0; i < SYND_BYTES; i++)
  {
    s[i] = eid[i] ^ bytes_bit_mul_block(pk_ptr, epk,
  PK_ROW_BYTES);
    pk_ptr += 8*PK_ROW_BYTES;
  } }
```

Listing 2. Revised syndrome implementation.

orting Comparator Bugs. We discovered bugs in the sorting functions used y the Classic McEliece implementation, which do not directly affect the implementation but could certainly present an issue in code reuse. The bugs we found ere in macros used by the sorting functions as element comparators. These acros take two variables, and place the minimum value in the first variable nd the maximum one in the second without performing a branch. The first acts two unsigned 64-bit integers, and the second acts on two signed 32-bit integers. In the former case, it simply does not produce the right output for certain inputs. In the latter, signed integer overflow can occur for certain inputs, which leads to implementation-defined and possibly undefined behaviour.

$$\mathsf{uint64\_MINMAX}(a,b) = \min(a,b),\ \max(a,b) \iff \left(\max(a,b) - \min(a,b) < 2^{63}\right) \vee \left((b < a) \wedge \left(a - b = 2^{63}\right)\right)$$

Fig. 2. Conditions for uint64_MINMAX to behave correctly.

The problem in both cases is the most significant bit; the sign bit in the signed case. Using a Cryptol implementation of the unsigned case, and careful, iterative use of its SMT-solving capabilities, we were able to isolate a condition (Fig. 2) for the first macro to work correctly. That is, the first macro only works when the inputs have the same most significant bit.

We did not detect the bug with the second macro Cryptol directly, but instead when verifying the sorting algorithm in SAW. This is because Cryptol's behaviour for integer overflow is always that it wraps, which is also the assumption of the macro. However, SAW's symbolic execution models the C specification itself, in which it is implementation-defined whether signed integers are treated as modular or if they overflow, and an overflow is undefined behaviour. Therefore, SAW detects the possibility of undefined behaviour and terminates the symbolic execution. The condition for avoiding any possibility of overflow is exactly that $b - a$ can be stored in a 32-bit integer, which admits a similar condition to that for the 64-bit case.

By looking at where these functions are used and what is stored in them, it appears that the troublesome bit will only ever be set to 0 in practice, and thus these bugs appear to be of limited, if at all, impact to Classic McEliece. However, another implementor might re-use these sorting functions in another context. Indeed, these functions are derived from a separate library, the `djbsort` library [11], and thus the bugs could have a wider impact. These functions could be fixed by applying input validation to check for the problematic cases.

This sort of subtle issue is one that is very hard to see with casual human review, but was easy to spot once the formal tool drew our attention to it. Thus this example further motivates the use of formal verification tools in the development of cryptographic schemes.

4 Verifying Aspects of Classic McEliece with Lean

In this section, we report on our efforts to apply the interactive theorem prover Lean 3 and its mathlib library [27] to produce verified proofs relating to Classic McEliece. Lean aims to be both a functional programming language, in which it is easy to write correct and maintainable code; and also an interactive theorem prover, similar to Coq [17]. Like Coq and its MathComp library, Lean has its own mathematical components library, mathlib. The mathlib library has enjoyed extensive interest from the pure mathematics community and has been growing and updating at a rapid pace in the last few years. The style in Lean and mathlib is generalised and abstract; in contrast to Coq formalisations, which tend towards a concrete approach [7].

Verification of Control Bit Constructions. In [13], Bernstein uses the HOL Light tool to gives proofs, and formal verifications of those proofs, for the control bit constructions used in Classic McEliece. As a proof of concept, we decided to attempt to re-implement the same proofs in Lean. The proofs we were able to obtain verified more theorems than the verifications in [13]; in addition, unlike HOL Light, it is relatively easy in Lean to talk about permutations of $\{0, 1, ..., n\}$ rather than permutations of $\{0, 1, ...\}$ that fix $\{n, n+1, ..., \}$, or indeed permutations defined on any well-ordered type. As such, unlike the verifications in HOL Light, the theorems we verified were closer to the original mathematical statements, with no translations required.

However, these proofs are not compatabile in the most recent version of Lean and mathlib, because the library itself has advanced since then. While they are available [2], they would require further work to update to the latest version of the library. This illustrates an issue with formal methods in general and ones based on unstable libraries in particular: they create an extra technical debt as they require maintenance. Nevertheless, the relative ease at which our work proceeded made us optimistic to try more experiments in proving aspects of Classic McEliece's design using Lean in future.

Verification of Coding Theory. We also investigated the use of Lean to verify the correctness of the decoding methods used in Classic McEliece. We targeted a recent monograph of Bernstein [12] setting out the necessary theorems of coding theory used in the proof of correctness. In theory, Lean's mathlib contains all the mathematics necessary to prove these theorems. In practice, there were a number of hurdles to overcome, for example in edge cases that need to be formally specified even though they may appear not to matter on paper, and this work is still in progress.

Towards this goal, we have provided to mathlib a refactor of theorems about Lagrange interpolation, and an implementation of the Hamming distance and theorems around it. These theorems are a building block towards verifying Goppa codes and Classic McEliece. Given the recent publishing of a Lean 4 specification of Classic McEliece [3], the possibility (even if a difficult one) of joining this work with proofs about the abstract design of the scheme is an interesting and potentially exciting one. This would be 'first strand' verification—in that it is verifying the mathematical correctness of the design itself—combined with 'second strand' verification—as it would be verifying an implementation against the constraints of a design.

Conclusions and Perspectives

.1 Recommendations

Our work adds to the increasing body of work showing that formal approaches can and should be incorporated into cryptographic design evaluation. In particular, we demonstrate that it is meaningful to talk of the verifiability of a particular implementation, and, by extension, of a particular design. Such verifiability can be treated as evidence in favour of a proposed design or implementation. Advocates for the use of computer-aided cryptography should aim to play a role in the setting of common standards around verifiability.

Designers and implementers of cryptographic schemes can follow two main approaches to incorporate computer-aided cryptography techniques. The first approach is using tools that aim to verify existing code. In this case, we recommend engaging with the limits of the chosen tool before beginning implementation. For instance, with SAW/Cryptol, we found that large loops that carried large amounts of state between each loop iteration were not feasibly verifiable. Other tools will have different limitations. Such tools can be incorporated into the software development cycle, as prior work has demonstrated [19,23]. It is easier to adjust the design of an implementation at an earlier stage in its development, and our experience in this study demonstrates that seemingly-small alterations in a design can make a real difference to verifiability.

The second approach is for implementors to choose a synthesis-first approach [9,18]. Novel cryptography has the advantage that it is necessarily based on "fresh" code, and has the flexibility to support verified code synthesis. Moreover, such implementations can be as efficient as hand-written code, if not more so.

5.2 Future Work Using Similar Approaches

Verification of Classic McEliece. The functions that we could verify or partially verify with SAW/Cryptol constitute the core of the decryption and encryption operations of Classic McEliece. It would be interesting to extend this to the higher-level encapsulation or decapsulation functions. For example, their memory safety could be determined by checking that SAW could symbolically execute them. In addition, some components of the implementation were technically challenging to specify in Cryptol. For instance, whilst we were able to produce a specification for the function that calculates permutation control bits, we were not successful at using it in verification. Prior work has explored formally proving the design of the formulae used for the control bit calculation [13]. Future work should seek to explore this further, perhaps porting these proofs to a language like Project Everest's F* [18] which has the facility for code synthesis.

Verification Using Lean. Lean is a relatively new theorem prover, and as such has seen relatively little attention from the cryptographic community. Lean's strong support for Unicode and the tendency of mathlib towards abstraction and generality means that statements and even proofs in mathlib can look closer to their "pen and paper" equivalents in, say, Coq. This is of interest for forms of cryptography in which the underlying constructions are often abstract and mathematical, even though the instantiations are necessarily concrete. The rapid development of Lean and mathlib means there is an opportunity for cryptographers to "get in at the ground floor" and shape the implementation choices behind key concepts. We see this as an important direction for future work.

References

1. Announcing four candidates to be standardized, plus fourth round candidates: CSRC. https://csrc.nist.gov/News/2022/pqc-candidates-to-be-standardized-and-round-4. NIST Accessed 07 Sept 2022
2. Control Bits Verification. https://github.com/linesthatinterlace/verif-cb. Wrenna Robson Accessed 12 Sept 2022
3. Cryptography in Lean 4. https://github.com/joehendrix/lean-crypto. Joe Hendrix Accessed 7 Sept 2022
4. Cryptol-Specs. https://github.com/GaloisInc/cryptol-specs. Galois Incorporated Accessed 7 Jan 2022
5. Post-quantum cryptography: CSRC. https://csrc.nist.gov/projects/post-quantum-cryptography. NIST Accessed 18 Jan 2022
6. PQC Verification. https://github.com/linesthatinterlace/pqc-verification. Wrenna Robson Accessed 7 Sept 2022
7. Affeldt, R.: A Coq formalization of information theory and linear error correcting codes (2022). https://github.com/affeldt-aist/infotheo
8. Albrecht, M.R., et al.: Classic McEliece: conservative code-based cryptography (2020). https://classic.mceliece.org/nist/mceliece-20201010.pdf
9. Almeida, J.B., et al.: The last mile: high-assurance and high-speed cryptographic implementations. In: 2020 IEEE Symposium on Security and Privacy (SP), pp. 965–982. IEEE (2020)
10. Barbosa, M., et al.: SoK: computer-aided cryptography. In: 2021 IEEE Symposium on Security and Privacy (SP), pp. 777–795. IEEE (2021)
11. Bernstein, D.J.: djbsort (2019). https://sorting.cr.yp.to
12. Bernstein, D.J.: Understanding binary-Goppa decoding (2019). https://cr.yp.to/papers/goppadecoding-20220320.pdf
13. Bernstein, D.J.: Verified fast formulas for control bits for permutation networks (2020). https://ia.cr/2020/1493. Cryptology ePrint Archive, Report 2020/1493
14. Bernstein, D.J.: Fast verified post-quantum software. In: International Cryptographic Module Conference 2021 (2021)
15. Bernstein, D.J., et al.: NTRU Prime: round 3 (2020). https://ntruprime.cr.yp.to/nist/ntruprime-20201007.pdf
16. Bernstein, D.J., Chou, T., Schwabe, P.: McBits: fast constant-time code-based cryptography. In: Bertoni, G., Coron, J.-S. (eds.) CHES 2013. LNCS, vol. 8086, pp. 250–272. Springer, Heidelberg (2013). https://doi.org/10.1007/978-3-642-40349-1_15
17. Bertot, Y., Huet, G., Castéran, P., Paulin-Mohring, C.: Interactive Theorem Proving and Program Development: Coq'Art: The Calculus of Inductive Constructions. Texts in Theoretical Computer Science An EATCS Series. Springer, Berlin (2013)
18. Bhargavan, K., et al.: Everest: towards a verified, drop-in replacement of HTTPS. In: 2nd Summit on Advances in Programming Languages (SNAPL 2017). Schloss Dagstuhl-Leibniz-Zentrum fuer Informatik (2017)
19. Boston, B., et al.: Verified cryptographic code for everybody. In: Silva, A., Leino, K.R.M. (eds.) CAV 2021. LNCS, vol. 12759, pp. 645–668. Springer, Cham (2021). https://doi.org/10.1007/978-3-030-81685-8_31
20. Carter, K., Foltzer, A., Hendrix, J., Huffman, B., Tomb, A.: SAW: the software analysis workbench. In: Proceedings of the 2013 ACM SIGAda Annual Conference on High Integrity Language Technology, pp. 15–18 (2013)

21. Castryck, W., Decru, T.: An efficient key recovery attack on SIDH (preliminary version). Cryptology ePrint Archive, Paper 2022/975 (2022). https://eprint.iacr.org/2022/975
22. Chou, T.: McBits revisited. In: Fischer, W., Homma, N. (eds.) CHES 2017. LNCS, vol. 10529, pp. 213–231. Springer, Cham (2017). https://doi.org/10.1007/978-3-319-66787-4_11
23. Chudnov, A., et al.: Continuous formal verification of amazon s2n. In: Chockler, H., Weissenbacher, G. (eds.) CAV 2018. LNCS, vol. 10982, pp. 430–446. Springer, Cham (2018). https://doi.org/10.1007/978-3-319-96142-2_26
24. Erbsen, A., Philipoom, J., Gross, J., Sloan, R., Chlipala, A.: Simple high-level code for cryptographic arithmetic – with proofs, without compromises. In: 2019 IEEE Symposium on Security and Privacy (SP), pp. 1202–1219. IEEE (2019)
25. Erkök, L., Carlsson, M., Wick, A.: Hardware/software co-verification of cryptographic algorithms using Cryptol. In: 2009 Formal Methods in Computer-Aided Design, pp. 188–191. IEEE (2009)
26. Fu, Y.F., Liu, J., Shi, X., Tsai, M.H., Wang, B.Y., Yang, B.Y.: Signed cryptographic program verification with typed cryptoline. In: Proceedings of the 2019 ACM SIGSAC Conference on Computer and Communications Security, pp. 1591–1606 (2019)
27. The mathlib Community: The Lean mathematical library. In: Proceedings of the 9th ACM SIGPLAN International Conference on Certified Programs and Proofs, CPP 2020, pp. 367–381, New York. Association for Computing Machinery (2020)
28. McEliece, R.J.: A public-key cryptosystem based on algebraic coding theory. DSN Progress Report, 4244:114–116 (1978)
29. Mouha, N., Hailane, A.: The application of formal methods to real-world cryptographic algorithms, protocols, and systems. Computer **54**(01), 29–38 (2021)
30. Moura, L., Ullrich, S.: The Lean 4 theorem prover and programming language. In: Platzer, A., Sutcliffe, G. (eds.) CADE 2021. LNCS (LNAI), vol. 12699, pp. 625–635. Springer, Cham (2021). https://doi.org/10.1007/978-3-030-79876-5_37
31. Robson, W.: Classic McEliece Verification (2022). https://github.com/linesthatinterlace/pqc-verification
32. Zinzindohoué, J.K., Bhargavan, K., Protzenko, J., Beurdouche, B.: HACL*: a verified modern cryptographic library. In: Proceedings of the 2017 ACM SIGSAC Conference on Computer and Communications Security, pp. 1789–1806 (2017)

Key-Recovery Fault Injection Attack on the Classic McEliece KEM

Sabine Pircher[1,2(✉)], Johannes Geier[3], Julian Danner[4], Daniel Mueller-Gritschneder[3], and Antonia Wachter-Zeh[1]

[1] Institute for Coding and Cryptography, Technical University of Munich, München, Germany
{sabine.pircher,antonia.wachter-zeh}@tum.de

[2] HENSOLDT Cyber GmbH, Research and Development, Taufkirchen, Germany

[3] Chair of Electronic Design Automation, Technical University of Munich, München, Germany
{johannes.geier,daniel.mueller}@tum.de

[4] Chair of Symbolic Computation, University of Passau, Passau, Germany
julian.danner@uni-passau.de

Abstract. We present a key-recovery fault injection attack on the Classic McEliece Key Encapsulation Mechanism (KEM). The fault injections target the error-locator polynomial of the Goppa code and the validity checks in the decryption algorithm, making a chosen ciphertext attack possible. Faulty decryption outputs are used to generate a system of polynomial equations in the secret support elements of the Goppa code. After solving the equations, we can determine a suitable Goppa polynomial and form an alternative secret key. To demonstrate the feasibility of the attack on hardware, we simulate the fault injections on virtual prototypes of two RISC-V cores at register-transfer level.

Keywords: Post-Quantum Cryptography · Key Recovery · Fault Attack · Laser Fault Injections · Classic McEliece · Key Encapsulation Mechanism

1 Introduction

Post-Quantum Cryptography (PQC) is an important research topic due to the imminent development of large-scale quantum computers. If capable quantum computers become available, cryptographic systems based on the integer factorization problem and the discrete logarithm problem over finite fields and elliptic curves can be attacked in polynomial time due to the work of Shor [23] in 1997. Therefore, the currently employed public-key cryptographic schemes like RSA and ECC are no longer secure. In 2017, the U.S. National Institute of Standards and Technology (NIST) initiated a competition for post-quantum cryptography to replace their current FIPS 186 and SP 800-56A/B recommendations [6]. PQC includes algorithms that run on classical computers but are resistant against attacks from quantum computers. The hardness of PQC is based on computationally hard problems that are expected to be resistant against attacks

C. Deneuville (Ed.): CBCrypto 2022, LNCS 13839, pp. 37–61, 2023.
ps://doi.org/10.1007/978-3-031-29689-5_3

performed by quantum computers for the next tens or hundreds of years. Currently proposed algorithms rely on, e.g., lattice problems, the syndrome decoding problem of error-correcting codes, the solving of multivariate equations and isogenies between elliptic curves.

The McEliece cryptosystem is a code-based public-key encryption (PKE) scheme that relies on the syndrome decoding problem (SDP) for decoding error-correcting codes [14]. The McEliece cryptosystem was introduced in 1978 [14] and its dual version, the Niederreiter cryptosystem, in 1986 [18]. In general, every PKE can be transformed into a key encapsulation mechanism (KEM) that encapsulates and decapsulates a symmetric secret session key for a key exchange procedure and is IND-CCA2 secure. The Classic McEliece KEM [3] is a code-based cryptosystem among the finalists of the PQC competition based on the Niederreiter PKE. It needs a large public key size compared to lattice-based KEMs, but is free from decryption failures and has a long history of research. With the efforts towards standardization, the security of implementations is an important issue and fault attacks are an interesting field of research. Fault injections are physical attacks on hardware which lead to computation errors that are exploited to extract secret information from the device. To produce such errors one may use highly focused laser beams that achieve good spatial and temporal precision in order to set and reset single and adjacent bits on a chip [22].

Cayrel et al. [4] present a message-recovery fault attack on Classic McEliece by attacking the syndrome computation that changes the syndrome from $\mathbb{F}_2$ to the integers $\mathbb{N}$. The resulting syndrome decoding problem in $\mathbb{N}$ can be easily solved by integer linear programming. In [5] they present a similar message-recovery attack using only side-channel information on power consumption of the chip. This attack also gathers information on the syndrome in $\mathbb{N}$ but is more tolerant to noise. Very recently, Guo et al. [10] published a key-recovery side-channel attack on Classic McEliece KEM. They use chosen ciphertexts and exploit a side-channel leakage in the additive Fast Fourier Transform (FFT) that evaluates the ELP during decoding. Xagawa et al. [27] demonstrate a single-fault injection attack that works for all NIST PQC Round 3 KEM candidates except Classic McEliece. The single-fault injection attacks presented in [27] are executed by skipping instructions on a chip using glitching of the power supply. The skipping circumvents the IND-CCA2 security of the KEM and enables chosen-chiphertext attacks on the vulnerable PKE. In the course of this work, we found useful relations for completing partially known support sets of a Goppa code, as independently reported by [11].

In this paper, we show that we can obtain an alternative secret key of Classic McEliece by adapting and combining the skipping attacks of Xagawa et al. [27] with the fault injection attack on the PKE by Danner and Kreuzer [6]. We additionally investigated our fault attack on two Open Source RISC-V processors.

The structure of the paper is as follows: Sect. 2 reviews the Classic McEliece KEM. In Sect. 3 we define our hardware fault model and give a mathematical description of the key-recovery attack. In Sect. 4 we present our implementation details and simulation results that validate our attack, together with a feasibility study for two RISC-V processors using RTL simulations. We conclude in Sect. 5. All algorithms can be found in the Appendix.

We use the following notation: The finite field of size q is denoted by $\mathbb{F}_q$. Row vectors are denoted by bold lower-case letters (e.g., $\mathbf{e}$) and column vectors by $\mathbf{e}^\top$. Denote $\mathrm{supp}(\mathbf{e}) := \{i \in \{1, \ldots, n\} \mid e_i \neq 0\}$ for $\mathbf{e} \in \mathbb{F}_q^n$, and the Hamming weight of $\mathbf{e}$ by $\mathrm{wt}(\mathbf{e})$. We denote matrices by bold capital letters (e.g., $\mathbf{H}$). We consider the Hamming metric for weight and distance. Let $\mathbb{F}_q[x]$ denote the univariate polynomial ring in x with coefficients in $\mathbb{F}_q$. For a polynomial $f \in \mathbb{F}_q[x]$ we denote its degree by $\deg(f)$, and the ideal generated by f with $\langle f \rangle$.

2 Classic McEliece KEM

The Classic McEliece KEM specified in [3] is designed as a quantum-resistant public-key encapsulation mechanism based on the Niederreiter cryptosystem [18]. The security relies on the syndrome-decoding problem (SDP) which is NP-complete for random linear codes [2]. The core idea of the Niederreiter cryptosystem in the KEM is to choose a binary irreducible Goppa code which allows efficient correction of errors when the algebraic structure is known, while a systematic parity check matrix of the code appears to be random. The algebraic structure is part of the secret key and the legitimate user thereby has access to an efficient decoder. For everyone else, the linear code appears to be a random code. It is believed that not only traditional computers, but also quantum computers require an exponential number of operations to correct errors without knowledge of the underlying algebraic structure.

Classic McEliece is extremely efficient in encoding and decoding at the cost of a large public key. For the CAT-5 proposed parameters the public key size is about 1 MB. This large public key makes its generation and storage more expensive compared to other PQC cryptosystems. We work with the Classic McEliece KEM implementation [3] submitted to NIST Round 3 and explain its key functionalities in the remainder of this section.[1] The current proposed parameter sets for Classic McEliece are listed in Table 4 in the appendix.

Classic McEliece consists of three main functions: key generation, encapsulation and decapsulation. They use the public parameters $n, m, t \in \mathbb{N}$ with $n \leq 2^m$, and a monic irreducible polynomial $f(z) \in \mathbb{F}_2[z]$ of degree m. The latter is used to fix a representation of elements in the field $\mathbb{F}_{2^m} \cong \mathbb{F}_2[z]/\langle f(z) \rangle$ as bit-tuples, i.e., elements in $\mathbb{F}_2^m$. The identification is given by the bijective map $\phi\colon \mathbb{F}_2^m \to \mathbb{F}_2[z]/\langle f(z) \rangle \cong \mathbb{F}_{2^m}$ where $(c_0, \ldots, c_{m-1}) \mapsto c_0 + c_1 z + \cdots + c_{m-1} z^{m-1}$.

Classic McEliece uses the SHA-3 Keccak SHAKE-256 hash function, defined in [17]. We denote it by $\mathcal{H}$, and its output is always 256 bits long, independent of its input length. In particular, we write $\mathcal{H}(2, \mathbf{v})$ and $\mathcal{H}(i, \mathbf{v}, C)$ for the hash of the concatenation of an initial byte valued $i \in \{0, 1\}$ or 2, vector $\mathbf{v} \in \mathbb{F}_2^n$ and ciphertext C, see also [3, Sec. 2.5.2].

[1] In this paper we do not consider the accelerated variant of the key generation in Classic McEliece that also accepts a semi-systematic form of the parity-check matrix. We expect the attack to work also on this variant after minor modification.

2.1 Key Generation

In this paper we understand the secret key[2] as a tuple $(\mathbf{s}, \gamma)$ where $\mathbf{s}$ is a bit-vector in $\mathbb{F}_2^n$ and $\gamma = (g, \alpha) \in \mathbb{F}_{2^m}[x] \times \mathbb{F}_{2^m}^n$ is a generator tuple of the **binary irreducible Goppa code**

$$\Gamma(\alpha, g) = \left\{ (c_1, \ldots, c_n) \in \mathbb{F}_2^n \mid \sum_{i \in \mathrm{supp}(c)} (x - \alpha_i)^{-1} = 0 \text{ in } \mathbb{F}_{2^m}[x]/\langle g \rangle \right\} \subseteq \mathbb{F}_2^n,$$

with $\deg(g) = t$ and $\alpha = (\alpha_1, \ldots, \alpha_n)$.

Then g is a monic irreducible polynomial and called the **Goppa polynomial** of the code, and $\alpha = (\alpha_1, \ldots, \alpha_n) \in \mathbb{F}_{2^m}^n$ satisfies $\alpha_i \neq \alpha_j$ for $i \neq j$ and $g(\alpha_i) \neq 0$ and is called the **support** of the code. Key generation ensures that the linear code $\Gamma(\alpha, g)$ has dimension $k = n - mt$, length n and allows efficient correction of up to t errors. Moreover, one can compute a parity-check matrix in systematic form $\mathbf{H}_{sys} = (\mathbf{I}_{n-k} | \mathbf{T})$, where $\mathbf{I}_{n-k}$ is the identity matrix of size $n - k$. The public key is then given by the matrix $\mathbf{T} \in \mathbb{F}_2^{(n-k) \times k}$. Note that in particular the code $\Gamma(\alpha, g)$ itself is public knowledge since $\mathbf{T}$ is public. However, the algebraic structure, i.e., the Goppa polynomial and the support, are part of the secret key. Algorithm 1 summarizes the construction of the secret and public keys in Classic McEliece.

2.2 Encapsulation

The encapsulation (Algorithm 3) takes a random plaintext and uses the public key to generate a ciphertext from which only the holder of the secret key can extract the random plaintext again. This can be used to establish a common secret session key. In particular, the encapsulation party chooses a vector $\mathbf{e} \in \mathbb{F}_2^n$ of Hamming weight t at random. The ciphertext $C = (\mathbf{c_0}, C_1)$ is generated by encoding the vector $\mathbf{e}$ using the public key such that $\mathbf{c_0} = \mathbf{e}\mathbf{H_{sys}}^\top$ and by calculating the hash $C_1 = \mathcal{H}(2, \mathbf{e})$. The secret session key K is then the hash of $\mathcal{H}(1, \mathbf{e}, C)$. Details can be found in Algorithm 2 and Algorithm 3.

2.3 Decapsulation

The holder of the secret key can compute the same session key using Algorithm 5. This is done by splitting the received ciphertext into the two parts $\mathbf{c_0} \in \mathbb{F}_2^{n-k}$ and the hash C_1, decoding $\mathbf{c_0}$ to a vector $\mathbf{e}' \in \mathbb{F}_2^n$ of weight t using knowledge of the generator tuple (α, g) of the Goppa code. Then the result is checked by calculating $C_1' = \mathcal{H}(2, \mathbf{e}')$ and ensuring that C_1' and C_1 are equal. (If no errors occurred during transmission and the computation is not faulted, this is the case.) Then the output is given by the (reconstructed) session key $K' = \mathcal{H}(1, \mathbf{e}', C)$. In this way both parties conclude with the same session key.

[2] In the actual implementation the secret key does not contain the support α explicitly but instead the seed of the random function that is used to generate it.

In case the input C_1 or C_2 is no valid ciphertext, the decoding step will fail, or the check of $C_1' = C_1$. In this case a predefined output $K' = \mathcal{H}(0, \mathbf{s}, C)$ is returned, where $\mathbf{s} \in \mathbb{F}_2^n$ is part of the secret key (see line 7 in Algorithm 1).

Our fault injections target the decapsulation algorithm in order to gain polynomial equations in the support α of the Goppa code. To decode a syndrome $\mathbf{c_0} = \mathbf{e}\mathbf{H_{sys}}^\top \in \mathbb{F}_2^{n-k}$ Algorithm 4 first forms the word $\mathbf{v} \in \mathbb{F}_2^n$ by appending zeros to $\mathbf{c_0}$. By construction the syndrome of $\mathbf{v}$ w.r.t. $\mathbf{H_{sys}}$ is exactly $\mathbf{c_0}$, i.e., $\mathbf{v}$ and $\mathbf{e}$ are in the same coset. This means that there is a codeword $\mathbf{c} \in \Gamma(\alpha, g)$ such that $\mathbf{v} = \mathbf{c} + \mathbf{e}$. This word is computed in Line 2. Different algorithms have been suggested in literature for this decoding step: the Sugiyama Algorithm [25], the Berlekamp-Massey Algorithm [1,13], and the Patterson Algorithm [21]. All of them explicitly compute the **error-locator polynomial** (ELP) of $\mathbf{e} \in \mathbb{F}_2^n$ defined as

$$\sigma_e(x) = \prod_{i \in \mathrm{supp}(\mathbf{e})} (x - \alpha_i) \in \mathbb{F}_{2^m}[x].$$

The error $\mathbf{e}$ can then be reconstructed directly from the zeros of $\sigma_e(x)$, since we have for all $i \in \{1, \ldots, n\}$: $\mathbf{e}_i = 1$ if and only if $\sigma_e(\alpha_i) = 0$. For more details on Goppa codes we refer the reader to [12, Ch. 12]. Figure 1a depicts the corresponding steps that are executed in the Classic McEliece implementations, which use the Berlekamp-Massey algorithm to find the ELP.

2.4 Implementation

The implementations submitted to NIST [3] contain a reference implementation, as well as several hardware accelerated implementations for x86/AMD64 processors. For our software simulation of the attack, we adapt the hardware accelerated implementation that makes use of vector arithmetics on the processor for faster runtime. To simulate the fault injections on RISC-V cores, we use the reference implementation.

The ELP $\sigma_e(x) \in \mathbb{F}_{2^m}[x]$ is represented differently in the reference and hardware accelerated code. The following remark summarizes how the implementations handle invalid inputs, i.e., syndromes corresponding to errors of smaller weight.

Remark 1 (ELP Implementation Details).

a) For any valid syndrome $\mathbf{c_0} = \mathbf{e}\mathbf{H_{sys}}^\top$ with $\mathrm{wt}(\mathbf{e}) \leq t$, the coefficients of the corresponding ELP $\sigma_e(x)$ are stored in such a way that it is read as the polynomial $\sigma_e(x) \cdot x^{t-\deg(\sigma_e)}$ of degree t.
b) This does not affect error correction as long as no α_i is zero, or $\mathrm{wt}(\mathbf{e}) = \deg(\sigma_e(x)) = t$. But, if there is $i \in \{1, \ldots, n\}$ with $\alpha_i = 0$ and $\mathrm{wt}(\mathbf{e}) < t$, then the output $\mathbf{e}' \in \mathbb{F}_2^n$ of line 2 in Algorithm 4 is indeed changed and we get $\mathrm{supp}(\mathbf{e}') = \mathrm{supp}(\mathbf{e}) \cup \{i\}$.
c) In particular, $\mathbf{e} \neq \mathbf{e}'$ only if there is an $i \in \{1, \ldots, n\}$ with $\alpha_i = 0$ and $\mathbf{e}_i = 0$, and we have $\mathrm{wt}(\mathbf{e}') \leq \mathrm{wt}(\mathbf{e}) + 1$.

Later, this allows us to quickly find the index $i \in \{1, \ldots, n\}$ with $\alpha_i = 0$, if there is such (see Remark 4).

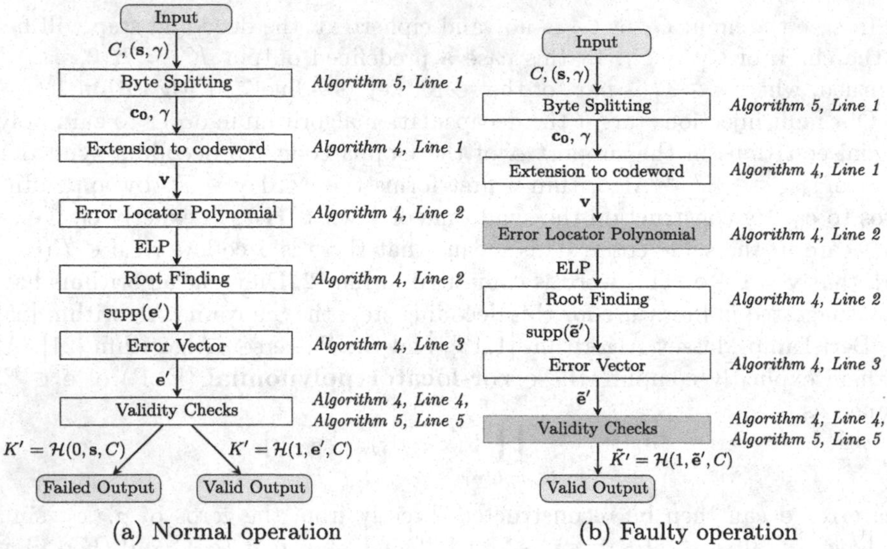

Fig. 1. Flowchart showing the decapsulation and decoding steps indicating the differences between normal and faulty operation. Fault injections target the steps marked in red. (Color figure online)

3 Key-Recovery Attack

This section describes our key-recovery attack. It targets the decapsulation function and can find an alternative secret key. This key can be used in place of the original secret key, i.e., it can be used to find session keys generated with the corresponding public key. Three steps are necessary: First, we inject a fault in the decoding procedure on the ELP coefficients so that it leaks information about the secret key, adapting the work of [6]. Second, we inject a fault to bypass the validity check (VCB) ensuring the faulty decoding result is not rejected. This is done similar to [27]. Third, we demonstrate that under given circumstances the information about the secret key contained in the hashed output can be retrieved. The injections in the decapsulation algorithm necessary for the attack are illustrated in Fig. 1b. We describe two kinds of faults in the ELP coefficients: ELP coefficient bit corruption (ELPB) and ELP coefficient zeroing (ELPZ). Both lead to successful key recovery, with ELPZ being more efficient. ELPZ further has synergy with the validity check bypass (VCB), as both can be achieved by fault injections at the same position on the chip (see Sect. 4.3).

3.1 Fault Model

We consider the setting that the secret key is stored in a Trusted Execution Environment (TEE) so that its memory location is well protected. Only the TEE itself has access to the secret key, i.e., the key cannot be physically accessed or retrieved by any other means.

Assumption 1. *The attacker has access to the input and output of the decapsulation function (Algorithm 5). We can freely choose the input of the decapsulation function (chosen ciphertext attack).*

Assumption 2. *We can inject faults on the physical device during decapsulation changing the transistor states at specific positions and times. To be precise, we assume that single and adjacent bits can be set or reset.*

Such faults are achievable e.g. by a laser fault injection [22].

On the computational level, the following is achieved by fault injections: The validity check in line 4 of Algorithm 4 and line 5 of Algorithm 5 is bypassed (VCB), and the ELP is corrupted either by setting or resetting one or more adjacent bits in a single coefficient (ELPB) or by setting a coefficient to zero (ELPZ).

To simplify the theoretic analysis of fault injections into the ELP, consider the following remark.

Remark 2. We model the faults on a coefficient $a \in \mathbb{F}_{2^m}$ of the ELP as an addition in the field $\mathbb{F}_{2^m}$, i.e., write the faulty coefficient $\tilde{a} \in \mathbb{F}_{2^m}$ as $\tilde{a} = a + \xi$ for some appropriately chosen $\xi \in \mathbb{F}_{2^m}$. Note that for our attack we do not need to know the fault value ξ.

3.2 Fault Attack on the Validity Checks (VCB)

The validity checks confirm whether the decoding function provides a valid output and compares the corresponding hashes. If not, a predefined session key is returned ("Failed Output" in Fig. 1a). After fault injection into the ELP, the faulty output $\tilde{\mathbf{e}}'$ in general does not pass the check $\tilde{\mathbf{e}}'\mathbf{H}_{sys}^{\top} = \mathbf{e}\mathbf{H}_{sys}^{\top}$ and $\mathrm{wt}(\tilde{\mathbf{e}}') = t$ in Algorithm 4 line 4 and the check $\mathcal{H}(2, \mathbf{e}) = \mathcal{H}(2, \tilde{\mathbf{e}}')$ in Algorithm 5 line 5. Therefore, we need an additional fault injection to bypass these checks such that we are able to retrieve the faulty session key $\tilde{K}' = \mathcal{H}(1, \tilde{\mathbf{e}}', C)$, which contains information about $\tilde{\mathbf{e}}'$, see Fig. 1b.

A faulty session key $\tilde{K}' = \mathcal{H}(1, \tilde{\mathbf{e}}', C)$ is a hash of the input ciphertext $C = (\mathbf{c}_0, \mathcal{H}(2, \mathbf{e}))$ and the output $\tilde{\mathbf{e}}' \in \mathbb{F}_2^n$ of the decode algorithm. According to our fault model the attacker has full control over C. It is feasible to extract $\tilde{\mathbf{e}}'$ from $\tilde{K}'$ by exhaustive search if the weight of $\tilde{\mathbf{e}}'$ is small enough.

Remark 3 (De-hash Session Key).

a) If C and hash $\tilde{K}' = \mathcal{H}(1, \tilde{\mathbf{e}}', C)$ are known for some $\tilde{\mathbf{e}}' \in \mathbb{F}_2^n$ with $\mathrm{wt}(\tilde{\mathbf{e}}') \leq 2$, then one can find $\tilde{\mathbf{e}}'$ with less than $\binom{n}{2} + \binom{n}{1} + \binom{n}{0}$ hash computations and comparisons via exhaustive search.
b) The statement in (a) is also true if $\mathrm{wt}(\tilde{\mathbf{e}}') \leq 3$ and one index $i \in \mathrm{supp}(\tilde{\mathbf{e}}')$ is known.
c) For the parameters (Table 4), we have $n \leq 2^{13}$, this means that less than $2^{25} + 2^{12} + 1$ hash computations and comparisons are required to find the output of the decoding algorithm $\tilde{\mathbf{e}}'$ from a faulty session key $\tilde{K}'$, given that $\mathrm{supp}(\tilde{\mathbf{e}}')$ contains at most two unknown indices.

3.3 Fault Attack on the ELP Coefficients

The goal is to inject faults into certain coefficients of the error-locator polynomial (ELP) during the decoding process of chosen words $\mathbf{e} \in \mathbb{F}_2^n$ of Hamming weight 2 such that the evaluation of that polynomial is erroneous. If we have access to the faulty output $\tilde{\mathbf{e}}' \in \mathbb{F}_2^n$ of the decoding step, we can obtain polynomial equations in the secret support α. A set of such equations eventually leads to an alternative support $\tilde{\alpha} \in \mathbb{F}_{2^m}^n$ for which there is an irreducible polynomial $\tilde{g} \in \mathbb{F}_{2^m}[x]$ of degree t with $\Gamma(\alpha, g) = \Gamma(\tilde{\alpha}, \tilde{g})$. This allows efficient correction of up to t errors in the code $\Gamma(\alpha, g)$. Hence, for every $\mathbf{s} \in \mathbb{F}_2^n$ the tuple $(\mathbf{s}, (\tilde{g}, \tilde{\alpha}))$ can be used as an alternative secret key with Algorithm 5.

The fault injections on the ELP are mainly based on the ideas of the fault attack presented in [6], but a handful of adjustments had to be made to accommodate the different fault model and the peculiarities of the implementation. Also the solving process was refined to decrease the number of required fault injections.

Before we discuss how corrupting coefficients of the ELP can lead to polynomial equations in the unknown support $\alpha \in \mathbb{F}_{2^m}^n$ of the Goppa code, we show that one can easily check if zero is one of the support elements and if so, find its index.

Locating Zero in the Support. In the previous section we have seen that we can choose the input of the decoding algorithm as well as read the output, if it is of small weight (Remark 3). So instead of syndromes corresponding to errors $\mathbf{e} \in \mathbb{F}_2$ of weight t, we may select errors of smaller weight, e.g. the all-zero vector. This allows us to decide whether zero is contained in the support, and if it is, find the index $i \in \{1, \ldots, n\}$ for which $\alpha_i = 0$.

Remark 4 (Finding Zero). Let $\mathbf{e} = \mathbf{0} \in \mathbb{F}_2^n$, and consider $\mathbf{c_0} = \mathbf{e}\mathbf{H_{sys}}^\top$ as input for the decoding algorithm. If there is a $j \in \{1, \ldots, n\}$ with $\alpha_j = 0$, then the decoding algorithm evaluates the polynomial x^t and outputs $\mathbf{e}' \in \mathbb{F}_2^n$ where $\mathrm{supp}(\mathbf{e}') = \{j\}$ by Remark 1; otherwise we have $\mathbf{e}' = \mathbf{e} = \mathbf{0}$. Since $\mathrm{wt}(\mathbf{e}') \leq 1$ we can quickly access $\mathbf{e}'$ from the hash output of the decapsulation function, see Remark 3, and from $\mathbf{e}'$ read off whether there is $j \in \{1, \ldots, n\}$ with $\alpha_j = 0$ and in that case deduce this index j.

From now on, we assume that we know $j \in \{1, \ldots, n\}$ with $\alpha_j = 0$, if there is such an index; as this information can be gathered with just a single run of the decapsulation algorithm where the validity checks are skipped.

Corrupting Bits of Coefficients (ELPB). For the fault injections on the ELP that eventually provide the polynomial equations in the support α, we choose syndromes corresponding to vectors $\mathbf{e} \in \mathbb{F}_2^n$ of weight 2 as input to the decoding algorithm. This way the ELP has the form $\sigma_{\mathbf{e}}(x) = (x - \alpha_{i_1})(x - \alpha_{i_2}) \in \mathbb{F}_{2^m}[x]$ for chosen $i_1, i_2 \in \{1, \ldots, n\}$ with $i_1 \neq i_2$. The idea is to set or rese single or adjacent bits in one of the two coefficients such that it is replaced b $\tilde{\sigma}_{\mathbf{e}}(x) = \xi x^d + \sigma_{\mathbf{e}}(x)$ for $d \in \{0, 1\}$ and some (unknown) $\xi \in \mathbb{F}_{2^m}$ (see Remark 2 Recall that the output of the decode algorithm, say $\tilde{\mathbf{e}}' \in \mathbb{F}_2^n$, is constructed nc from the zeros of $\tilde{\sigma}_\mathbf{e}(x)$ but from the zeros of $x^{t-2}\tilde{\sigma}_\mathbf{e}(x)$, see Remark 1. The next remark summarizes the information about the zeros of $\tilde{\sigma}_\mathbf{e}(x)$ that can be obtained from $\tilde{\mathbf{e}}'$.

Remark 5. Let $\mathbf{e} \in \mathbb{F}_2^n$ with $\operatorname{supp}(\mathbf{e}) = \{i_1, i_2\}$ and $i_1 \neq i_2$. Assume that a fault $\xi \in \mathbb{F}_{2^m}$ is injected into the d-th coefficient of $\sigma_\mathbf{e}(x)$ with $d \in \{0, 1\}$. Let $\tilde{\mathbf{e}}' \in \mathbb{F}_2^n$ be the output of the decoding algorithm when the polynomial for the root finding is given by $x^{t-2}\tilde{\sigma}_\mathbf{e}(x)$ where $\tilde{\sigma}_\mathbf{e}(x) = \xi x^d + \sigma_\mathbf{e}(x)$.

(a) If $\alpha_j \neq 0$ for all $j \in \{1, \ldots, n\}$, then we have $\operatorname{wt}(\tilde{\mathbf{e}}') \leq 2$, and

$$\operatorname{supp}(\tilde{\mathbf{e}}') = \{i \in \{1, \ldots, n\} \mid \alpha_i \text{ is a zero of } \tilde{\sigma}_\mathbf{e}(x)\}.$$

(b) If there is $j \in \{1, \ldots, n\}$ with $\alpha_j = 0$, then $\operatorname{wt}(\tilde{\mathbf{e}}') \leq 3$ and $j \in \operatorname{supp}(\tilde{\mathbf{e}}')$ is known. Moreover, we have

$$\operatorname{supp}(\tilde{\mathbf{e}}') = \{i \in \{1, \ldots, n\} \mid \alpha_i \text{ is a zero of } \tilde{\sigma}_\mathbf{e}(x)\} \cup \{j\}.$$

By Remark 4 we can distinguish those two cases, and Remark 3 tells us how we can then gain access to $\tilde{\mathbf{e}}' \in \mathbb{F}_2^n$.

Definition 6. *Let* $d \in \{0, 1\}$, $\mathbf{e} \in \mathbb{F}_2^n$ *with* $\operatorname{supp}(\mathbf{e}) = \{i_1, i_2\} \subseteq \{1, \ldots, n\}$, $i_1 \neq i_2$, *and let* $\tilde{\mathbf{e}}' \in \mathbb{F}_2^n$ *be the output of Algorithm 4 where*

(1) a fault was injected such that the d-th coefficient of $\sigma_\mathbf{e}(x)$ *is corrupted by* $\xi \in \mathbb{F}_{2^m}$, *i.e., the ELP is replaced by* $\tilde{\sigma}_\mathbf{e}(x) = \xi x^d + \sigma_\mathbf{e}(x)$,
(2) the output $\tilde{\mathbf{e}}'$ *is constructed from the roots of* $x^{t-2}\tilde{\sigma}_\mathbf{e}(x)$ *(see Remark 1), and*
(3) a fault injection ensures that the validity checks in line 4 pass.

Then we call the tuple $(\mathbf{e}, \tilde{\mathbf{e}}')$ *a* ***fault injection****. If* $d = 0$ *it is also called a* ***constant injection****, and a* ***linear injection*** *for* $d = 1$*, respectively.*

Our fault model allows to generate arbitrary many such fault injections. Also note that we assume no control over the unknown fault ξ.

Not all fault injections lead to polynomial equations, only those where the faulty ELP has two zeros among the support α. In view of Remark 5, a sufficient condition is given by the following definition.

Definition 7. *A fault injection* $(\mathbf{e}, \tilde{\mathbf{e}}')$ *is called* ***successful****, if*

(1) for all $j \in \{1, \ldots, n\}$ *we have* $\alpha_j \neq 0$ *and* $\operatorname{wt}(\tilde{\mathbf{e}}') = 2$, *or*
(2) there is $j \in \{1, \ldots, n\}$ *with* $\alpha_j = 0$ *and* $\operatorname{wt}(\tilde{\mathbf{e}}') = 3$.

For every successful fault injection the set $\{i \in \{1, \ldots, n\} \mid \alpha_i \text{ is a zero of } \tilde{\sigma}_\mathbf{e}(x)\}$ can be deduced from $\tilde{\mathbf{e}}'$ with Remark 5 and contains exactly two elements.

Next we explain why the term *successful* is adequate.

Proposition 8. *Let* $(\mathbf{e}, \tilde{\mathbf{e}}')$ *be a successful fault injection with* $\operatorname{supp}(\mathbf{e}) = \{i_1, i_2\}$ *and* $\{i \in \{1, \ldots, n\} \mid \alpha_i \text{ is a zero of } \tilde{\sigma}_\mathbf{e}(x)\} = \{j_1, j_2\}$.

(1) If $(\mathbf{e}, \tilde{\mathbf{e}}')$ *is a successful constant injection, then* $\alpha_{i_1} + \alpha_{i_2} = \alpha_{j_1} + \alpha_{j_2}$, *and* α *is a zero of the linear polynomial* $x_{i_1} + x_{i_2} + x_{j_1} + x_{j_2} \in \mathbb{F}_{2^m}[x_1, \ldots, x_n]$.

(b) *If* $(\mathbf{e}, \tilde{\mathbf{e}}')$ *is a successful linear injection, then* $\alpha_{i_1}\alpha_{i_2} = \alpha_{j_1}\alpha_{j_2}$*, and* α *is a zero of the quadratic polynomial* $x_{i_1}x_{i_2} + x_{j_1}x_{j_2} \in \mathbb{F}_{2^m}[x_1, \ldots, x_n]$.

Proof. Denote the ELP by $\sigma_e(x) = (x - \alpha_{i_1})(x - \alpha_{i_2})$ and the faulty ELP by $\tilde{\sigma}_e(x) = \xi x^d + \sigma_e(x)$ for $d \in \{0, 1\}$ and $\xi \in \mathbb{F}_{2^m}$. By Remark 5 and Definition 7, we get that α_{j_1} and α_{j_2} are the roots of $\tilde{\sigma}_e(x)$, i.e., $\tilde{\sigma}_e(x) = (x - \alpha_{j_1})(x - \alpha_{j_2})$. Both statements are now shown by comparing the coefficients in $\xi x^d + \sigma_e(x) = \tilde{\sigma}_e(x)$:

$$\xi x^d + (x - \alpha_{i_1})(x - \alpha_{i_2}) = (x - \alpha_{j_1})(x - \alpha_{j_2}).$$

For (a) we get $x^2 + (\alpha_{i_1} + \alpha_{i_2})x + (\alpha_{i_1}\alpha_{i_2} + \xi) = x^2 + (\alpha_{j_1} + \alpha_{j_2})x + \alpha_{j_1}\alpha_{j_2}$, as $d = 0$. Comparing the linear coefficients yields $\alpha_{i_1} + \alpha_{i_2} = \alpha_{j_1} + \alpha_{j_2}$. For (b) we get $x^2 + (\alpha_{i_1} + \alpha_{i_2} + \xi)x + \alpha_{i_1}\alpha_{i_2} = x^2 + (\alpha_{j_1} + \alpha_{j_2})x + \alpha_{j_1}\alpha_{j_2}$, as $d = 1$. So in particular $\alpha_{i_1}\alpha_{i_2} = \alpha_{j_1}\alpha_{j_2}$ follows from the constant coefficients. □

Remark 9. The probability to have a successful fault injection increases with the ratio $\frac{n}{2^m}$. This follows simply from the fact that the number of support elements increases with n and by that also the number of possible roots for the faulty ELP $\tilde{\sigma}_e(x)$ increases.

Zeroing Coefficients (ELPz). Instead of targeting the General Purpose Register (GPR) holding the ELP coefficients directly, one may also aim at the instructions operating on them. For example, by skipping the instruction storing the ELP coefficient to memory, the resulting coefficient will be equal to zero. This is the case because the algorithm sets the ELP vector to zero before calculating its coefficients. Such fault injections also fit well with Definition 6, where the fault value $\xi \in \mathbb{F}_{2^m}$ has the same value as the targeted coefficient of the ELP such that the coefficient cancels out. Using coefficient-zeroing fault injections can also provide polynomial equations as follows.

Proposition 10. *Let* $(\mathbf{e}, \tilde{\mathbf{e}}')$ *be a fault injection on the* d*-th coefficient of* $\sigma_e(x)$ *s.t. the* d*-coefficient of* $\tilde{\sigma}_e(x)$ *is zero. Write* $\mathrm{supp}(\mathbf{e}) = \{i_1, i_2\}$*, and let* $j \in \mathrm{supp}(\tilde{\mathbf{e}}')$ *with* $\alpha_j \neq 0$.

(a) *If* $(\mathbf{e}, \tilde{\mathbf{e}}')$ *is a constant fault injection, then we have* $\alpha_{i_1} + \alpha_{i_2} = \alpha_j$*, and* α *is a zero of the linear polynomial* $x_{i_1} + x_{i_2} + x_j \in \mathbb{F}_{2^m}[x_1, \ldots, x_n]$.

(b) *If* $(\mathbf{e}, \tilde{\mathbf{e}}')$ *is a linear fault injection, then we have* $\alpha_{i_1}\alpha_{i_2} = \alpha_j^2$*, and* α *is a zero of the quadratic polynomial* $x_{i_1}x_{i_2} + x_j^2 \in \mathbb{F}_{2^m}[x_1, \ldots, x_n]$.

Proof. Note that we have $\sigma_e(x) = (x - \alpha_{i_1})(x - \alpha_{i_2}) = x^2 + (\alpha_{i_1} + \alpha_{i_2})x + \alpha_{i_1}\alpha_{i_2}$.

In the situation of (a) we have $\tilde{\sigma}_e(x) = x^2 + (\alpha_{i_1} + \alpha_{i_2})x$. By Remark 1 the implementation constructs $\tilde{\mathbf{e}}'$ from the zeros of $x^{t-2}\tilde{\sigma}_e(x) = x^{t-1}(x + \alpha_{i_1} + \alpha_{i_2}$ which has only one non-zero root, $\alpha_{i_1} + \alpha_{i_2}$. Now $j \in \mathrm{supp}(\tilde{\mathbf{e}}')$ and $\alpha_j \neq 0$ implies that α_j is exactly this non-zero root. Thus we get $\alpha_j = \alpha_{i_1} + \alpha_{i_2}$. For (b) we have $\tilde{\sigma}_e(x) = x^2 + \alpha_{i_1}\alpha_{i_2}$. Now we know that α_j is non-zero and a zero of $x^{t-2}\tilde{\sigma}_e(x)$ i.e., it is a zero of $\tilde{\sigma}_e(x)$. This gives $\alpha_j^2 = \alpha_{i_1}\alpha_{i_2}$. □

Recall that the attacker knows exactly if there is $j \in \mathrm{supp}(\tilde{\mathbf{e}}')$ with $\alpha_j \neq 0$ by virtue of Remark 4. As such the above proposition can be applied directly.

Remark 11. If the support elements $\alpha_1, \dots, \alpha_n$ and $\mathbf{e} \in \mathbb{F}_2^n$ with $\mathrm{wt}(\mathbf{e}) = 2$ are chosen uniformly at random, then the probability that there exists an α_j with $\alpha_j = \alpha_{i_1} + \alpha_{i_2}$ or $\alpha_j^2 = \alpha_{i_1}\alpha_{i_2}$ for $\mathrm{supp}(\mathbf{e}) = \{i_1, i_2\}$ is $\frac{n}{2^m}$. This means that the *success rate* for obtaining a polynomial equation for a zeroing fault injection (ELPZ) is about $\frac{n}{2^m}$.

This probability is significantly greater than the success rate of the injections that directly target single or adjacent bits of the coefficients (ELPB), especially if $n \ll 2^m$. Our simulations confirm this observation.

The first step of the attack is now straightforward: generate constant and linear fault injections (where each injection requires two fault injections to (1) corrupt/zero a coefficient in the ELP and (2) skip the validity checks) and deduce linear and quadratic equations which have the common zero α.

3.4 Computing Alternative Secret Keys

Using many fault injections, we collect polynomial equations using Proposition 8 and Proposition 10 in a so-called **fault equation system** $L \subseteq \mathbb{F}_{2^m}[x_1, \dots, x_n]$ with the common zero α. Note that all these polynomials are either linear or quadratic. We require both linear and quadratic equations, as shown in Proposition 18. The first goal is to find a **support candidate set** $S_L \subseteq \mathbb{F}_{2^m}^n$ that is a subset of the set of the common zeros of L and contains a **support candidate** $\tilde{\alpha} \in S_L$ for which an irreducible polynomial $\tilde{g}$ of degree t exists with $\Gamma(\alpha, g) = \Gamma(\tilde{\alpha}, \tilde{g})$. To find such a support candidate set we follow the core solving process of the fault attack in [6, Section 6], summarized in the following proposition. Denote the **set of zeros** of $L \subseteq \mathbb{F}_{2^m}[x_1, \dots, x_n]$ by

$$\mathcal{Z}(L) = \{a \in \mathbb{F}_{2^m}^n \mid f(a) = 0 \text{ for all } f \in L\}.$$

Proposition 12 (Solving Fault Equations). *Let $L \subseteq \mathbb{F}_{2^m}[x_1, \dots, x_n]$ be a fault equation system. Consider the following sequence of instructions.*

1) *Reduce the linear polynomials in L (via Gaussian elimination).*
2) *Substitute the leading terms in the quadratic polynomials, call the set of reduced quadratic equations $L_{red} \in \mathbb{F}_{2^m}[x_{i_1}, \dots, x_{i_s}]$.*
3) *Fix one of the remaining indeterminates to 1, i.e., for some $i \in \{i_1, \dots, i_s\}$ add $x_i - 1$ to L_{red}.*
4) *Find the set of zeros $\mathcal{Z}(L_{red}) \subseteq \mathbb{F}_{2^m}^s$ of L_{red} via Gröbner basis techniques.*
5) *Extend the zeros in $\mathcal{Z}(L_{red})$ to elements of $\mathcal{Z}(L \cup \{x_i - 1\}) \subseteq \mathbb{F}_{2^m}^n$ using the linear polynomials, construct and return*

$$S_L = \{\tilde{\alpha} \in \mathcal{Z}(L \cup \{x_i - 1\}) \mid \tilde{\alpha}_{j_1} \neq \tilde{\alpha}_{j_2} \text{ for } j_1 \neq j_2\}.$$

his computes a support candidate set S_L for L.

soon as support candidates have been found, we check one by one, if they n be extended with an irreducible Goppa polynomial $\tilde{g}$ to generate the Goppa code $\Gamma(\alpha, g)$. One approach to do this, based upon [6, Algorithm 6.7], uses the fact that for every $c \in \Gamma(\alpha, g)$ we have

$$g \mid \sum_{i\in \mathrm{supp}(c)} \prod_{k\in \mathrm{supp}(c)\setminus\{i\}} (x - \alpha_k).$$

Proposition 13 (Finding Goppa Polynomials). *Let $\tilde{\alpha} \in \mathbb{F}_{2^m}^n$ with $\tilde{\alpha}_i \neq \tilde{\alpha}_j$ for $i \neq j$. For $s \geq 1$, consider the following sequence of instructions.*

(1) Let $\tilde{g} = 0$. Choose codewords $c_1, \ldots, c_s \in \Gamma(\alpha, g)$, for $j \in \{1, \ldots, s\}$ set $f_j = \sum_{i\in \mathrm{supp}(c)} \prod_{k\in \mathrm{supp}(c)\setminus\{i\}}(x - \alpha_k)$, and compute $h = \gcd(f_1, \ldots, f_s)$.
(2) Factorize h and collect all irreducible factors of degree t in a set G.
(3) For every $\hat{g} \in G$, check if $\Gamma(\tilde{\alpha}, \hat{g}) = \Gamma(\alpha, g)$ by comparing parity check matrices in systematic form. In that case let $\tilde{g} = \hat{g}$.
(4) Return $\tilde{g}$.

This is an algorithm that returns a non-zero $\tilde{g}$ if and only if there exists an irreducible polynomial $g' \in \mathbb{F}_{2^m}[x]$ with $\Gamma(\tilde{\alpha}, g') = \Gamma(\alpha, g)$. In that case we have $\Gamma(\tilde{\alpha}, \tilde{g}) = \Gamma(\alpha, g)$.

Proof. If $\tilde{g}$ is non-zero, by step (3), we have $\Gamma(\tilde{\alpha}, \tilde{g}) = \Gamma(\alpha, g)$. Conversely, if there is an irreducible $g' \in \mathbb{F}_{2^m}[x]$ of degree t with $\Gamma(\tilde{\alpha}, g') = \Gamma(\alpha, g)$, then g' is an irreducible factor of h, i.e., $g' \in G$. This g' is processed in step (3) and ensures $\tilde{g} \neq 0$. This proves the claim. □

With $s = 5$ our simulations showed that, in practice, we always have two cases in step (2): either $\deg(h) = 2t$ and G contains exactly one element, or $h = 1$ and $G = \emptyset$. Our implementation is optimized for this observation.

Improvements. While the above already summarizes the overall solving procedure, we make a few additional remarks and optimizations.

The first observation is that in the first two steps of the Algorithm in Proposition 13 for finding Goppa polynomials only support elements $\tilde{\alpha}_j$ where $j \in \mathrm{supp}(c_i)$ with $i \in \{1, \ldots, s\}$ are used, i.e., to get a Goppa polynomial candidate $\tilde{g}$ not all elements $\tilde{\alpha}_i$ need to be known.

Remark 14 (Support Candidate Completion). Let $\tilde{\alpha} \in \mathbb{F}_{2^m}^n$ be a support candidate with irreducible Goppa polynomial $\tilde{g} \in \mathbb{F}_{2^m}[x]$ where $\Gamma(\alpha, g) = \Gamma(\tilde{\alpha}, \tilde{g})$. Let $J \subseteq \{1, \ldots, n\}$ be a set where $\tilde{\alpha}_j$ is known for $j \in J$.

(a) Let $c \in \Gamma(\alpha, g)$ be a code-word with $\mathrm{supp}(c)\setminus J = \{i\}$ for some $i \in \{1, \ldots, n\}$ Then one can determine $\tilde{\alpha}_i$ as the unique zero of the linear polynomial

$$1 + (x - y) \cdot \sum_{j\in \mathrm{supp}(c)\setminus\{i\}} (x - \tilde{\alpha}_j)^{-1} \in (\mathbb{F}_{2^m}[x]/\langle \tilde{g}(x)\rangle)[y],$$

since $\sum_{j\in \mathrm{supp}(c)} (x - \tilde{\alpha}_j)^{-1} = 0$ in $\mathbb{F}_{2^m}[x]/\langle \tilde{g}\rangle$ by definition of $\Gamma(\tilde{\alpha}, \tilde{g})$.

(b) In order to find (all) codewords $c \in \Gamma(\alpha, g)$ with $\mathrm{supp}(c) \setminus J = \{i\}$ one can compute an affine $\mathbb{F}_2$-basis of the intersection of the (affine) vector subspaces $\Gamma(\alpha, g)$ and $\{c \in \mathbb{F}_2^n \mid c_i = 1, c_j = 0 \text{ for } j \notin J \cup \{i\}\}$ by linear algebra.
(c) This allows us to exclude all indeterminates x_{i_k} that do not occur in L_{red} in step (2) of the solving procedure (Proposition 12) such that $\mathcal{Z}(L_{red})$ decreases in size by a factor of 2^m for every removed indeterminate. Then we find Goppa polynomial candidates $\tilde{g}$ using the first two steps of Proposition 13, where only known support elements are used (find appropriate code-words $c_1, \dots, c_s$ similar to (b)). Using part (a), one can now find the missing support elements and construct support candidates $\tilde{\alpha}$. Finally, one can check if $\Gamma(\alpha, g) = \Gamma(\tilde{\alpha}, \tilde{g})$ as in Proposition 13, step (3).

This optimization only works if codewords as in (b) actually exist. Since many linear equations are required to make the solving of the quadratic polynomials in L_{red} feasible in the first place, only a few elements of the support candidates need to be found in the above way, i.e., the set J is rather large in practice. This also makes the existence of the required codewords highly likely. Recently, [11] followed the same approach, and showed that it suffices to know as little as $mt+1$ support elements to find both - the corresponding Goppa polynomial and the remaining support elements - under mild conditions.

Denote the *Frobenius automorphism* by $\psi\colon \mathbb{F}_{2^m} \to \mathbb{F}_{2^m}, a \mapsto a^2$ and consider the related automorphism $\Psi\colon \mathbb{F}_{2^m}[x_1, \dots, x_n] \to \mathbb{F}_{2^m}[x_1, \dots, x_n]$ where $\Psi(x_i) = x_i$ for $i \in \{1, \dots, n\}$ and $\Psi|_{\mathbb{F}_{2^m}} = \psi$. For $\alpha \in \mathbb{F}_{2^m}$ we also write in the following $\varphi(\alpha) := (\varphi(\alpha_1), \dots, \varphi(\alpha_n))$.

Remark 15. Let $L \subseteq \mathbb{F}_{2^m}[x_1, \dots, x_n]$ be a fault equation system. Then all polynomials in L are homogeneous, their coefficients are contained in $\mathbb{F}_2$, and $\alpha \in \mathcal{Z}(L)$ is a common zero. In particular $\Psi(f) = f$ for all $f \in L$.

(a) For $a \in \mathbb{F}_{2^m}$ we have $a \cdot \alpha \in \mathcal{Z}(L)$, as for all $f \in L$: $f(a \cdot \alpha) = a^{\deg(f)} f(\alpha) = 0$.
b) For $i \in \{0, \dots, m-1\}$ we have $\psi^i(\alpha) \in \mathcal{Z}(L)$, since for all $f \in L$:

$$0 = \psi^i(0) = \psi^i(f(\alpha)) = \Psi^i(f)(\psi^i(\alpha)) = f(\psi^i(\alpha)).$$

his highlights that $\mathcal{Z}(L)$ contains quite many elements derived from α, and in act all these are as useful to us as the support itself. This is a direct consequence f the following remark, proven in [9]. Let Ψ now operate on $\mathbb{F}_{2^m}[x]$.

emark 16. Remember that $\Gamma(\alpha, g)$ is a binary irreducible Goppa code with eg$(g) = t$ as before.

) For every $a \in \mathbb{F}_{2^m} \setminus \{0\}$ we have $\Gamma(\alpha, g(x)) = \Gamma(a \cdot \alpha, g(a^{-1}x))$.
) For every $i \in \{0, \dots, m-1\}$ we have $\Gamma(\alpha, g(x)) = \Gamma(\psi^i(\alpha), \Psi^i(g))$

oreover, $g(a^{-1}x)$ and $\Psi^i(g)$ are both irreducible polynomials of degree t.

all these zeros in $\mathcal{Z}(L)$ only a single one of them is sufficient to construct an ernative secret key, as for all of those $\tilde{\alpha}$ there is an irreducible $\tilde{g}$ of degree t with

$\Gamma(\alpha, g) = \Gamma(\tilde{\alpha}, \tilde{g})$. In the following we discuss how one can decrease the size of the support candidate set S_L while still ensuring that one of these support candidates is present. Note that step (3) of our solving procedure (Proposition 12) already uses part (a) of the above remarks by fixing the coordinate of x_i to 1. This shrinks the support candidate set by a factor of 2^m. The next observation allows us to reduce this set by another factor of almost m.

Remark 17. Let $U \subseteq \mathbb{F}_{2^m}$ such that for every $a \in \mathbb{F}_{2^m}$ there exists $u \in U$ and $i \in \{0, \ldots, m-1\}$ with $a = \psi^i(u)$. By Remark 15.(b) and Remark 16.(b) for every $s \in \{1, \ldots, n\}$ there is $\tilde{\alpha} \in \mathcal{Z}(L)$ with $\tilde{\alpha}_i \neq \tilde{\alpha}_j$ for $i \neq j$ and $\tilde{\alpha}_s \in U$.

Instead of $\mathcal{Z}(L_{red})$ we can thus compute

$$\bigcup_{u \in U} \mathcal{Z}(L_{red} \cup \{x_{i_1} - u\}) = \{\tilde{\alpha} \in \mathcal{Z}(L_{red}) \mid \tilde{\alpha}_{i_1} \in U\}$$

in step (4) of Proposition 12.

To find such a set $U \subseteq \mathbb{F}_{2^m}$ consider the following greedy algorithm: Choose $u \in \mathbb{F}_{2^m}$ and add it to U. Then repeat with $\mathbb{F}_{2^m} \setminus \{u, u^2, \ldots, u^{2^{m-1}} \mid u \in U\}$. For the proposed parameter sets, this gave sets U of size very close to $\frac{2^m}{m}$.

Our implementation computes each individual set of zeros with Gröbner basis techniques, to be precise it uses the SageMath function `variety`.

The following proposition indicates the necessity of the quadratic equations in our solving procedure by showing that it is impossible to find a small set of support candidates only from linear fault equations.

Proposition 18. *Assume that* $n > 2^{m-1}$. *Let* $L \subseteq \mathbb{F}_{2^m}[x_1, \ldots, x_n]$ *be a fault equation system consisting only of linear polynomials. Then* L *contains less than* $n - m$ *linearly independent polynomials.*

Proof. We know from Remark 15 that for all $j \in \{0, ..., m-1\}$ the tuple $z_j = \psi^j(\alpha)$ is a zero of the polynomials in L. We show that $(z_0, ..., z_{m-1})$ is $\mathbb{F}_2$-linear independent in $\mathbb{F}_{2^m}^n$. The rank theorem then shows that L contains less than $n - m$ linearly independent polynomials. Let $b_0, ..., b_{m-1} \in \mathbb{F}_2$ with $b_0 z_0 + ... + b_{m-1} z_{m-1} = 0$. Then we have $b_0 \alpha_i + ... + b_{m-1} \alpha_i^{2^{m-1}} = 0$ for $i \in \{1, \ldots, n\}$. Consider the polynomial $f(x) = b_0 x + b_1 x^2 + ... + b_{m-1} x^{2^{m-1}} \in \mathbb{F}_{2^m}[x]$. Suppose f is non-zero, then it has at most $\deg(f) \leq 2^{m-1}$ roots, but $f(\alpha_i) = 0$ for all $i \in \{1, \ldots, n\}$. With $n > 2^{m-1}$ we get a contradiction. This shows $f = 0$, and thus $b_0 = \cdots = b_{m-1} = 0$ and the linear independence follows by definition. □

Note that the condition $n > 2^{m-1}$ is satisfied by all proposed parameter sets (see Table 4). So for the set of reduced quadratic polynomials $L_{red} \in \mathbb{F}_{2^m}[x_{i_1}, \ldots, x_{i_s}]$ in step (2) of Proposition 12 we have $s \geq m$.

4 Fault Attack Implementation and Simulation

In this section, we demonstrate the viability of the key-recovery attack. We first use a C-implementation to simulate the attack (Sect. 4.1). For this we inject faulty variable values directly in software. We simulate the inputs and corresponding hashed outputs of the faulty decapsulation procedure. The de-hashing of these is described separately in Sect. 4.2, leading to the system of polynomial equations. This is solved to obtain an alternative secret key as described in Sect. 3.4 by a program written in Python3 using SageMath [26].

An attacker cannot directly modify the software execution. Instead, there are different ways to conduct a fault attack, e.g., using a laser to corrupt hardware memory elements in a processor. To investigate whether this allows to inject the specific faults required for the presented attack as were identified at software-level, we execute the cryptosystem as software on a virtual prototype (VP) (Sect. 4.3). The VP implements the RISC-V Instruction Set Architecture (ISA) and allows us to inject faults into the hardware of the processor in order to study how they impact the executing software. For our software-error-model-based fault injection attack, we first analyze the binary to find the program sections calculating the ELP and processing the validity checks. The disassembly and its required alteration gives us the fault positions necessary to produce the identified faulty variable values. The necessary hardware fault attacks are then simulated on two levels; First, a fast ISA-level simulation assures that the hardware faults produce exploitable output. Second, a Register Transfer Level (RTL) simulation yields practicability of the fault attack w.r.t. a real CPU core's micro-architecture.

4.1 Key-Recovery Simulation

We simulated the attack of Sect. 3 in C and SageMath code. To speed up that simulation at C-level we work on AMD64 machines with the vector-accelerated AVX-2 implementation. An overview of the software simulation is given in Algorithm 6.

To model the attack, we adapt the implementation of the cryptosystem to include the effects of the ELPB, ELPZ and VCB faults. For the fault injections on the ELP, we have identified the following lines of code as injection points. The fault injection on the ELP happens between the function calls `bm(locator, s)` and `root(images, locator, L)` in `decrypt.c`. Fault injections on the ELP are modelled as bitwise operations on one of its coefficients. This way, the ELPB fault injection that sets two adjacent bits is implemented by setting one coefficient $a \to a \,\mathrm{OR}\, \zeta$, where ζ is an m-bit array containing only zeros except for two adjacent entries. The ELPZ fault injection is implemented by replacing all entries of one ELP coefficient with zeroes. Note that the fault value ξ corresponding to these injections as defined in Remark 2 is unknown, as it depends on the value a. To skip the validity checks the variable `m` in file `operations.c` and in function `crypto_kem_dec_faulty` in the line `m = ret_decrypt | ret_confirm` are forced to 0. This gives $\mathcal{H}(1, \tilde{\mathbf{e}}', C)$ as output of the C-code for further analysis (see next Sect. 4.2).[3]

[3] For the purposes of verifying the fault attack, the simulator also directly gives $\tilde{\mathbf{e}}'$ as output, sparing us the computational effort of de-hashing $\mathcal{H}(1, \tilde{\mathbf{e}}', C) \to \tilde{\mathbf{e}}'$.

The simulation code is called repeatedly for different chosen ciphertexts and faults ζ to build a system of equations using Propositions 8 and 10, that can be solved with the methods from Sect. 3.4 to obtain an (alternative) secret key. To obtain linear equations in the support elements, faults are injected into the constant term of the ELP. In ELPB mode, we start with ζ having the two least significant bits non-zero. Then we generate faulty session keys from ciphertexts corresponding to plaintext vectors $\mathbf{e}$ with $\mathrm{wt}(\mathbf{e}) = 2$ and $\mathrm{supp}(\mathbf{e}) \in \{\{n-1, 0\}, \{0, 1\}, \{1, 2\}, \dots\}$. This is repeated for faults ζ with non-zero bits in other adjacent positions, until the resulting system of equations contains equations involving all the support elements. In ELPZ mode, there is only one way of injecting a fault, so that instead of different fault values ζ, ciphertexts corresponding to plaintext vectors $\mathbf{e}$ with $\mathrm{wt}(\mathbf{e}) = 2$ with increasing distance between the non-zero support elements $\mathrm{supp}(\mathbf{e}) \in \{\{n-1, 1\}, \{0, 2\}, \{1, 3\}, \dots\}$ are used to obtain a sufficiently large system of equations (this is also done in the ELPB-case if the number of possible ζ is exhausted before finding sufficiently many equations). The same procedure is used to inject faults on the linear term of the ELP in order to obtain quadratic equations in the support elements, finishing after an empirically determined fixed number of equations has been obtained. To confirm that the attack is working, we ran simulations of 100 random public/private key pairs, for several sets of parameters where $n \in \{3488, 6688, 8192\}$ (see Table 4). The average number of required fault injections for a successful attack on the different parameter sets are shown in Tables 1 and 2 for the fault modes ELPB and ELPZ respectively. The ELPZ-mode requires significantly fewer fault injections to complete the attack (compare with Remark 11). Parameter sets with smaller ratio $\frac{n}{2^m}$ also require more injections, as indicated by Remark 9. We find that the SageMath code usually takes only minutes to obtain an alternative secret key from the system of polynomial equations on an office computer.

Table 1. Arithmetic Mean out of 100 simulations for ELPB.

	CAT I $n = 3488$, $m = 12, t = 64$	CAT V $n = 6688$, $m = 13, t = 128$	CAT V $n = 8192$, $m = 13, t = 128$
# of constant injections	31759	70700	56991
# of linear equations	8627	17649	21343
# of linear injections	293	564	266
# of quadratic equations	80	140	100

Table 2. Arithmetic Mean out of 100 simulations for ELPz.

	CAT I $n = 3488$, $m = 12$, $t = 64$	CAT V $n = 6688$, $m = 13$, $t = 128$	CAT V $n = 8192$, $m = 13$, $t = 128$
# of constant injections	8030	16516	8944
# of linear equations	6836	13482	8941
# of linear injections	94	121	100
# of quadratic equations	80	100	100

4.2 De-hashing: Obtaining the Faulty Error Vector from Hash Output

As output of the simulation in Sect. 4.1 we generate two files containing hashes $\tilde{K}' = \mathcal{H}(1, \tilde{\mathbf{e}}', C)$ with $(\mathbf{e}, \tilde{\mathbf{e}}')$ defining linear or quadratic equations in the support elements. Thanks to the small weight of the error vectors $\tilde{\mathbf{e}}'$, we can determine them from the hashes in a brute-force manner as follows.

First, we determine whether the zero element is part of the support set (Remark 1) and determine its index if present, according to Remark 4. This requires only one fault injection, giving the output $\mathcal{H}(1, \mathbf{e}', C)$ for $C = (\mathbf{0}, \mathcal{H}(2, \mathbf{0}))$, with $\text{wt}(\mathbf{e}') \in \{0, 1\}$. The support $\text{supp}(\mathbf{e}')$ specifies the index of the zero element in the support set, if it is present. It is determined from the hash by calculating all $n+1$ possible hashes until the match with the output is found. Next, for every $\tilde{K}'$ we calculate the hashes $\mathcal{H}(1, \mathbf{v}, C)$ for the chosen ciphertext $C = (\mathbf{c_0}, \mathcal{H}(2, \mathbf{e}))$ and all possible $\tilde{\mathbf{e}}'$, as described in Remark 3. When a match is found, $\tilde{\mathbf{e}}'$ has been determined.

We run the de-hashing on a computer with AMD EPYC 7543P processor running up to 3.3 GHz using 32 cores (64 threads) on Arch Linux with kernel 5.19.7. For the ELPB case we have about $\binom{n}{2}$ different $\tilde{\mathbf{e}}'$ to check for every hash output (number of constant injections plus number of linear injections in Table 1). Depending on the cryptosystem and its parameters, the total runtime in our system spans a few hours up to a few days. For the ELPz case we have about $\binom{n}{1} = n$ different $\tilde{\mathbf{e}}'$ to check for every hash output (number of constant injections plus number of linear injections in Table 2). The running time on our system is a few seconds.

.3 Simulation at Register Transfer Level

fault injection simulation campaign and its cost w.r.t. simulation time is pendent on the abstraction level, such that limiting the fault space is crucial. gure 2a shows our approach to identify the fault injection points to further aluate the feasibility of an attack by exhaustive search campaign on RTL. haustive search means applying the fault model (single bit set/reset) to all ssible bits at all possible simulation steps (clock cycles). To gain more detailed results quicker, we align the simulation abstraction level with the fault abstraction level: We start by formulating a software test for *Exploit*, so that we have a defined faulty reference output of the targeted system. This can be directly manipulated to the source code on C-level. We continue on the *ISA Error Model* level where we run the attacked system on the VP with a fast ISA Level Simulation (RISC-V) to transfer the source code faults into ISA specific errors. This is basically assembly level. From there we gain a more narrow timing information as to where faults in the processor core can result in the wanted exploit, e.g., instruction data manipulations or register value modifications. After that, we take this set of narrow program sections and feed it into an RTL fault simulation, a specific micro architecture, to evaluate the *Manifestation*. This gives us the benefit to do an exhaustive search on bit level to reproduce the exploits while focusing on program sections that were earlier identified as critical. Depending on the *Physical Attack* we want to mimic, we can directly transfer the findings from the RTL simulation (Laser Fault analogue) or make predictions (vulnerable micro architecture) that could become an attack scenario for other physical attacks, e.g., clock or voltage glitches.

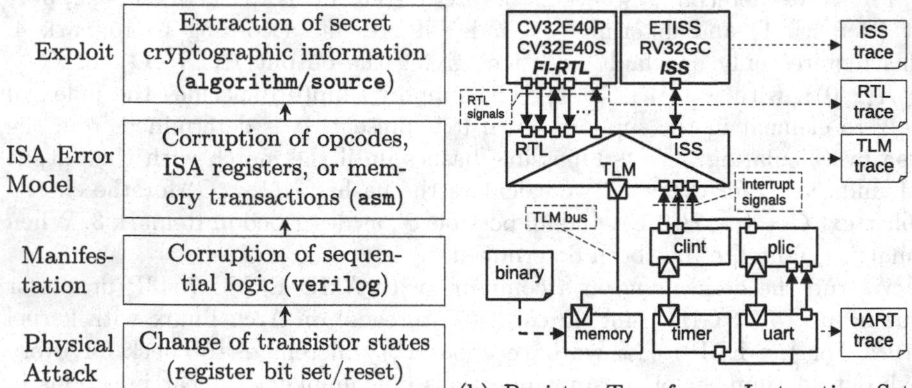

(a) Fault Attack Effect Abstraction (b) Register Transfer or Instruction Set Level Fault Injection Virtual Prototype

Fig. 2. Experimental Setup for ISS/RTL Fault Injection Evaluation.

Figure 2b shows the fault injection VP used to evaluate the vulnerability of two open source RISC-V cores, the OpenHWGroup's CV32E40P [19], formerly known as RI5CY [7,8], and its security focused derivative CV32E40S [20]. The RTL model is generated with the open source Verilog hardware description language to C++/SystemC synthesis tool Verilator [24]. The generated RTL is then modified with a LLVM-based automated source code transformation tool. The modified RTL yields a clock cycle accurate simulation with fault injection capability into sequential storage elements, i.e., flip-flop and latch equivalents. The RTL's SystemC ports are connected to the Transaction Level Modeling (TLM) peripherals and memory through an RTL to TLM transactor that implemen

Table 3. Single-Bit RTL Fault Injection Results.

(a) Validity Check Fault Scenario

core: CV32E40-	P	S
clock cycles[a]	301	301
micro-arch. bits	4,351	12,938
ISA register bits[b]	1,650	3,648
# experiments	1,806,301	4,992,386
exploits output mask reset N_{VCB}	114	57
# unique faulty bits	93	39

[a] identified by ISA simulation
[b] without performance counters

(b) ELP Coefficient Fault Scenario

core: CV32E40-	P	S
clock cycles[a]	521	521
micro-arch. bits	4,351	12,938
ISA register bits[b]	1,650	3,648
# experiments	3,126,521	8,641,306
# experiments coeff. bit corruption N_{ELPB}	69	57
# unique faulty bits	35	29
# experiments coeff. zeroing N_{ELPZ}	508	212
# unique faulty bits	225	94

the required bus protocol. The VP's memory may host any cross-compiled RISC-V binary suitable for the used core and is initialized before simulation start by an binary loader. TLM transactions, certain RTL signals, and the peripheral output are logged in respective trace files. This allows to evaluate the effect an injected fault has on the system's behavior compared to a reference simulation executing the same binary without fault injection. Through the RTL fault injection, we are able to simulate faults on the manifestation level of our fault attack abstraction model as shown in Fig. 2a. We deem a fault attack experiment as successful in a security scenario, if its manifestation results in an undetected exploit defined by the first step of our simulations, see Sect. 4.1.

Table 3a shows the simulation results for the output mask fault attack to ypass the cryptosytem's validity check. For CV32E40P, in total 4,351 micro rchitectural and 1,650 ISA related bits were faulted over a clock cycle period f 301 cycles. The cycle range reflects vulnerable sections of the cryptosystem. 3 unique bits were found to be capable to result in a bypass of the validity heck in 114 experiments. None of which resemble ISA registers, e.g. RISC-V PRs. Although CV3240S contains more sequential logic, thus, injectable bits, he number of successful fault experiments is much lower at 57. Table 3b shows he simulation results for the ELP fault attacks over a clock cycle period of 521 ycles. 69 experiments on 35 unique bits resulted in a faulted ELP coefficient of hich a small number was directly injected into GPRs. For the ELP coefficient roing exploit, 225 unique bits were the reason for a total number of 508 faulty enarios in CV32E40P. Most of these fault injections, all of which in the core's icro architecture, manifested as manipulation of the memory store instructions the respective ELP coefficient. Furthermore, 47 bits and 17 bits, for CV3240P d CV32E40S respectively, are equal for the validity check bypass and the ELP efficient zeroing attack. This can result in a significantly less complex fault ection setup, e.g., by only requiring one laser injection source.

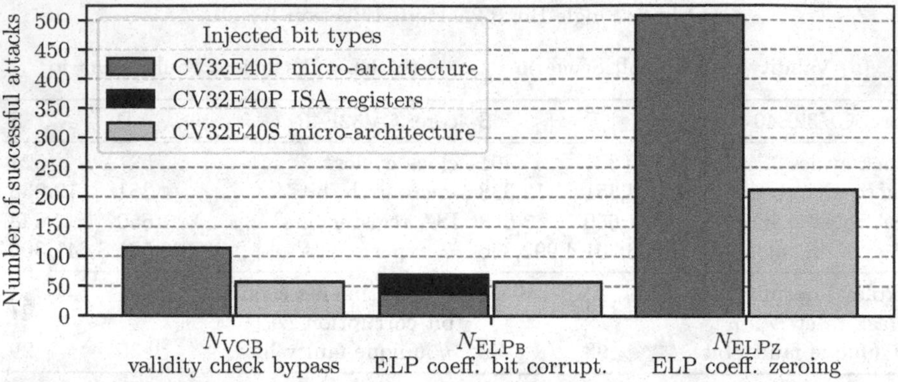

Fig. 3. Single-Bit RTL Fault Injection Results.

Figure 3 shows a plot of the three scenarios for both cores. Overall, the more secure CV32E40S is harder to fault. Reasons for this can be found in its hardware-based countermeasures, such as an ECC protected register file eliminating all bit errors up to two by raising a security alert. The remaining faults can be mostly traced back to in-pipeline faults, e.g., modified instruction code or operands for which no error protection is deployed. Furthermore, in both cores faulting the fetch instruction address can result in replacing the original instruction code without modifying the in-pipeline program counter, thus, bypassing the program counter validity checks of CV32E40S. Here, configuring the Memory Protection Unit (MPU) with executable memory ranges can help to mitigate this easy instruction replacement. For our RTL fault analysis, we did not make use of CV32E40S's side-channel countermeasure that randomly inserts dummy instructions in the executed code, but would consider it as viable countermeasure. Feeding this unit with a true random seed, would make our proposed attack significantly harder. The attack requires delicate timing of the fault injection which would become harder due to the unpredictable execution time.

5 Summary

We have presented a key-recovery fault injection attack on Classic McEliece. Two fault injections are necessary for the attack. CCA2-security is bypassed by one fault injection in combination with brute-force de-hashing of possible faulty session keys. The other fault injection targets the error-locator polynomial (ELP) to find the support set of the Goppa code, which is part of the secret key. We use the faulty output of the decapsulation function to construct a polynomial system of equations whose unknowns are the elements of the support set. Solving these equations, we obtain their values, which can be used with the public key to generate a matching Goppa polynomial. Together, this can be used as an alternative secret key that generates valid session keys. We have verified the attack simulating it using C and SageMath code. Simulations for several instances of Classic McEliece show that parameters with n close to 2^m are particularly easy to attack. We evaluated the vulnerability of two RISC-V cores, simulating the fault injections on virtual prototypes at RTL. On specific hardware and with knowledge of the core structure, the two required faults may be injected at the same location, simplifying the execution of the attack. The next steps are to deploy our attack on real hardware.

The simulation code in C and SageMath can be found online at GitHub: https://www.github.com/sahpir/attackFI-ClassicMcEliece.

Acknowledgements. This research was partly funded by the Bavarian State Ministry for Economic Affairs as part of the funding program *Information and Communication Technology* through the project MITHRIL, grant no. IUK623.

A Appendix

A.1 Classic McEliece KEM Algorithms and Parameters

Here we show the parameters and algorithms used in Classic McEliece KEM [3]. In Algorithm 6 we list the steps executed for the attack simulation.

Table 4. Parameter sets of Classic McEliece KEM [3].

Security Category[a]	n	m	t
CAT 1	3488	12	64
CAT 3	4608	13	96
CAT 5	6688	13	128
CAT 5	6960	13	119
CAT 5	8192	13	128

[a]NIST defines security categories in [15] with the requirement "Any attack that breaks the relevant security definition must require computational resources comparable to or greater than those required for key search on a block cipher with a 128-bit key (e.g. AES128)" with 128/192/256-bit key size corresponding to CAT-1/3/5, respectively.

Algorithm 1. Key Generation

Input: Parameters $m, t, n \leq 2^m$, $f(z) \in \mathbb{F}_2[z]$ irreducible of degree m.
Output: Secret key (s, γ), public key $\mathbf{T}$.

1: Generate a uniform random monic irreducible polynomial $g(x) \in \mathbb{F}_{2^m}[x]$ of degree t.
2: Select a uniform random sequence $L = (\alpha_1, \alpha_2, \ldots, \alpha_n)$ of n distinct elements in $\mathbb{F}_{2^m}$.
3: Compute the $t \times n$ matrix $\mathbf{H} = \{h_{ij}\}$ over $\mathbb{F}_{2^m}$ where $h_{ij} = \alpha_j^{i-1}/g(\alpha_j)$ for $i \in [t], j \in [n]$, i.e.,

$$\mathbf{H} = \begin{pmatrix} \frac{1}{g(\alpha_1)} & \frac{1}{g(\alpha_2)} & \cdots & \frac{1}{g(\alpha_n)} \\ \frac{\alpha_1}{g(\alpha_1)} & \frac{\alpha_2}{g(\alpha_2)} & \cdots & \frac{\alpha_n}{g(\alpha_n)} \\ \vdots & \vdots & \ddots & \vdots \\ \frac{\alpha_1^{t-1}}{g(\alpha_1)} & \frac{\alpha_2^{t-1}}{g(\alpha_2)} & \cdots & \frac{\alpha_n^{t-1}}{g(\alpha_n)} \end{pmatrix}.$$

4: Form matrix $\hat{\mathbf{H}} \in \mathbb{F}_2^{mt \times n}$ by replacing each entry $c_0 + c_1 z + ... + c_{m-1} z^{m-1} \in \mathbb{F}_2[z]/\langle f(z) \rangle \cong \mathbb{F}_{2^m}$ of $\mathbf{H} \in \mathbb{F}_{2^m}^{t \times n}$ with a column of m bits $c_0, c_1, ..., c_{m-1}$.
5: Reduce $\hat{\mathbf{H}}$ to systematic form $(\mathbf{I_{n-k}}|\mathbf{T})$ where $\mathbf{I_{n-k}}$ is an identity matrix of $(n-k) \times (n-k)$ and $k = n - mt$
6: If Step 5 fails, go back to Step 1
7: Generate a uniform random n-bit string s (needed if decapsulation fails).
8: Output secret key: (s, γ) with $\gamma = (g(x), \alpha_1, \alpha_2, ..., \alpha_n)$
9: Output public key: $\mathbf{T} \in \mathbb{F}_2^{(n-k) \times k}$

Algorithm 2. Encoding

Input: Weight-t row vector $\mathbf{e} \in \mathbb{F}_2^n$, public key $\mathbf{T}$
Output: Syndrome $\mathbf{c_0}$

1: Construct $\mathbf{H_{sys}} = (\mathbf{I_{n-k}}|\mathbf{T})$.
2: Compute and output $\mathbf{c_0} = \mathbf{e}\mathbf{H_{sys}}^\top \in \mathbb{F}_2^{n-k}$

Algorithm 3. Encapsulation

Input: Public key $\mathbf{T}$
Output: Session key K, chiphertext C

1: Generate a uniform random vector $\mathbf{e} \in \mathbb{F}_2^n$ of Hamming weight t.
2: Use the encoding subroutine defined in Algorithm 2 on $\mathbf{e}$ and public key $\mathbf{T}$ to compute $\mathbf{c_0}$
3: Compute $C_1 = \mathcal{H}(2, \mathbf{e})$ (input to hash function is a concatenation of 2 and $\mathbf{e}$ as a 1-byte and $\lceil n/8 \rceil$-byte string representation).
4: Put $C = (C_0, C_1)$.
5: Compute $K = \mathcal{H}(1, \mathbf{e}, C)$ (input to hash function is a concatenation of 1, $\mathbf{e}$ and C as a 1-byte, $\lceil n/8 \rceil$-byte and $\lceil mt/8 \rceil + \lceil \ell/8 \rceil$ string representation).

Algorithm 4. Decoding

Input: vector $\mathbf{c_0} \in \mathbb{F}_2^{n-k}$, private key (s, γ)
Output: Weight-t vector $\mathbf{e}' \in \mathbb{F}_2^n$ or Failure

Extend $\mathbf{c_0}$ to $\mathbf{v} = (\mathbf{c_0}, 0, ..., 0) \in \mathbb{F}_2^n$ by appending k zeros.
Find the unique codeword $\mathbf{c}$ in the Goppa code defined by γ that is at distance $\leq t$ from $\mathbf{v}$. If there is no such codeword, return failure.
Set $\mathbf{e}' = \mathbf{v} + \mathbf{c}$.
If $w(\mathbf{e}') = t$ and $\mathbf{c_0} = \mathbf{e}'\mathbf{H_{sys}}^\top$, return $\mathbf{e}'$, otherwise return Failure.

Algorithm 5. Decapsulation

Input: Ciphertext C, Private key $(\mathbf{s}, \gamma)$
Output: Session key K'

Split the ciphertext C as $(\mathbf{c_0}, C_1)$ with $\mathbf{c_0} \in \mathbb{F}_2^{n-k}$ and hash C_1.
Set $b \leftarrow 1$.
Use the decoding subroutine defined in Algorithm 4 on $\mathbf{c_0}$ and private key γ to compute $\mathbf{e}'$. If the subroutine returns Failure, set $\mathbf{e}' \leftarrow \mathbf{s}$ and $b \leftarrow 0$.
Compute $C_1' = \mathcal{H}(2, \mathbf{e}')$ (input to hash function is concatenation of 2 and $\mathbf{e}'$ as a 1-byte and $\lceil n/8 \rceil$-byte string representation).
If $C_1' \neq C_1$, set $\mathbf{e}' \leftarrow \mathbf{s}$ and $b \leftarrow 0$.
Compute $K' = \mathcal{H}(b, \mathbf{e}', C)$ (input to hash function is concatenation of b, $\mathbf{e}'$ and C as a 1-byte, $\lceil n/8 \rceil$-byte and $\lceil mt/8 \rceil + \lceil \ell/8 \rceil$ string representation).
Output session key K'.

Algorithm 6. Attack Simulation on C-level

Specify a ciphertext C as input for the decapsulation function as follows:
  i. Choose a plaintext $\mathbf{e}$ of Hamming weight wt($\mathbf{e}$)$= 2$.
  ii. Calculate the ciphertext $C = (\mathbf{c_0}, C_1) = (\mathbf{eH_{sys}}^\top, \mathcal{H}(2, \mathbf{e}))$
Inject a fault into the error locator polynomial (ELP) as follows:
  i. Fix a fault value of $\zeta \in \mathbb{F}_{2^m}$
  ii. Start the decapsulation process and let the Berlekamp-Massey algorithm calculate the ELP (in file *decrypt.c*).
  iii. Inject a constant or quadratic fault into the ELP (see Definition 6).
Inject a fault and reset the variable called m during decapsulation such that the following comparisons are bypassed (in file *operations.c*)
  a) Skip the comparison $\tilde{\mathbf{e}}'\mathbf{H_{sys}}^\top = \mathbf{eH_{sys}}^\top$ (Alternative: in file *decrypt.c* clear 8-bit variable *ret_decrypt* during decapsulation).
  b) Skip the comparison $C_1' = \mathcal{H}(2, \tilde{\mathbf{e}}') = \mathcal{H}(2, \mathbf{e}) = C_1$ (Alternative: in file *operations.c* clear 8-bit variable *ret_confirm*).
Reconstruct $\tilde{\mathbf{e}}'$ from the output $\tilde{K'} = \mathcal{H}(1, \tilde{\mathbf{e}}', (\mathbf{eH_{sys}}^\top, \mathcal{H}(2, \mathbf{e})))$ of the decapsulation function as described in Section 4.2.
Calculate an alternative secret key as described in Section 3.4.

References

1. Berlekamp, E.R.: Nonbinary BCH decoding (Abstr.). IEEE Trans. Inf. Theory **14**(2), 242–242 (1968). https://doi.org/10.1109/TIT.1968.1054109
2. Berlekamp, E.R., McEliece, R.J., van Tilborg, H.C.A.: On the inherent intractability of certain coding problems. IEEE Trans. Inf. Theory **24**(3), 384–386 (1978). https://doi.org/10.1109/TIT.1978.1055873
3. Bernstein, D.J., et al.: Classic McEliece: NIST submission (2020). https://classic.mceliece.org/nist.html. Accessed 19 Sept 2022
4. Cayrel, P.-L., Colombier, B., Drăgoi, V.-F., Menu, A., Bossuet, L.: Message-recovery laser fault injection attack on the *Classic McEliece* cryptosystem. In: Canteaut, A., Standaert, F.-X. (eds.) EUROCRYPT 2021. LNCS, vol. 12697, pp. 438–467. Springer, Cham (2021). https://doi.org/10.1007/978-3-030-77886-6_15
5. Colombier, B., Dragoi, V.F., Cayrel, P.L., Grosso, V.: Message-recovery profiled side-channel attack on the Classic McEliece cryptosystem. Cryptology ePrint Archive, Paper 2022/125 (2022). https://eprint.iacr.org/2022/125
6. Danner, J., Kreuzer, M.: A fault attack on the Niederreiter cryptosystem using binary irreducible Goppa codes. J. Groups Complex. Cryptol. **12**(1), 2:1–2:20 (2020). https://doi.org/10.46298/jgcc.2020.12.1.6074. https://arxiv.org/abs/2002.01455
7. Davide Schiavone, P., et al.: Slow and steady wins the race? A comparison of ultra-low-power RISC-V cores for Internet-of-Things applications. In: International Symposium on Power and Timing Modeling, Optimization and Simulation (PATMOS), vol. 27, pp. 1–8 (2017). https://doi.org/10.1109/PATMOS.2017.8106976
8. Gautschi, M., et al.: Near-threshold RISC-V core with DSP extensions for scalable IoT endpoint devices. IEEE Trans. Very Large Scale Integr. (VLSI) Syst. **25**(10), 2700–2713 (2017). https://doi.org/10.1109/TVLSI.2017.2654506
9. Gibson, J.K.: Equivalent Goppa codes and trapdoors to McEliece's public key cryptosystem. In: Davies, D.W. (ed.) EUROCRYPT 1991. LNCS, vol. 547, pp. 517–521. Springer, Heidelberg (1991). https://doi.org/10.1007/3-540-46416-6_46
10. Guo, Q., Johansson, A., Johansson, T.: A key-recovery side-channel attack on Classic McEliece. Cryptology ePrint Archive, Paper 2022/514 (2022). https://eprint.iacr.org/2022/514
11. Kirshanova, E., May, A.: Decoding McEliece with a hint - secret Goppa key parts reveal everything. Cryptology ePrint Archive, Paper 2022/525 (2022). https://eprint.iacr.org/2022/525
12. MacWilliams, F., Sloane, N.: The Theory of Error-Correcting Codes, vol. 16, 1st edn. North-Holland (1983). ISBN 978-0-444-85193-2
13. Massey, J.L.: Shift-register synthesis and BCH decoding. IEEE Trans. Inf. Theory **15**(1), 122–127 (1969). https://doi.org/10.1109/TIT.1969.1054260
14. McEliece, R.J.: A public-key cryptosystem based on algebraic coding theory. Deep Space Netw. Progress Rep. **44**, 114–116 (1978)
15. National Institute for Standards and Technology: Submission Requirements and Evaluation Criteria for the Post-Quantum Cryptography Standardization Process (2016). https://csrc.nist.gov/CSRC/media/Projects/Post-Quantum-Cryptography/documents/call-for-proposals-final-dec-2016.pdf. Accessed 19 Sept 2022
16. National Institute for Standards and Technology - Computer Security Division, Information Technology Laboratory: Post-Quantum Cryptography Standardization (2017). https://csrc.nist.gov/Projects/post-quantum-cryptography/post-quantum-cryptography-standardization. Accessed 19 Sept 2022

17. National Institute of Standards: SHA-3 Standard: Permutation-Based Hash and Extendable-Output Functions. Technical report. Federal Information Processing Standard (FIPS) 202, U.S. Department of Commerce (2015). https://doi.org/10.6028/NIST.FIPS.202. https://csrc.nist.gov/publications/detail/fips/202/final
18. Niederreiter, H.: Knapsack-type cryptosystems and algebraic coding theory. Probl. Control Inf. Theory **15**(2), 159–166 (1986)
19. OpenHW Group: CV32E40P - GitHub. https://github.com/openhwgroup/cv32e40p. Accessed 25 Aug 2022
20. OpenHW Group: CV32E40S - GitHub. https://github.com/openhwgroup/cv32e40s. Accessed 25 Aug 2022
21. Patterson, N.: The algebraic decoding of Goppa codes. IEEE Trans. Inf. Theory **21**(2), 203–207 (1975). https://doi.org/10.1109/TIT.1975.1055350
22. Selmke, B., Heyszl, J., Sigl, G.: Attack on a DFA protected AES by simultaneous laser fault injections. In: Workshop on Fault Diagnosis and Tolerance in Cryptography (FDTC), pp. 36–46 (2016). https://doi.org/10.1109/FDTC.2016.16
23. Shor, P.W.: Polynomial-time algorithms for prime factorization and discrete logarithms on a quantum computer. SIAM J. Comput. **26**(5), 1484–1509 (1997). https://doi.org/10.1137/S0097539795293172. https://arxiv.org/abs/quant-ph/9508027
24. Snyder, W.: Verilator. https://www.veripool.org/verilator/. Accessed 25 Aug 2022
25. Sugiyama, Y., Kasahara, M., Hirasawa, S., Namekawa, T.: A method for solving key equation for decoding Goppa codes. Inform. Control **27**(1), 87–99 (1975). https://doi.org/10.1016/S0019-9958(75)90090-X
26. The Sage Developers: SageMath, the Sage Mathematics Software System (Version 9.5) (2022). https://www.sagemath.org
27. Xagawa, K., Ito, A., Ueno, R., Takahashi, J., Homma, N.: Fault-injection attacks against NIST's post-quantum cryptography round 3 KEM candidates. In: Tibouchi, M., Wang, H. (eds.) ASIACRYPT 2021. LNCS, vol. 13091, pp. 33–61. Springer, Cham (2021). https://doi.org/10.1007/978-3-030-92075-3_2

Towards Automating Cryptographic Hardware Implementations: A Case Study of HQC

Carlos Aguilar-Melchor[1], Jean-Christophe Deneuville[2], Arnaud Dion[3], James Howe[1], Romain Malmain[4], Vincent Migliore[5], Mamuri Nawan[6], and Kashif Nawaz[6](✉)

[1] SandboxAQ, Palo Alto, USA
{carlos.aguilar,james.howe}@sandboxaq.com
[2] ENAC, University of Toulouse, Toulouse, France
jean-christophe.deneuville@enac.fr
[3] ISAE-SupAero, University of Toulouse, Toulouse, France
arnaud.dion@isae-supaero.fr
[4] EURECOM, Biot, France
romain.malmain@eurecom.fr
[5] INSA/LAAS-CNRS, University of Toulouse, Toulouse, France
vincent.migliore@laas.fr
[6] Cryptography Research Centre, Technology Innovation Institute, Abu Dhabi, UAE
{mamuri,kashif.nawaz}@tii.ae

Abstract. While hardware implementations allow the production of highly efficient and performance-oriented designs, exploiting features such as parallelization, their longer time to code and implement often bottlenecks rapid prototyping. On the other hand, high-level synthesis (HLS) tools allow for faster experimentation of software code to a hardware platform while demonstrating a reasonable extrapolation of the expected hardware behavior. In this work, we attempt to show a rapid prototyping of the well known HQC algorithm, using HLS, and show how with a modification of certain parameters, varying degrees of comparable results can be obtained. These results, in turn, could be used as a guide for HDL (Hardware Description Language)-RTL (Register-transfer Level) developers to enhance their designs and better prototyping time in the future. Additionally, we also demonstrate that it is possible to benefit from HQC's versatility; by achieving a low hardware footprint whilst also maintaining good performances, even on low-cost FPGA devices, which we demonstrate on the well-known Artix-7 xc7a100t-ftg256-1.

1 Introduction

Quantum-resistant cryptography, more colloquially known as Post-Quantum Cryptography (PQC), has emerged as one of the leading research fields in the broader scope of theoretical and applied cryptography. This research field has appeared due to the likely realization of quantum computers in the next fe

J.-C. Deneuville (Ed.): CBCrypto 2022, LNCS 13839, pp. 62–76, 2023.
https://doi.org/10.1007/978-3-031-29689-5_4

decades, which threaten the current public-key cryptography standards ubiquitously used today. Indeed, with a large fault-tolerant quantum computer, quantum algorithms are able to trivially solve discrete logarithms and factor very large numbers, which has been the cornerstone of our public-key cryptography standards for the last few decades. In 2016, the National Institute of Standards and Technology (NIST) [15] initiated an open call for post-quantum cryptographic algorithms for public evaluation. This standardization process started with having 69 accepted submissions for either a key encapsulation mechanism (KEM) or a digital signature scheme (DSS) to in 2022 where we received the first PQC standards; one KEM selection, CRYSTALS-Kyber, and three DSS selections, CRYSTALS-Dilithium, SPHINCS$^+$, and Falcon [4]. Additionally, four KEM candidates were promoted to a fourth round for further analysis, with the potential of them being standardized in the future. Three of these KEMs are based on code-based cryptography, being seen as a good alternative to CRYSTALS-Kyber, a lattice-based cryptography scheme, and which would add diversity to NIST's PQC suite of standards. These three candidates are BIKE, HQC and Classic McEliece. NIST have stated that at the end of the fourth round they intend to standardize at most one of the two former candidates, and also that they are in no rush to standardize the latter [4].

This standardization process partially motivates the purpose of this research. Since the beginning, NIST has stated their desire for hardware designs of these PQC candidates, and has in the past used these results to compare similar proposals in their decision process. We add to this line of research by proposing hardware designs for the code-based KEM HQC, specifically for HQC-128. We utilize tools and techniques for the rapid prototyping of schemes in hardware, specifically high-level synthesis (HLS), which has proven in the past to significantly increase design time for hardware engineers by converting especially designed software code to hardware languages such as VHDL. This strategy was recently shown successfully by Guerrieri, Da Silva, Regazzoni, and Upegui for PQC candidates based on lattice-based cryptography [11].

1.1 Design Artifacts

The source code for the HLS designs can be downloaded under an open source license at https://pqc-hqc.org/implementation.html.

1.2 Outline of the Paper

The remainder of the paper is structured as follows. Section 2 gives some mathematical preliminaries and a background on the HQC algorithm. Section 3 details the HLS synthesis design and implementation. Section 4 presents our results and compares this HQC design to other, existing designs, both in hardware and software. Section 5 concludes the paper and provides future research directions.

2 Preliminaries and Background

Hamming Quasi-Cyclic (HQC) is a public-key encryption scheme that relies on the hardness of —as its name suggests— decoding random quasi-cyclic codes in Hamming metric. The construction itself shares similarities with Alekhnovich's cryptosystem [5], which uses random linear codes, making it inefficient in practice. HQC was originally proposed in 2016 by Aguilar *et al.* using BCH codes tensored with a repetition code [2,3]. Aragon *et al.* later proposed an improved version using Reed-Muller concatenated with Reed-Solomon codes [6] named HQC-RMRS. The version that is currently considered in the NIST standardization process is an IND-CCA2 KEM variant (see [1, Section 2.3.2]) of HQC-RMRS, obtained by applying the Fujisaki- Okamoto ($FO^{\perp}$) transform to the IND-CPA public-key encryption scheme [12].

This section describes the notations used throughout this paper, and recalls the description of the HQC encryption scheme. For conciseness, we refer the reader:

- to [13] for additional details on Reed-Muller and Reed-Solomon codes;
- to [10] for an introduction to code-based cryptography;
- to [3,6] for full details about HQC (original and RMRS versions), including the security proof and decryption failure analysis; and
- to [12] for full details about the PKE-KEM conversion.

2.1 Notations

Throughout this document, $\mathbb{Z}$ denotes the ring of integers and $\mathbb{F}_2$ the binary field. Additionally, we denote by $\omega(\cdot)$ the Hamming weight of a vector *i.e.* the number of non-zero coordinates, and by $\mathcal{S}_w^n(\mathbb{F}_2)$ the set of words in $\mathbb{F}_2^n$ of weight w. Formally:

$$\mathcal{S}_w^n(\mathbb{F}_2) = \{\boldsymbol{v} \in \mathbb{F}_2^n, \text{ such that } \omega(\boldsymbol{v}) = w\}.$$

$\mathcal{V}$ denotes the vector space $\mathbb{F}_2^n$ of dimension n over $\mathbb{F}_2$ for some positive $n \in \mathbb{Z}$. Elements of $\mathcal{V}$ can be interchangeably considered as row vectors or polynomials in $\mathcal{R} = \mathbb{F}_2[X]/(X^n - 1)$. Vectors/Polynomials (resp. matrices) will be represented by lower-case (resp. upper-case) bold letters. For a vector $\boldsymbol{v}$, v_k denotes its k-th coordinate. For the sake of conciseness, we will say that a prime integer n is primitive if 2 is a primitive n-th root of unity, equivalently if the polynomial $(X^n - 1)/(X - 1)$ is irreducible in $\mathbb{F}_2[X]$.

For $\boldsymbol{u}, \boldsymbol{v} \in \mathcal{V}$, we define their product similarly as in $\mathcal{R}$, *i.e.* $\boldsymbol{uv} = \boldsymbol{w} \in \mathcal{V}$ with

$$w_k = \sum_{i+j \equiv k \mod n} u_i v_j, \text{ for } k \in \{0, 1, \ldots, n-1\}. \quad (1)$$

HQC takes great advantage of matrices with a cyclic structure. Following [3], $\mathbf{rot}(\boldsymbol{v})$ for $\boldsymbol{v} \in \mathcal{V}$ denotes the circulant matrix whose i-th column is the vector corresponding to $\boldsymbol{v}X^i$. This is captured by the following definition.

Definition 1 (Circulant Matrix). *Let* $\boldsymbol{v} = (v_0, \dots, v_{n-1}) \in \mathbb{F}_2^n$. *The* circulant matrix *induced by* $\boldsymbol{v}$ *is defined and denoted as follows:*

$$\mathbf{rot}(\boldsymbol{v}) = \begin{pmatrix} v_0 & v_{n-1} & \cdots & v_1 \\ v_1 & v_0 & \cdots & v_2 \\ \vdots & \vdots & \ddots & \vdots \\ v_{n-1} & v_{n-2} & \cdots & v_0 \end{pmatrix} \in \mathbb{F}_2^{n \times n} \tag{2}$$

As a consequence, it is easy to see that the product of any two elements $\boldsymbol{u}, \boldsymbol{v} \in \mathcal{R}$ can be expressed as a usual vector-matrix (or matrix-vector) product using the $\mathbf{rot}(\cdot)$ operator as

$$\boldsymbol{u} \cdot \boldsymbol{v} = \boldsymbol{u} \times \mathbf{rot}(\boldsymbol{v})^\top = \left(\mathbf{rot}(\boldsymbol{u}) \times \boldsymbol{v}^\top\right)^\top = \boldsymbol{v} \times \mathbf{rot}(\boldsymbol{u})^\top = \boldsymbol{v} \cdot \boldsymbol{u}. \tag{3}$$

Finally, the HQC version considered for standardization in the NIST PQC process has been modified to use Reed-Muller codes concatenated with Reed-Solomon codes, between the 2nd and 3rd rounds.

Definition 2 [Concatenated codes [1, Section 2.5.1]]. *A concatenated code consists of an external code* $[n_e, k_e, d_e]$ *over* $\mathbb{F}_q$ *and an internal code* $[n_i, k_i, d_i]$ *over* $\mathbb{F}_2$, *with* $q = 2^{k_i}$. *We use a bijection between elements of* $\mathbb{F}_q$ *and the words of the internal code, this way we obtain a transformation:*

$$\mathbb{F}_q^{n_e} \to \mathbb{F}_2^N$$

where $N = n_e n_i$. *The external code is thus transformed into a binary code of parameters* $[N = n_e n_i, K = k_e k_i, D \geqslant d_e d_i]$.

2.2 Background on HQC

We now recall the HQC scheme in Fig. 1. In [3], code $\mathcal{C}$ used for decoding is a tensor product of BCH and repetition codes. But since this code is public, its structure has no incidence on security, and one can choose any code family, influencing only the DFR and the parameter sizes.

- $\mathsf{Setup}(1^\lambda)$: generates and outputs the global parameters $\mathsf{param} = (n, k, \delta, w, w_r, w_e)$.
- $\mathsf{KeyGen}(\mathsf{param})$: samples $\boldsymbol{h} \overset{\$}{\leftarrow} \mathcal{R}$, the generator matrix $\boldsymbol{G} \in \mathbb{F}_2^{k \times n}$ of the public code $\mathcal{C}$, $\mathsf{sk} = (\boldsymbol{x}, \boldsymbol{y}) \overset{\$}{\leftarrow} \mathcal{R}^2$ such that $\omega(\boldsymbol{x}) = \omega(\boldsymbol{y}) = w$, sets $\mathsf{pk} = (\boldsymbol{h}, \boldsymbol{s} = \boldsymbol{x} + \boldsymbol{hy})$, and returns $(\mathsf{pk}, \mathsf{sk})$.
- $\mathsf{Encrypt}(\mathsf{pk}, \mathbf{m})$: generates $\boldsymbol{e} \overset{\$}{\leftarrow} \mathcal{R}$, $\boldsymbol{r} = (\boldsymbol{r}_1, \boldsymbol{r}_2) \overset{\$}{\leftarrow} \mathcal{R}^2$ such that $\omega(\boldsymbol{e}) = w_e$ and $\omega(\boldsymbol{r}_1) = \omega(\boldsymbol{r}_2) = w_r$, sets $\boldsymbol{u} = \boldsymbol{r}_1 + \boldsymbol{h} \cdot \boldsymbol{r}_2$ and $\boldsymbol{v} = \boldsymbol{mG} + \boldsymbol{sr}_2 + \boldsymbol{e}$, returns $\boldsymbol{c} = (\boldsymbol{u}, \boldsymbol{v})$.
- $\mathsf{Decrypt}(\mathsf{sk}, \boldsymbol{c})$: returns $\mathcal{C}.\mathsf{Decode}(\boldsymbol{v} - \boldsymbol{uy})$.

Fig. 1. Description of HQC.

Based on this observation, Aragon *et al.* suggested using Reed-Muller concatenated with Reed-Solomon codes to reduce the size of the resulting parameters, yielding HQC-RMRS.

For the external code, HQC-RMRS uses a Reed-Solomon code of dimension 32 over $\mathbb{F}_{256}$ and for the internal code, a Reed-Muller code $[128, 8, 64]$ duplicated 3 or 5 times (*i.e.* duplicating each bit to obtain codes of parameters $[384, 8, 192]$ and $[640, 8, 320]$).

For decoding, a maximum likelihood decoding algorithm is first performed onto the internal code, yielding a (noisy) vector in $\mathbb{F}_q^{n_e}$, that is hence decoded using an algebraic decoder for the external Reed-Solomon code.

All technical details regarding the encoding and decoding of Reed-Muller and (shortened) Reed-Solomon are provided in the NIST submission package of HQC [1, Sections 2.5.2 to 2.5.7].

3 HLS Design Implementation of the HQC

In this section, we detail the High-level synthesis (HLS) and the Software (SW) implementations that we optimize. We describe this synthesis and optimizations for HQC with parameters that target NIST Level 1 security, that is 128 bits of security, i.e., HQC-128.

3.1 HLS Implementation: Basics

Traditional RTL development, using an HDL-based language, most commonly Verilog or VHDL dates back a few decades providing a robust and concrete methodology in which almost all (if not all) digital designs are conceived, written (in code) and implemented. Clearly, these languages have been resilient and have resisted much change (compared to their more dynamic counterparts in the corresponding software world) and are the *de-facto* jargon of all digital designers and engineers alike. The final implementation of code developed using these languages finds implementations in devices like FPGAs and ASICs, for prototyping or production. The design cycle from concept to the final bitstream (in case of the FPGA) or the GDSII (in case of ASIC) often involves considerable time and design effort[1] and hence, correspondingly a higher time-to-market. Additionally, if there are changes required to be made on the design, post-routing and post-implementation, it involves considerable debugging in case of FPGAs to understand the nuances of the proprietary synthesizer engines, whereas in the case of ASICs, if these are detected post-fabrication, it involves a complete reversal to the RTL design phase.

Although digital designers have ways to circumvent and prevent such catastrophic failures, software engineers, or hardware-software co-designers/system architects, cannot simply afford the time to port their software code to RT

[1] We note here that compared to FPGAs, ASICs have a much higher and long tun-around time.

design based flow and debug back. High-level synthesis offers a cheap, quick and versatile design flow methodology that allows the software designer to predict what their code would perform like in a hardware setting, what will be the resources and performance numbers etc. Nevertheless acknowledging, that hand-crafted RTL could outperform HLS based designs, but at the cost of increased time and effort. We now briefly review some terminologies specific to the HLS design methodology.

1. Initiation-Interval, II, is defined as the minimum number of clock cycles between any two successive operations. In the case of HLS, the initiation interval is defined w.r.t the loop iterations, i.e., the number of clock cycles between any given two loop iterations. In an ideal pipelined based flow, the expected value of the II=1 [11].
2. Loop iteration, n, is defined as the number of counts an operation is repeated; in a design implementing pipelines, the loop iteration is simply number of times a pipeline is full when performing operations.
3. Iteration latency, t_{il}, the number of (minimum) clock cycles required to complete one loop iteration (i.e., for $n = 1$).
4. Latency-Area Product (LAP), the classical LAP metric, in the context of HLS methodology [11], can be defined as

$$LAP = (t_{ii} \times (n - 1) + t_{il}) \times Area \tag{4}$$

where $(t_{ii} \times (n - 1) + t_{il})$ represents the total latency and $Area$, the number of Slices (or LUTs).

3.2 Methodology and Implementation

The NIST submission package for the HQC, available online[2], contains refer-ence, optimized and the hardware implementations available for download. The eference implementation is the NIST KEM submitted version which contains he source C-files from the authors of the algorithm. The README file details he conversion requirements as per NIST FAQ #13 and describes the different ariants of the submission, which we omit here for brevity. Additionally, the sub-ission provides the reference implementations for all the 3 proposed versions f the HQC-algorithm, namely, hqc-128, hqc-192, and hqc-256. During the build, e corresponding binaries are generated in the build folder.

The optimized implementation consists of the AVX2 implementation and is nstant time (as per the latest submission specification) and avoids any secret y dependent memory access [1].

The hardware implementation consists of an HLS-compatible C implemen-tion (although the authors explicitly specify the C++ extension) which can compiled standalone as a C code (with the same functionality as the golden erence implementation) or translated into a VHDL implementation using the S design flow methodology.

See https://pqc-hqc.org/implementation.html.

Additionally, we provide an area-friendly `compact` and a performance-oriented `perf` version to allow for trade-offs between an area-footprint and throughput.

In addition to the above, the vanilla (or the pure) version also adds an optimized version, wherein we manually refactor some of the HLS-synthesized VHDL-generated code to remove possible duplications of the modules (as in the case of keccak which we explore in the next section) (Fig. 2).

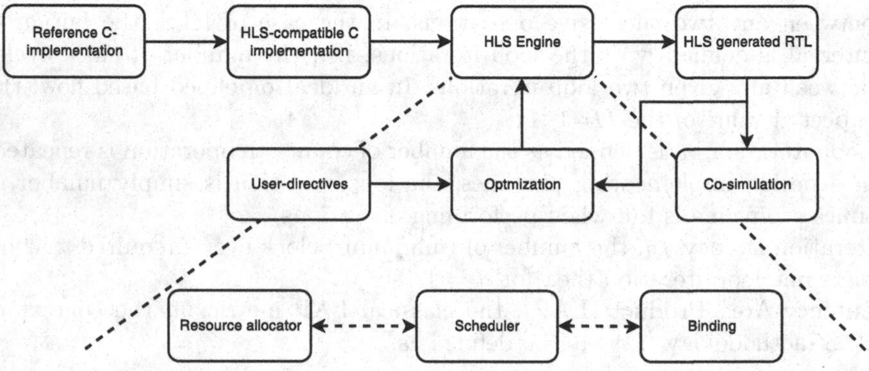

Fig. 2. A highly simplified overview of the HLS flow. Adapted from [17]

Design Flow Methodology. The methodology consists of converting a design, written in a high-level programming language such as C/C++, to a hardware description language (HDL), such as Verilog or VHDL. HLS consists of 3 main steps: resource allocation (or sharing), scheduling (using a scheduler) and binding [8]. As the name implies, the resource allocator allocates or allows sharing of multiple resources (such as functional blocks like Block-RAMs, DSP units, LUTs, registers etc.) between different code blocks. The scheduler is responsible for the actual implementation of the target operation, corresponding to the operation defined in the C-code. For instance, a multiplier operation between, any two variables, x and y, and the corresponding product, z would entail, retrieval of x and y, from their corresponding stored locations (which may be ROM, RAM, or simply registers holding on to those values), determining their bit widths, looking for optimizations (if they can be applied such as using a DSP unit) computing the product z, and finally writing back to the specified target location (in RAM) or holding onto the value for subsequent computations. For all of these enumerated operations, the scheduler determines (or rather estimates) the number of clock cycles required and schedules the operation either in a single clock cycle or over a span of multiple clock cycles. This then allows the scheduler to determine if parallelism can be exploited to reduce the number of clock cycles by computing the number of available resources at hand and checking for any instructions that could (potentially) have some data-dependencies [8]. Binding allows for the variable to be linked to a functional unit (storage or otherwise) to allow for better optimization.

HLS Implementation of HQC. The HQC algorithm submission package consists of 3 main algorithms, as defined in the preceding section, namely the keypair generation, the encapsulation function and the decapsulation functions. These can be categorized according to the top level functions, first introduced in [17], namely, the `crypto_kem_keygen`, `crypto_kem_enc` and `crypto_kem_dec` functions. Each of these functions could then be further divided into smaller functions based on their respective modules; for instance, `crypto_kem_enc` would consist of the `crypto_kem_pke_ind_cpa`. As mentioned above, the IND-CPA scheme is transformed into a secure CCA-2 KEM, thanks to the FO transform.

1. `crypto_kem_keygen` outputs the public key, pk and the secret key sk
2. `crypto_kem_enc` outputs the shared key K and the ciphertext ck taking the public key pk as input
3. `crypto_kem_dec` outputs the key K, taking in the secret key sk and the ciphertext ck as inputs

While HLS allows for rapid prototyping and outputs an HDL netlist, it must be highlighted that the tool in itself is restricted in terms of the functionalities it can implement; for instance, converting recursive functions or using unspecified lengths of execution loops, which are currently not supported by the HLS synthesis engines. Additionally, integration of open source libraries, which software implementations usually rely upon, for instance, in the case of random number generation, presents further scope for optimizations and enhancing the synthesis capabilities of such tools [11].

4 Results and Comparisons

In this section, we present and describe our synthesis, implementation and simulation results for the High-level synthesis of the HQC algorithm. Although the results described here are for HQC-128, we hypothesize similar trends for the other variants, i.e., HQC-192 and HQC-256 and leave these implementations for future works.

.1 Target Settings

he HLS has been synthesized and implemented for a target frequency of ≥125 IHz (i.e., a clock period of 8 ns). In principle, achieving higher target clock equencies (especially for performance-oriented applications) is desirable, nevtheless, our goal is to demonstrate the versatility of HLS in general and a st-pass at the design, so as to benchmark the overall performance/area of a sign over a broad range of applications quickly, rather than elaborate into timg closure and optimizations issues (which require finer tuning of the directives tings and the code itself). The target FPGA for these settings is the Xilinx ix7 xc7a100t-ftg256-1.

4.2 Synthesis Results

In this section, we present our HLS results for the given target FPGA for each module (i.e., individual functions). This allows for a granular understanding of how the HLS engine is able to resource allocate and share similar blocks across different operations. Note, for brevity, we present only the values for the optimized perf version of our implementation.

1) **crypto_kem_keygen**: Table 1 presents the synthesis and implementation results for the modules (functions) comprising the keypair generation module. For the sake of brevity, we report the minimum values of the latency (both in terms of the number of clock cycles required and the absolute time) to demonstrate the competitiveness of the HLS based designs. Additionally, we provide the post-implementation results to highlight the optimizations the tool (in this case Vivado, and not the Vitis or HLS tool) is able to implement the HLS synthesized netlist. We also compare our design with the state-of-art for the available modules, for instance, the polynomial multiplier and adder module from [9] are compared with our vector multiplier and adder module. Although handcrafted RTL is superior in terms of the number of clock cycles (required for the computation), nevertheless it provides a close enough approximation for a software designer to optimize the design. We also note that the RTL design (from [9]) uses four BRAM modules compared to zero from the HLS design.

Table 1. Post-synthesis latency and area results for the individual crypto_kem_keygen functions.

Module (function)	Latency		BRAM	DSP	FF	LUT
	Clocks	Time				
seedexpander_init	51	0.337 μs	0	0	3 384	9 552
seedexpander_mult_ty	3048	20.117 μs	0	0	3 723	9 240
shake_prng	4	26.40 ns	0	0	3 380	9 055
shake_prng_init	70	0.462 μs	1	0	3 572	10 311
vect_mul_add	21418	0.141 ms	0	0	3 701	6 175
poly_mult & add module[a] [9]	18976	83 μs	4	-	906	2137
vect_set_random_fixe	2573	16.982 μs	0	0	4 354	9 942
vect_set_random_fixe_1	2478	16.335 μs	0	0	72	225
fixed weight generator module [9]	3649	16.39 μs	2	0	124	316

[a] includes the sum of the poly_mult and the adder modules.

2) **crypto_kem_enc**: Table 2 presents the synthesis and implementation result for the modules (functions) comprising the encapsulation module. Agair for the sake of brevity, we report the minimum values of the latency (bot in terms of the number of clock cycles required and the absolute tim to demonstrate the competitiveness of the HLS based designs like abov

Additionally, we omit the modules which are shared across the different functions for instance, the `shake_prng_init`, and the `vect_set_random_fixe` functions described above.

Table 2. Post-synthesis latency and area results for the individual `crypto_kem_enc` functions.

Module (function)	Latency		BRAM	DSP	FF	LUT
	Clocks	Time				
reed_solomon_encode	803	5.3 µs	0	0	423	1 523
reed_muller_encode	6 441	42.511 µs	0	0	180	496
vect_add	2 211	14.593 µs	0	0	54	112
shake256_512_ds	238	1.57 µs	0	0	3 721	10 343
shake256 [7]	270	1.80 µs	0	0	270	2017
hqc_ciphertext_to_st	4 489	29.627 µs	0	0	177	483
hqc_public_key_from_s	559	3.689 µs	0	0	118	164

From Table 2, specifically for the SHAKE256 module, HLS outperforms the handcrafted RTL design in terms of latency. Although, the reader may be tempted to point to the larger usage area using HLS, which indeed can be further optimized, the design from [7] uses a parallel slice-based design, and the total area is computed using the LUTs as both logic and memory, which amortizes the total overall area cost.

3) `crypto_kem_dec`: Table 3 presents the synthesis and implementation results for the modules (functions) comprising the encapsulation module. Again, for the sake of brevity, we report the minimum values of the latency (both in terms of the number of clock cycles required and the absolute time) to demonstrate the competitiveness of the HLS based designs as above. Additionally, we omit the modules which are shared across the different functions for instance, the `shake_prng_init`, the `vect_set_random_fixe` functions described above.

able 3. Post-synthesis latency and area results for the individual `crypto_kem_dec` nctions.

Module (function)	Latency		BRAM	DSP	FF	LUT
	Clocks	Time				
reed_solomon_decode	12 774	0.11 ms	3	0	1 910	7 894
reed_muller_decode	55 845	0.482 ms	0	0	659	2260
vect_compare_64	18	0.115 µs	0	0	13	100
vect_compare	2 210	19.070 µs	0	0	19	143
hqc_ciphertext_from_s	4 465	38.528 µs	0	0	152	413
hqc_public_key_from_s	559	4.824 µs	0	0	118	164

4.3 Modular Comparisons Among Different Versions

To the best of our knowledge, this is the first work that targets a high-level synthesis hardware implementation of the HQC algorithm, although a very recent work that targets a complete handcrafted Hardware implementation of HQC is available from [9].

In this subsection, we provide a detailed breakdown of the hardware components utilized for all the 3 functions, for the sake of completeness of our results, in Table 4.

Table 4. Implementation comparisons of HQC-128 across the different implementation variants with state-of-the-art.

Target	Alg.	Design		Freq (MHz)	Slices	LUT	FF	BRAM	Latency	
									Clocks	*ms*
HLS (this work)	keygen	pure	Perf	153	8 359	24 746	21 746	7	40 427	0.27
			Comp	132	2 470	7 907	9 544	7	626 589	5.01
		optimized	Perf	150	3 921	11 484	8 798	6	40 427	0.27
			Comp	130	1 541	4 676	9 544	6	626 589	5.01
	encaps	pure	Perf	148	9 955	29 496	26 333	11	89 131	0.59
			Comp	131	3 075	9 544	9 544	11	1 482 332	11.85
		optimized	Perf	152	5 575	16 487	13 390	10	89 110	0.59
			Comp	129	2 122	9 544	9 544		1 482 332	11.85
	decaps	pure	Perf	150	8 434	24 898	21 680	18	193 004	1.27
			Comp	129	3 168	9 544	9 544	21	2 152 313	17.21
		optimized	Perf	152	6 223	18 739	15 243	18	193 082	1.27
			Comp	130	2 678	9 544	9 544	21	2 152 313	17.21
RTL [9]	keygen	single clock	-	164	-	2 350	1 106	9.5	23 480	0.14
		dual clock	-	242	-	3 094	879	14.5	27 013	0.12
	encaps	single clock	-	164	-	2 725	2 060	15.5	52 757	0.32
		dual clock	-	218	-	2 609	2 070	15.5	45 739	0.30
	decaps	single clock	-	164	-	8 426	6 642	36	78 233	0.48
		dual clock	-	204	-	8 434	6 652	36	71 199	0.43

Figure 3 provides a comparison of the area (measured in the number of LUTs) between the different variants the HLS HQC-128 design offers. Clearly,

- The area utilization of the perf version is ×2 - ×3 the comp version, which is expected. This is further elaborated in the difference (both in terms of absolute latency (measured in ms and the number of clock cycles) and the frequency of operation, as detailed in Table 4.
- The optimized version clearly outperforms the pure or the baseline version for both the perf and comp variants, across all the functional modules, i.e. keygen, encapsulation and decapsulation.
- Interestingly, the gain (in terms of area, higher is better) is better for the optimized version across the perf and comp variants compared to the base-line implementation. This demonstrates that irrespective of the architecture deployed, (i.e., round-based or performance-oriented), HLS is able to optimize the overall design in a better fashion.

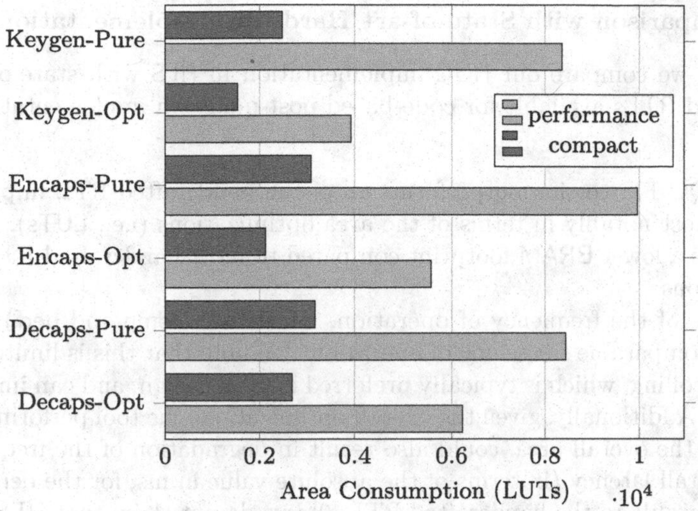

Fig. 3. Area (measured in LUTs) optimizations between perf and compact for the pure (baseline) and optimized versions.

4.4 Comparisons with Software Implementations

In Table 5 we provide results for our proposed HLS designs of HQC-128 compared to those in software, taken from SUPERCOP [18]. For variety, the table shows results from a variety of different CPU targets, and thus provides an overall indicator of how performant the proposed implementations are in comparison. Our performance-enhanced design makes significant savings in clock cycles compared to high-end CPUs, with savings between 4–7× on average. Our compact enhanced design has at least a 2× saving in clock cycles compared to the low-end CPU results. Overall we see that HLS designs are a viable option for implementing HQC, for both high-end and low-end devices and applications.

Table 5. Benchmarking results of HQC-128, comparing those in software, taken from SUPERCOP-20220506 (using 50% median values), to our results for HLS.

Platform	**Clock Cycles**		
	Keygen	**Encaps**	**Decaps**
Intel Xeon Skylake (2015)	202 120	351 273	645 728
AMD Ryzen 7 (2017)	307 486	661 913	1 259 627
ARM Cortex A53 (2018)	1 509 404	3 029 021	5 179 020
Artix 7 FPGA (perf)	40 427	89 110	193 082
Artix 7 FPGA (comp)	626 589	1 482 332	2 152 313

4.5 Comparison with State-of-art Hardware Implementations

In Table 6, we compare our HQC implementation in HLS with state-of-the-art handcrafted RTLs available for code-based post-quantum implementations. We note that

1. HLS-HQC-128 version outperforms all of the handcrafted RTL implementations, most notably in terms of the area optimizations (i.e., LUTs). Notably, HLS has a lower BRAM footprint compared to most handcrafted RTL implementations.
2. In terms of the frequency of operation, HLS (both comp and perf) variants offer a comparable frequency of operation. We note that this is limited to the loop unrolling, which is typically preferred in HLS design, and can impact frequency. Additionally, given the overall optimizations the tool performs, trying to limit the overall area, could also result in degradation of the frequency.
3. The overall latency (in terms of the absolute value in ms, for the perf version is comparable to the handcrafted RTL [9] (we do not claim that HLS outperforms them) but rather point out that such values, if obtained very earlier in the design cycle, allow for a better optimization of the existing code. A similar argument can be made for the clock cycles required for each operation. Nevertheless, we clearly see our HLS based design outperforms the existing BIKE (level 1) and classic McEliece and the SIKE RTL-based implementations.

Table 6. FPGA design comparisons of post-quantum code-based KEMs at NIST L1 security level across implementation variants lightweight (LW) and high-speed (HS), for our works this corresponds to comp and perf, respectively. For HQC-128-RTL we provide single- (SC) and dual-clock (DC).

PQC Scheme	Imp.	LUT	FF	BRAM	DSP	Freq (MHz)	Latency (cc/10^6, ms)					
							keygen		encaps		decaps	
HLS-HQC-128	LW	8 876	6 405	28	0	132	0.62	5.01	1.48	11.85	2.15	17.21
(this work)	HS	20 169	16 374	25	0	148	0.04	0.27	0.09	0.59	0.19	1.27
Classic	LW	23 890	45 658	139	5	112	8.88	79.20	0.13	1.10	0.17	1.50
McEliece [7]	HS	40 018	61 881	178	4	113	0.97	8.60	0.03	0.30	0.10	0.90
BIKE-L1 [16]	LW	12 868	5 354	17	7	121	2.67	21.90	0.20	1.20	1.62	13.30
	HS	52 967	7 035	49	13	96	0.26	2.60	0.01	0.10	0.19	1.90
HQC-128-RTL [9]	SC	16 320	10 044	61	0	164	0.02	0.14	0.05	0.32	0.08	0.48
	DC	16 956	9 837	66	0	204	0.03	0.12	0.06	0.30	0.08	0.43
SIKE [14]	LW	11 943	7 202	21	57	145	-	25.60	-	27.20	-	15.10
	HS	22 673	11 661	37	162	109	-	15.30	-	16.30	-	9.10

5 Conclusions

Given the interesting results HLS has generated, the importance of HLS in rap prototyping and in HW-SW co-designs cannot be understated, although t authors note that HLS cannot be a (complete) alternative to RTL developed using handwritten code. Rather, we emphasize that for certain designs where a quick understanding of the bottleneck parts of a larger algorithm need to be identified and quickly reworked upon, then HLS is the perfect candidate for such. We would also like to extend our work to the hqc-192 and hqc-256 versions, in addition to HLS implementations of other code-based cryptographic schemes as open future works. Additionally, this paves the way for further design automation in hardware based designs and allows for designing better and efficient implementations with minimal effort and time [11].

References

1. Aguilar Melchor, C., et al.: HQC (2020). updated 06/06/2021) NIST Round 3 submission for Post-Quantum Cryptography
2. Aguilar Melchor, C., Blazy, O., Deneuville, J.C., Gaborit, P., Zémor, G.: Efficient encryption from random quasi-cyclic codes. CoRR abs/1612.05572 (2016)
3. Aguilar Melchor, C., Blazy, O., Deneuville, J., Gaborit, P., Zémor, G.: Efficient encryption from random quasi-cyclic codes. IEEE Trans. Inform. Theory **64**(5), 3927–3943 (2018)
4. Alagic, G., et al.: NIST IR 8413: status report on the third round of the NIST post-quantum cryptography standardization process (2022)
5. Alekhnovich, M.: More on average case vs approximation complexity. In: 44th Annual IEEE Symposium on Foundations of Computer Science, 2003. Proceedings, 298–307. IEEE (2003)
6. Aragon, N., Gaborit, P., Zémor, G.: HQC-RMRS, an instantiation of the HQC encryption framework with a more efficient auxiliary error-correcting code (2020)
7. Chen, P., et al.: Complete and improved FPGA implementation of classic MCEliece. IACR Trans. Cryptogr. Hardw. Embed. Syst. **2022**(3), 71–113 (2022)
8. Coussy, P., Gajski, D.D., Meredith, M., Takach, A.: An introduction to high-level synthesis. IEEE Design Test Comput. **26**(4), 8–17 (2009)
9. Deshpande, S., Nawan, M., Nawaz, K., Szefer, J., Xu, C.: Towards a fast and efficient hardware implementation of HQC. Cryptology ePrint Archive, Paper 2022/1183 (2022). https://eprint.iacr.org/2022/1183

0. Gaborit, P., Deneuville, J.C.: Code-based cryptography. In: Concise Encyclopedia of Coding Theory. Chapman and Hall/CRC, pp. 799–822 (2021)
1. Guerrieri, A., Marques, G.D.S., Regazzoni, F., Upegui, A.: Design exploration and code optimizations for fpga-based post-quantum cryptography using high-level synthesis (2022)
2. Hofheinz, D., Hövelmanns, K., Kiltz, E.: A modular analysis of the fujisaki-okamoto transformation. In: Kalai, Y., Reyzin, L. (eds.) TCC 2017. LNCS, vol. 10677, pp. 341–371. Springer, Cham (2017). https://doi.org/10.1007/978-3-319-70500-2_12

. Huffman, W.C., Kim, J.L., Solé, P.: Basics of coding theory. In: Concise Encyclopedia of Coding Theory. Chapman and Hall/CRC, pp. 3–44 (2021)

. Massolino, P.M.C., Longa, P., Renes, J., Batina, L.: A compact and scalable hardware/software co-design of SIKE. IACR Trans. Cryptogr. Hardw. Embed. Syst. **2020**(2), 245–271 (2020)

NIST: Submission requirements and evaluation criteria for the post-quantum cryptography standardization process (2016). https://csrc.nist.gov/CSRC/media/Projects/Post-Quantum-Cryptography/documents/call-for-proposals-final-dec-2016.pdf

16. Richter-Brockmann, J., Mono, J., Güneysu, T.: Folding BIKE: scalable hardware implementation for reconfigurable devices. IEEE Trans. Comput. **71**(5), 1204–1215 (2022)
17. Soni, D., Basu, K., Nabeel, M., Karri, R.: A hardware evaluation study of NIST post-quantum cryptographic signature schemes. In: Second PQC Standardization Conference, NIST (2019)
18. SUPERCOP: System for unified performance evaluation related to cryptographic operations and primitives. https://bench.cr.yp.to/supercop.html

Software Implementation of a Code-Based Key Encapsulation Mechanism from Binary QD Generalized Srivastava Codes

Boly Seck[1,3](✉), Cheikh Thiécoumba Gueye[2], Gilbert Ndollane Dione[2], Jean Belo Klamti[4], Pierre-Louis Cayrel[3], Idy Diop[1], and Ousmane Ndiaye[2]

[1] École Eupérieure Polytechnique, Laboratoire d'imagerie médicale et de Bio-informatique, Dakar, Senegal
seck.boly@ugb.edu.sn, idy.diop@esp.sn

[2] Université Cheikh Anta Diop, Dakar, Senegal
{cheikht.gueye,gilbertndollane.dione,ousmane3.ndiaye}@ucad.edu.sn

[3] Univ Lyon, UJM-Saint-Etienne, CNRS, Laboratoire Hubert Curien UMR 5516, 42023 Saint-Etienne, France
pierre.louis.cayrel@univ-st-etienne.fr

[4] Department of Electrical and Computer Engineering, University of Waterloo, Waterloo, Canada
jbklamti@uwaterloo.ca

Abstract. In the NIST Post-Quantum Cryptography (PQC) standardization process, among 17 candidates for code-based public-key encryption (PKE), signature or key encapsulation mechanism (KEM), only three are in the 4th evaluation round. The remaining code-based candidates are Classic McEliece [CCUGLMMNPP+20], BIKE [ABBBBDGGGM+17] and HQC [MABBBBDDGL+20]. Cryptographic primitives from coding theory are some of the most promising candidates and their security is based on the well-known problems of post-quantum cryptography. In this paper, we present an efficient implementation of a secure KEM based on binary quasi-dyadic generalized Srivastava (QD-GS) codes. With QD-GS codes defined for an extension degree $m > 2$, this key establishment scheme is protected against the attacks of Barelli-Couvreur Bardet *et al.*. We also provide parameters that are secure against folding technique and FOPT attacks. Finally, we compare the performance of our implementation in runtime with the NIST finalists based on codes for the 4th round.

Keywords: NIST PQC Standardization · QD-GS codes · Code-based KEM · Binary DAGS

Introduction

a reminder, Faugère *et al.* had introduced an attack known in the litera-
‹e as FOPT against scheme using quasi-cyclic or quasi-dyadic algebraic codes

. Deneuville (Ed.): CBCrypto 2022, LNCS 13839, pp. 77–89, 2023.
s://doi.org/10.1007/978-3-031-29689-5_5

[FOPT10]. Their attack exploits the algebraic structure to build a system of equations and then uses the Grobnër bases techniques to solve it efficiently. Therefore, with FOPT attack, proposals based on quasi-cyclic algebraic codes are compromised. However, techniques using a quasi-dyadic approach need to be treated with caution for a proper choice of parameters concerning the dimension of space of solutions. That means that it is possible to design secure schemes using for instance binary Goppa codes, or Generalized Srivastava (GS) codes. Separately, note that, during the first round of the NIST PQC standardization process, Banegas *et al.* [BBBCDGGHKN+18] introduced a KEM scheme based on nonbinary QD-GS codes. This scheme was broken by Barelli and Couvreur [BC18]. They used in their attack the norm and trace codes technique which works only for code designed on an extension field with extension degree m equal to 2. It was shown that a simple parameters variation of the base field could avoid this attack [BC18, Section 5.3]. Lately, Banegas *et al.* introduced a new version of their scheme called DAGS reloaded [BBBCDGGHKN+19]. At the same time, Bardet *et al.* [BBCO19] introduced a hybrid version of the Barelli-Couvreur attack against the updated parameters. However, due to a proper choice of parameters, their attack worked only for the parameters of NIST security level 1 and not for the two others.

As part of this work, we show that the Barelli-Couvreur and Bardet *et al.* attacks have no effect against the code-based KEM using binary QD-GS codes that we call binary DAGS. We provide parameters that are secure against folding technique [FOPDPT15] and FOPT attacks. The main difference between the binary DAGS and the version submitted to the first round of NIST PQC standardization process [BBBCDGGHKN+18] is that the base fields are nonbinary. In addition, the underlying cryptosystem in the binary DAGS is that of Niederreiter instead of McEliece.

Contribution: In this work, we focus on the fast software implementation of the secure binary DAGS.

First, we show that the Barelli-Couvreur and Bardet *et al.* attacks have no effect against the code-based KEM using binary QD-GS codes that we called binary DAGS. We provide parameters that are secure against folding technique [FOPDPT15] and FOPT attacks.

Second, we perform an efficient software implementation of the binary DAGS. For that, we use techniques from [BBPS20] that specifically aim to improve the multiplication of QD matrices. These involve a version of the Karatsuba multiplication algorithm and an application of the LUP version in order to compute the product and inverse of matrices more efficiently. These improvements allow us to achieve better runtimes than previous DAGS implementations.

Finally, we show that our implementation is competitive in terms of executio time with the NIST candidates for advanced evaluation.

Organisation: The paper is organized as follows. In Sect. 2, we focus on th required prerequisites for this paper. In Sect. 3, we give the description of tl code-based KEM from binary QD-GS codes. We also propose a set of parameter In Sect. 4, we present the technical details about the software implementatic and results. Finally, we conclude this paper in Sect. 5.

2 Prerequisites

2.1 Notations

In this paper we use the following notations:

$\mathbb{F}_q$	finite field of size $q = 2^m$
$\boldsymbol{A}$	matrix
$\boldsymbol{I}_r$	identity matrix of size $r \times r$
$\boldsymbol{a}$	vector
$\mathsf{wt}(\boldsymbol{a})$	Hamming weight of $\boldsymbol{a}$
$d(\boldsymbol{x}, \boldsymbol{y})$	Hamming distance between $\boldsymbol{x}$ and $\boldsymbol{y}$
$(\boldsymbol{x} \Vert \boldsymbol{y})$	concatenation of vector $\boldsymbol{x}$ and $\boldsymbol{y}$
$(\boldsymbol{A} \Vert \boldsymbol{B})$	concatenation of matrices $\boldsymbol{A}$ and $\boldsymbol{B}$
$\mathcal{H}$	hash function
$\mathbf{Diag}(\boldsymbol{a})$	Diagonal matrix from vector $\boldsymbol{a}$
$\mathcal{S}_{w,n}$	Set of binary vectors of length n and Hamming weight w

2.2 Coding Theory

Let $\mathbb{F}_q$ be a finite field with $q = 2^m$. A linear code $\mathcal{C}$ of length n and dimension k over $\mathbb{F}_q$ is a subspace of $\mathbb{F}_q^n$ of dimension k. Elements of $\mathcal{C}$ are called code words. A generator matrix of $\mathcal{C}$ is a matrix $\boldsymbol{G} \in \mathbb{F}_q^{k \times n}$ such that

$$\mathcal{C} = \{\boldsymbol{mG} \ \text{ s.t } \ \boldsymbol{m} \in \mathbb{F}_q^k\}$$

ınd a parity check matrix of $\mathcal{C}$ is a matrix $\boldsymbol{H}$ such $\boldsymbol{H}\boldsymbol{c}^T = \boldsymbol{0}$ for all $\boldsymbol{c} \in \mathcal{C}$.

Let $\boldsymbol{x}, \boldsymbol{y} \in \mathbb{F}_q^n$ be two vectors. The Hamming weight of $\boldsymbol{x}$ denoted by $\mathsf{wt}(\boldsymbol{x})$ orresponds to the number of nonzero components of $\boldsymbol{x}$. The Hamming distance etween $\boldsymbol{x}$ and $\boldsymbol{y}$ denoted by $d(\boldsymbol{x}, \boldsymbol{y})$ is the Hamming weight of the vector $\boldsymbol{x} - \boldsymbol{y}$. 'he minimal distance of a code $\mathcal{C}$ denoted by $d(\mathcal{C})$ is the minimal distance etween different code words. For more details on coding theory refer to [MS77].

Let $n = 2^r$ be an integer and $\boldsymbol{a} = (a_0, a_1, ..., a_{n-1}) \in \mathbb{F}_q^n$ be a nonzero vector. square matrix $\boldsymbol{A} = (a_{i,j}) \in \mathbb{F}_q^{n \times n}$ is said dyadic of signature $\boldsymbol{a} \in \mathbb{F}_q^n$ if it is fined by:

$$a_{i,j} = a_{i \oplus j}$$

ıere $\oplus$ is the bitwise operation. A matrix is said quasi-dyadic when it is a block atrix where each block is a dyadic matrix. A linear code $\mathcal{C}$ is said quasi-dyadic ıen one of its parity check matrices is in the quasi-dyadic form.

Let $\boldsymbol{u} = (u_0, ..., u_{n-1}) \in \mathbb{F}_{2^m}^n$ and $\boldsymbol{v} = (v_0, ..., v_{s-1}) \in \mathbb{F}_{2^m}^s$ be two vectors :h pairwise distinct coefficients such that $u_i - v_j \neq 0$ for all $0 \leq i \leq n-1$ l $0 \leq j \leq s-1$. The matrix $C(\boldsymbol{u}, \boldsymbol{v}) = (c_{ij})_{0 \leq i \leq n-1, 0 \leq j \leq s-1}$ such that

$c_{ij} = 1/(u_i - v_j)$ is called a Cauchy matrix. This matrix plays an important role in the design of quasi-dyadic Goppa codes. Indeed, it was shown that Goppa with a monic generator polynomial without multiple zeros has a parity check in the Cauchy form [MS77]. Moreover, recently, Barreto et Misoczki established how to design a binary Goppa code in Cauchy and dyadic form [MB09, Section 3].

A Generalized Srivastava code $\mathcal{C}$ over a $\mathbb{F}_{2^m}$ is an alternant code with a parity check matrix in the form:

$$\boldsymbol{H} = \begin{pmatrix} \boldsymbol{H}_0 \\ \boldsymbol{H}_1 \\ \vdots \\ \boldsymbol{H}_{s-1} \end{pmatrix}. \tag{1}$$

The matrices $\boldsymbol{H}_i$ are defined by (2) from $n+s$ different elements $\alpha_0, \alpha_1, ..., \alpha_{n-1}$ and $w_0, w_1, ..., w_{s-1}$ of $\mathbb{F}_{q^m}$, and n nonzero elements $z_0, z_1, ..., z_{n-1}$ of $\mathbb{F}_q$ with $n \leq q^m - s$.

$$\boldsymbol{H}_i = \begin{pmatrix} \frac{z_1}{\alpha_0 - w_i} & \cdots & \frac{z_{n-1}}{\alpha_{n-1} - w_i} \\ \frac{z_1}{(\alpha_0 - w_i)^2} & \cdots & \frac{z_{n-1}}{(\alpha_{n-1} - w_i)^2} \\ \vdots & & \vdots \\ \frac{z_1}{(\alpha_0 - w_i)^t} & \cdots & \frac{z_{n-1}}{(\alpha_{n-1} - w_i)^t} \end{pmatrix} \tag{2}$$

Dimension k and minimal distance d of $\mathcal{C}$ verify $k \geq n - mst$ and $d \geq st + 1$. It is important to note that when $t = 1$ GS codes are Goppa codes. Moreover, by reordering rows of the matrix $\boldsymbol{H}$ defined by (1) we can see that generalized Srivasta codes could be defined by a parity check matrix in the form

$$\tilde{\boldsymbol{H}} = \begin{pmatrix} \tilde{\boldsymbol{H}}_1 \\ \boldsymbol{H}_2 \\ \vdots \\ \tilde{\boldsymbol{H}}_t \end{pmatrix} \text{ where } \tilde{\boldsymbol{H}}_i = \begin{pmatrix} \frac{z_1}{(\alpha_0 - w_0)^i} & \cdots & \frac{z_{n-1}}{(\alpha_{n-1} - w_0)^i} \\ \frac{z_1}{(\alpha_0 - w_1)^i} & \cdots & \frac{z_{n-1}}{(\alpha_{n-1} - w_1)^i} \\ \vdots & & \vdots \\ \frac{z_1}{(\alpha_0 - w_{s-1})^i} & \cdots & \frac{z_{n-1}}{(\alpha_{n-1} - w_{s-1})^i} \end{pmatrix} \text{ for } i = 1, ..., t. \tag{3}$$

We can see that for constructing a generalized Srivastava code from (3), we need to compute the matrix $\tilde{\boldsymbol{H}}_1$ and the other matrices $\tilde{\boldsymbol{H}}_i$ could be obtained by raising each coefficient of $\tilde{\boldsymbol{H}}_1$ to the power of i. For more information about GS codes see [MS77].

2.3 Key Encapsulation Mechanism

A KEM is a set of four algorithms (Setup, KeyGen, Encapsulation, Decapsulation described as follows:

- Setup(1^λ): Setup is a probabilistic algorithm that takes as in input a securit parameter λ and returns public parameters PP
- KeyGen(PP): KeyGen is the key generation algorithm. It takes as input publ parameters and returns a couple (sk, pk) of secret and public keys.

- Encapsulation(PP, pk): This algorithm takes as input public parameters and public key. It first generates a session key $\boldsymbol{k}$ then computes its encapsulated value $\boldsymbol{c}$. Finally, it returns $\boldsymbol{c}$.
- Decapsulation(sk, $\boldsymbol{c}$): Decapsulation is the algorithm consisting to recover a session key from an encapsulation $\boldsymbol{c}$. It takes as input an encapsulation $\boldsymbol{c}$ and a secret key sk. It returns either a session key $\boldsymbol{k}$ or the failed symbol $\perp$.

3 KEM from Binary QD-GS Codes

In this section, we first describe the key encapsulation mechanism from binary QD-GS codes and then make its security analysis.

3.1 Description

It is important to note that the scheme is built upon the Niederreiter cryptosystem thus the public key is a systematic parity check matrix. In the key generation algorithm, the process is similar to that of DAGS reloaded [BBBCDGGHKN+19]. However, the main difference is in the fact that the base field is the binary field $\mathbb{F}_2$ instead of an extension $\mathbb{F}_{2^r}$. The key generation, encapsulation, and decapsulation algorithms of binary DAGS are defined as follows:

Algorithm 1. Key Generation

Input: A finite field $\mathbb{F}_{2^m}$, nonzero integers $n = n_0 s$ and t.
Output: A public key pk and a secret key sk

1. Generate the dyadic signature $\boldsymbol{h}$
2. Construct the Cauchy support $(\boldsymbol{u}, \boldsymbol{v})$
3. Compute the Cauchy matrix $\boldsymbol{H}_1 = C(\boldsymbol{u}, \boldsymbol{v})$
4. Compute $\boldsymbol{H}_i$ for $i = 2, ..., t$ by computing the power of i of each coefficient of the matrix $\boldsymbol{H}_1$
5. Compute a vector $\boldsymbol{z}$ by sampling uniformly at random elements in $\mathbb{F}_{2^m}$ with the restriction $z_{is+j} = z_{is}$ for $i = 0, ..., n_0 - 1$, $j = 0, ..., s - 1$.
6. Compute the matrix $\tilde{\boldsymbol{H}} = \begin{pmatrix} \boldsymbol{H}_1 \\ \boldsymbol{H}_2 \\ \vdots \\ \boldsymbol{H}_t \end{pmatrix} \mathbf{Diag}(\boldsymbol{z})$
7. Split $\boldsymbol{H}_{bin}$ as $(\boldsymbol{B} \| \boldsymbol{A})$ such that $\boldsymbol{A}$ is a $mst \times mst$ invertible matrix.
8. Compute the systematic form $\tilde{\boldsymbol{H}}_{bin} = (\boldsymbol{M} \| \boldsymbol{I}) = \boldsymbol{A}^{-1} \boldsymbol{H}_{bin}$
9. Choose randomly a binary string $\boldsymbol{r} \in \mathbb{F}_2^n$.
10. Return pk $= \boldsymbol{M}$ and sk $= (\boldsymbol{u}, \boldsymbol{A}, \boldsymbol{r}, \boldsymbol{M})$

In the key generation algorithm the dyadic signature $\boldsymbol{h}$ is computed according the work of Barreto and Misoczki [MB09]. The integer s represents the order the quasi-dyadic matrix $\boldsymbol{H}_1$. Finally, n is the length of the code and t is the mber of block rows in the parity check matrix of the generalized Srivastava le.

The Cauchy support $(\boldsymbol{u}, \boldsymbol{v})$ is constructed as follows:

- Choose a random offset $w \xleftarrow{\$} \mathbb{F}_{2^m}$;
- Compute $\boldsymbol{u}_i = \frac{1}{h_i} + w$ and $\boldsymbol{v}_j = \frac{1}{h_j} + \frac{1}{h_0} + w$ for $i = 0, \cdots, s-1$ and $j = 0, \cdots, n-1$;
- Set $u = (\boldsymbol{u}_0, \cdots, \boldsymbol{u}_{s-1})$ and $\boldsymbol{v} = (\boldsymbol{v}_0, \cdots, \boldsymbol{v}_{n-1})$.

Algorithm 2. Encapsulation

Input: The public key $\mathsf{pk} = \boldsymbol{M}$ where $\tilde{\boldsymbol{H}}_{bin} = (\boldsymbol{M} \| \boldsymbol{I})$ is a binary parity check matrix of a QD-GS code.
Output: A session key $\boldsymbol{k}$ and its encapsulation $\boldsymbol{c}$

1. Choose randomly an error vector $\boldsymbol{e} \xleftarrow{\$} \mathcal{S}_{w,n}$
2. Compute $\boldsymbol{c}_0 = \boldsymbol{e}_1 + \boldsymbol{M}\boldsymbol{e}_0$ and $\boldsymbol{c}_1 = \mathcal{H}(2, \boldsymbol{e})$ where $\boldsymbol{e}$ is parse as $(\boldsymbol{e}_0 \| \boldsymbol{e}_1)$.
3. Set $\boldsymbol{c} = (\boldsymbol{c}_0 \| \boldsymbol{c}_1)$
4. Compute $\boldsymbol{k} = \mathcal{H}(1, \boldsymbol{e}, \boldsymbol{c})$
5. Return the encapsulation $\boldsymbol{c}$

Algorithm 3. Decapsulation

Input: The secret key $\mathsf{sk} = (\boldsymbol{u}, \boldsymbol{A}, \boldsymbol{r}, \boldsymbol{M})$, encapsulation $\boldsymbol{c}$
Output: A session key $\boldsymbol{k}$

1. Parse $\boldsymbol{c}$ into $\boldsymbol{c} = (\boldsymbol{c}_0 \| \boldsymbol{c}_1)$
2. Obtain the syndrome $\boldsymbol{c}_0' \in \mathbb{F}_q$ from $\boldsymbol{c}_0$.
3. Compute $\boldsymbol{e}' = \mathsf{Decode}(\mathsf{sk}, \boldsymbol{c}_0')$ where Decode is a decoding algorithm for alternant code.
4. If decoding failed or $wt(\boldsymbol{e}') \neq w$ set $b = 0$ and $\eta = \boldsymbol{r}$
5. If $\tilde{\boldsymbol{H}}_{bin}\boldsymbol{e}' = \boldsymbol{c}_0$ and $\boldsymbol{c}_1 = \mathcal{H}(2, \boldsymbol{e}')$.
   Set $b = 1$ and $\eta = \boldsymbol{e}'$
6. Else:
   Set $b = 0$ and $\eta = \boldsymbol{r}$
7. Return $\boldsymbol{k} = \mathcal{H}(b, \eta, \boldsymbol{c})$

Description of the Decoding Algorithm
The input to the decoding algorithm is not, as commonly, a noisy codeword, but a syndrome.

The main step in the decoding algorithm involves reconstructing the alternant matrix $\boldsymbol{H}_{alt}$ and a syndrome $\boldsymbol{c}_0'$ corresponding to the alternant code. For this reconstruction, we first compute $\boldsymbol{A}\tilde{\boldsymbol{H}}_{bin} = \boldsymbol{H}_{bin}$; $\boldsymbol{A}\boldsymbol{c}_0 = \tilde{\boldsymbol{c}}_0$. Then we use the inverse of the co-trace function to transform respectively $\boldsymbol{H}_{bin}$ and $\tilde{\boldsymbol{c}}_0$ into matrix $\tilde{\boldsymbol{H}}$ and syndrome $\tilde{\boldsymbol{c}}$ with coefficients in the extension field $\mathbb{F}_{2^m}$. Finally, we compute $\boldsymbol{H}_{alt} = \boldsymbol{C}^{-1}\tilde{\boldsymbol{H}}$ and $\boldsymbol{c}_0' = \boldsymbol{C}^{-1}\tilde{\mathrm{c}}$, where $\boldsymbol{C}$ is a $r \times r$ matrix such that it

r rows correspond to the coefficients of the polynomials $g_1(x), g_2(x), \cdots, g_r(x)$ defined by:

$$g_{(l-1)t+i} = \frac{\prod_{j=1}^{s} (x - \boldsymbol{u}_j)^t}{(x - \boldsymbol{u}_l)^i}$$

for $l = 1, \cdots, s$ and $i = 1, \cdots, t$. For more details on the alternant matrix reconstruction and the corresponding alternant syndrome, refer to [BBBCDGGHKN+19].

3.2 Security Analysis

Decoding Attack. In code-based cryptography, the main efficient and known decoding attack is the information set decoding (ISD) technique introduced by E. Prange [Pra62]. Other approaches such as statistical decoding [Jab01] are considered as less efficient. For a given linear code of length n and dimension k, the main idea behind the information-set decoding algorithm is to find a set of k coordinates of a garbled vector that are error-free and such that the restriction of the code's generator matrix to these positions is invertible. Then, the original message can be computed by multiplying the encrypted vector by the inverse of the submatrix.

Thus, those k bits determine the codeword uniquely, and hence the set is called an information set. It is sometimes difficult to draw the exact resistance to this type of attack. However, they are always lower-bounded by the ratio of information sets without errors to total possible information sets, i.e.,

$$R_{\text{ISD}} = \frac{\binom{n-\omega}{k}}{\binom{n}{k}},$$

where ω is the Hamming weight of the error vector. Therefore, well-chosen parameters can avoid these non-structural attacks.

Algebraic Attack. In code-based cryptography, the main key recovery attack against schemes using structured codes are that of Faugère *et al.* denoted in the literature by FOPT attack [FOPT10]. Their attack was originally aimed at two variants of McEliece-like schemes, introduced respectively in [BCGO09] and [MB09]. The first scheme based on quasi-cyclic is completely broken. The second variant, instead, only considered quasi-dyadic Goppa codes. Most of the parameters proposed in [MB09], have also been broken very easily, except for the binary case code. This is not connected to the base field but is due to the fact that with a small base field, authors provided a higher extension degree. The extension degree m plays an important role in the attack, as it defines the dimension of the solution space, which is equal, in fact, exactly to $m - 1$. However, in [FOPT13], the authors provided a bound of the complexity of their attack and showed that schemes for which this dimension is less or equal to 20 would be within the scope of the attack.

In this paper, the underlying code is Generalized Srivastava code and in [Per12], the author showed that the dimension of the solution space is $mt - 1$ instead of $m-1$. Therefore the choice of a good parameter could avoid this attack. Recently, in [FOPDPT16] an improvement of FOPT attack was introduced. Authors introduced a new technique called folding to reduce the complexity of the FOPT attack to that of attacking a smaller code (i.e. the folded code) by using the strong properties of the automorphism group of the alternant codes. However, it is important to note that there is not a clear application of this attack against GS codes and furthermore, the authors do not propose a concrete bound, but only experimental results.

During the NIST process for standardization of post-quantum public key schemes, there is only one scheme based on quasi-dyadic generalized Srivastava code presented by Banegas *et al.* [BBBCDGGHKN+18]. The specificity of this scheme is that the authors used a non-binary based field and a small degree extension compared to the scheme of [MB09]. Some proposal parameters of Banegas *et al.*'s scheme were attacked by Barelli and Couvreur in [BC18].

The Barelli-Couvreur attack is based on a novel construction called Norm-Trace Code. The construction of these codes is given explicitly only for the specific case $m = 2$ which is the case in all parameters proposed in [BBBCDGGHKN+18]. However, it is possible to avoid this attack by modifying a single parameter, namely the size q of the base field i.e by changing this value from 2^6 to 2^8. To address of the Barelli-Couvreur attack, Banegas *et al.* provided updated parameters in [BBBCDGGHKN+19] while keeping the size of the base field corresponding to the level 1 of NIST security to $q = 2^6$. This leads to a new attack introduced by Bardet *et al.* [BBCO19].

In Bardet *et al.*'s paper, they first applied the Barelli-Couvreur attack and after, presented a hybrid attack combining exhaustive search and Gröbner basis to attack the updated parameters of level 1 in [BBBCDGGHKN+19]. However, note that their attack did not concern updated parameters of NIST security levels 2 and 3 where the size of the base field is $q = 2^8$. In addition, in [BBCO19] authors showed that when the reduced system is undetermined, both attacks (i.e. of [BC18] and [BBCO19]) have no effect. Note that among all aforementioned attacks only that of Faugère *et al.*'s [FOPT10] concerns binary codes. As it is mentioned, to avoid it we need to choose parameters to have a dimension of the solution space satisfying $mt - 1 > 20$.

Proposal Parameters. The parameters used for this implementation (Table 1 are that proposed in [BBBCDGGHKN+19]. These parameters are chosen to be secure against information decoding attack as well as the folding technique [FOPDPT15] and FOPT attacks. They are chosen as follows:

- *Information set decoding attack*: for avoiding the information set decoding attack, the parameters n and k are chosen such that the ration $\frac{n}{k}$ is close to $\frac{1}{2}$.

Table 1. Proposal parameters in [BBBCDGGHKN+19]

Security level	q	n	k	s	t	w
1	2^{13}	6400	3072	2^7	2	128
3	2^{14}	11520	4352	2^8	2	256
5	2^{14}	14080	6912	2^8	2	256

- *FOPT attack*: considering the fact that the underlying quasi-dyadic code is a generalized Srivastava code which is a generalization of Goppa code, the parameters m and t are chosen such that the dimension of solution space is larger than 20 as recommended in [FOPT13].
- *Folding technique attack*: for avoiding the folding technique attack, the quasi-dyadic order s of the underlying generalized Srivastava code is chosen such that it is not very large.
  Despite these parameter adjustments, binary DAGS still has a small public key size compared to Classic McEliece [CCUGLMMNPP+20] and BIKE [ABBBBDGGGM+17] (Table 2).

4 Efficient Implementation

In this software implementation for binary DAGS ($\mathsf{DAGS_{bin}}$), we will exploit the particular structure of QD matrices to improve the multiplication of two QD matrices. Some matrix operations, such as sum or inversion, can be performed efficiently in the dyadic case by simply considering the signatures as in [BBPS20]. The multiplication operations can be significantly improved by means of LUP decomposition and the Karatsuba multiplication in the QD case. This method provides a fast software implementation of key generation and decapsulation in the binary DAGS compared to the standard method.

4.1 Implementation Details

'or Key Generation. We realized that the systematization of the matrix $\boldsymbol{H}_{bin}$ epresents almost the total cost of the key generation. To reduce this, we first erformed a trick in our implementation. By combining Steps 6 and 7 into one nd with the projection of the matrix $\tilde{\boldsymbol{H}}$ onto $\mathbb{F}_2$, we obtain a QD matrix $mst \times n$ $\boldsymbol{I}_{bin}$. Then the systematic form $\tilde{\boldsymbol{H}}_{bin}$ of $\boldsymbol{H}_{bin}$ is also a QD matrix. Therefore, stead of considering the complete $mst \times n$ matrix $\boldsymbol{H}_{bin}$, we just need the gnature of each block. Thus, the first row of $\boldsymbol{H}_{bin}$ is composed of the signatures the first blocks, the second row is obtained from the signatures of the second ocks, and so on. Finally, $\boldsymbol{H}_{bin}$ is $mt \times n$ matrix, with n_0 block-rows, where $= n/s$. As a result, the time required to systematize the matrix $\boldsymbol{H}_{bin}$ decreases nificantly.

Second, in Step 9, we used the efficient inversion of the secret matrix $\boldsymbol{A}$ as [BBPS20] by merging the LUP decomposition and Karatsuba multiplication.

This improved inversion method reduces the execution time of the key generation by almost 10 times for the level security 1 ($\mathsf{DAGS_{bin}\_1}$) for example.

Table 2. Public key size in bytes for level security 3

Algorithm	BIKE [ABBBBDGGGM+17]	HQC [MABBBBDDGL+20]	Classic McEliece [CCUGLMMNPP+20]	DAGS reloaded	$\mathsf{DAGS_{bin}\_3}$
Public Key	24 659	4 522	524 160	11 264	15 232

For Encapsulation. This is faster than the key generation and the decapsulations algorithms. It is just composed by a binary matrix-vector product and hash computation. We just cleaned up the C code compared to the previous implementations.

For Decapsulation. For the decapsulation we need to reconstruct the alternant syndrome c_0' and the alternant secret matrix $\boldsymbol{H}_{alt}$ from the secret key [BBBCDGGHKN+19]. We observe that this step consumes almost half of the execution time in the decapsulation. Therefore, we first compute $\boldsymbol{H}_{bin} = \boldsymbol{A}\tilde{\boldsymbol{H}}_{bin}$. Here we use the Karatsuba multiplication technique in the QD case to save time in our implementation.

Then, from $\boldsymbol{H}_{bin}$, we apply the inverse of the co-trace function to obtain the matrix $\tilde{\boldsymbol{H}}$ with coefficients in the extension field. We compute the matrix $\boldsymbol{C}$ from the support $\boldsymbol{u}$.

Finally, we compute $\boldsymbol{H}_{alt} = \boldsymbol{C}^{-1}\tilde{\boldsymbol{H}}$ using the same technique in Step 9 in the key Generation. The LUP decomposition factorizes the matrix $\boldsymbol{C}$ as LUP. This procedure consists in using a block decomposition, which works directly on the signatures, to exploit the simple and efficient algebra of QD matrices. Once the factorization of $\boldsymbol{C}$ is obtained, it is sufficient to perform the computation of $\boldsymbol{C}^{-1}$ in an efficient way and use the Karatsuba method to perform the product.

All these techniques could have allowed us to make the decapsulation very fast. Unfortunately, we could not generate the session key correctly for some tests with the version of the binary DAGS ($\mathsf{DAGS_{bin}\_5}$) of level security 5. Therefore we cannot present the runtime for this version in the results.

In the following, we call the version of the binary DAGS with the application of the above techniques for key generation and decapsulation, $\mathsf{DAGS_{bin}}$ improved

Table 3. Timings with previous codes for security level 1

Algorithm	DAGS reloaded	$\mathsf{DAGS_{bin}\_1}$	$\mathsf{DAGS_{bin}\_1}$ improved
Key Generation	408 342 881	679 076 980	77 768 093
Encapsulation	5 061 697	6 564 782	4 641 252
Decapsulation	192 083 862	298 987 096	15 091 4566

Table 4. Timings with previous codes for security level 3

Algorithm	DAGS reloaded	$\text{DAGS}_{\text{bin}}\_3$	$\text{DAGS}_{\text{bin}}\_3$ improved
Key Generation	1 560 879 328	1 597 980 876	847 980 876
Encapsulation	14 405 500	15 200 232	8 020 732
Decapsulation	392 435 142	454 765 478	34 656 844

4.2 Results

In this section, we present the results obtained in our implementation in C. The timings were acquired by running the code 10 times and taking the average. We used CLANG compiler version 8.0.0 and the processor was an Intel(R) Core(TM) i5-5300U CPU @ 2.30 GHz.

We present below the number of cycles obtained for our binary DAGS implementation with the improvements in key generation and decapsulation compared to previous implementations (Table 3 and Table 4). Tables 5 and 6 compare our implementation with the other NIST finalists.

Table 5. Timings with NIST finalists for security level 1

Algorithm	BIKE [ABBBBDGGGM+17]	HQC [MABBBBBDDGL+20]	Classic McEliece [CCUGLMMNPP+20]	$\text{DAGS}_{\text{bin}}\_1$ improved
Key Generation	650 638	98 570	49 758 742	77 768 093
Encapsulation	247 976	356 980	56 672	4 741 252
Decapsulation	2 575 687	467 891	253 864	15 091 4566

Table 6. Timings with NIST finalists for security level 3

Algorithm	BIKE [ABBBBDGGGM+17]	HQC [MABBBBBDDGL+20]	Classic McEliece [CCUGLMMNPP+20]	$\text{DAGS}_{\text{bin}}\_3$ improved
Key Generation	3 674 894	267 983	364 756 564	847 980 876
Encapsulation	564 896	567 836	245 794	8 020 732
Decapsulation	4 298 673	947 920	387 678	34 656 844

Conclusion

his paper is an extension of the work of Banegas *et al.* [BBBCDGGHKN+19] DAGS. We first established that the Barelli-Couvreur and Bardet *et al.* tacks have no effect against binary DAGS. This is a code-based KEM heme using quasi-dyadic binary generalized Srivastava codes. We have proled parameters that are secure against folding technique and FOPT attacks *et* [BBBCDGGHKN+19]. Despite these parameter adjustments, binary DAGS ll has a small public key size. Then, we realized an efficient software implemenion of the binary DAGS using tricks to reduce the computational time mainly in the key generation and decapsulation algorithms. We also used LUP decomposition and Karatsuba multiplication techniques in the case of quasi-dyadic matrices. This allowed us to have a competitive runtime performance compared to other code-based NIST finalists. Finally, the high execution time in binary DAGS compared to DAGS reloaded is related to the choice of parameters that are very large (e.g. $n = 6400$ security level 1). We need to reduce the parameters in binary DAGS while being aware of existing attacks. In this way, we will be able to achieve even better performance. This work is currently in progress and the results will appear in our future work.

References

[ABBBBDGGGM+17] Aragon, N., et al.: BIKE: Bit Flipping Key Encapsulation (2017). https://bikesuite.org/files/v4.2/BIKE_Spec021.09.29.1.pdf. Accessed 09 Dec 2022

[BBBCDGGHKN+18] Banegas, G., et al.: DAGS: key encapsulation using dyadic GS codes. J. Math. Cryptol. **12**(4), 221–239 (2018)

[BBBCDGGHKN+19] Banegas, G., et al.: DAGS: reloaded revisiting dyadic key encapsulation. In: Baldi, M., Persichetti, E., Santini, P. (eds.) CBC 2019. LNCS, vol. 11666, pp. 69–85. Springer, Cham (2019). https://doi.org/10.1007/978-3-030-25922-8_4

[BBCO19] Bardet, M., Bertin, M., Couvreur, A., Otmani, A.: Practical algebraic attack on DAGS. In: Baldi, M., Persichetti, E., Santini, P. (eds.) CBC 2019. LNCS, vol. 11666, pp. 86–101. Springer, Cham (2019). https://doi.org/10.1007/978-3-030-25922-8_5

[BBPS20] Banegas, G., Barreto, P.S., Persichetti, E., Santini, P.: Designing efficient dyadic operations for cryptographic applications. J. Math. Cryptol. **14**(1), 95–109 (2020)

[BC18] Barelli, É., Couvreur, A.: An efficient structural attack on NIST submission DAGS. In: Peyrin, T., Galbraith, S. (eds.) ASIACRYPT 2018. LNCS, vol. 11272, pp. 93–118. Springer, Cham (2018). https://doi.org/10.1007/978-3-030-03326-2_4

[BCGO09] Berger, T.P., Cayrel, P.-L., Gaborit, P., Otmani, A.: Reducing key length of the McEliece cryptosystem. In: Preneel, B. (ed.) AFRICACRYPT 2009. LNCS, vol. 5580, pp. 77–97. Springer, Heidelberg (2009). https://doi.org/10.1007/978-3-642-02384-2_6

[CCUGLMMNPP+20] Chou, T., et al.: Classic McEliece: conservative code-based cryptography (2020). https://classic.mceliece.org/nist/mceliece-20201010.pdf. Accessed 09 Dec 2022

[FOPDPT15] Faugère, J.-C., Otmani, A., Perret, L., De Portzamparc, F., Tillich, J.-P.: Folding alternant and Goppa codes with nontrivial automorphism groups. IEEE Trans. Inf. Theory **62**(1), 184–198 (2015)

[FOPDPT16] Faugère, J.-C., Otmani, A., Perret, L., De Portzamparc, F., Tillich, J.-P.: Structural cryptanalysis of McEliece schemes with compact keys. Des. Codes Cryptography **79**(1), 87–1 (2016)

[FOPT10] Faugère, J.-C., Otmani, A., Perret, L., Tillich, J.-P.: Algebraic cryptanalysis of McEliece variants with compact keys. In: Gilbert, H. (ed.) EUROCRYPT 2010. LNCS, vol. 6110, pp. 279–298. Springer, Heidelberg (2010). https://doi.org/10.1007/978-3-642-13190-5_14

[FOPT13] Faugère, J.-C., Otmani, A., Perret, L., Tillich, J.-P.: Algebraic cryptanalysis of compact McEliece's variants- toward a complexity analysis. In: Conference on Symbolic Computation and Cryptography, p. 45 (2013)

[Jab01] Jabri, A.A.: A statistical decoding algorithm for general linear block codes. In: Honary, B. (ed.) Cryptography and Coding 2001. LNCS, vol. 2260, pp. 1–8. Springer, Heidelberg (2001). https://doi.org/10.1007/3-540-45325-3_1

[MABBBBDDGL+20] Melchor, C.A., et al.: Hamming quasi-cyclic (HQC) (2020). https://pqc-hqc.org/doc/hqc-specification_2020-10-01.pdf. Accessed 09 Dec 2022

[MB09] Misoczki, R., Barreto, P.S.L.M.: Compact McEliece keys from Goppa codes. In: Jacobson, M.J., Rijmen, V., Safavi-Naini, R. (eds.) SAC 2009. LNCS, vol. 5867, pp. 376–392. Springer, Heidelberg (2009). https://doi.org/10.1007/978-3-642-05445-7_24

[MS77] MacWilliams, F.J., Sloane, N.J.A.: The Theory of Error Correcting Codes, vol. 16. Elsevier (1977)

[Per12] Persichetti, E.: Compact McEliece keys based on quasidyadic Srivastava codes. J. Math. Cryptol. **6**(2), 149–169 (2012)

[Pra62] Prange, E.: The use of information sets in decoding cyclic codes. IRE Trans. Inf. Theory **8**(5), 5–9 (1962)

On Decoding High-Order Interleaved Sum-Rank-Metric Codes

Thomas Jerkovits[1,3](✉), Felicitas Hörmann[1,2], and Hannes Bartz[1]

[1] Institute of Communications and Navigation, German Aerospace Center (DLR), Wessling, Germany
{thomas.jerkovits,felicitas.hoermann,hannes.bartz}@dlr.de
[2] School of Computer Science, University of St. Gallen, St. Gallen, Switzerland
[3] Institute for Communications Engineering, Technical University of Munich (TUM), Munich, Germany

Abstract. We consider decoding of vertically homogeneous interleaved sum-rank-metric codes with high interleaving order s, that are constructed by stacking s codewords of a single constituent code. We propose a Metzner–Kapturowski-like decoding algorithm that can correct errors of sum-rank weight $t \leq d - 2$, where d is the minimum distance of the code, if the interleaving order $s \geq t$ and the error matrix fulfills a certain rank condition. The proposed decoding algorithm generalizes the Metzner–Kapturowski(-like) decoders in the Hamming metric and the rank metric and has a computational complexity of $O(\max\{n^3, n^2 s\})$ operations in $\mathbb{F}_{q^m}$, where n is the length of the code. The scheme performs linear-algebraic operations only and thus works for any interleaved linear sum-rank-metric code. We show how the decoder can be used to decode high-order interleaved codes in the skew metric. Apart from error control, the proposed decoder allows to determine the security level of code-based cryptosystems based on interleaved sum-rank metric codes.

1 Introduction

The development of quantum-secure cryptosystems is crucial in view of the recent advances in the design and the realization of quantum computers. As it is reflected in the number of submissions during the NIST's post-quantum cryptography standardization process for key encapsulation mechanisms (KEMs) many promising candidates belong to the family of code-based systems of which still three candidates are in the current 4th round [1]. Code-based cryptography is mostly based on the McEliece cryptosystem [11] whose trapdoor is that the public code can only be efficiently decoded if the secret key is known.

Variants of the McEliece cryptosystem based on interleaved codes in the Hamming and the rank metric were proposed in [4,7,19]. Interleaving is a well-known technique in coding theory that enhances a code's burst-error-correction capability. The idea is to stack a fixed number s of codewords of a constituent code over a field $\mathbb{F}_{q^m}$ in a matrix and thus to transform burst errors into errors occurring at the same position in each codeword. Equivalently, these errors can

J.-C. Deneuville (Ed.): CBCrypto 2022, LNCS 13839, pp. 90–109, 2023.
https://doi.org/10.1007/978-3-031-29689-5_6

be seen as symbol errors in a vector code over the extension field $\mathbb{F}_{q^{ms}}$. There exist list and/or probabilistic unique decoders for interleaved Reed–Solomon (RS) codes in the Hamming metric [8] as well as for interleaved Gabidulin codes in the rank metric [9] and for interleaved Reed–Solomon (LRS) codes in the sum-rank metric [2].

All of the mentioned decoders are tailored to a particular code family and explicitly exploit the code structure. In contrast, Metzner and Kapturowski proposed a decoder which works for interleaved Hamming-metric codes with *any* linear constituent code. The decoding algorithm only requires a high interleaving order s as well as a linear-independence constraint on the error [14]. Variants of the linear-algebraic Metzner–Kapturowski algorithm were further studied in [5,6,12,13,15,21], often under the name vector-symbol decoding (VSD). Moreover, Puchinger, Renner and Wachter-Zeh adapted the algorithm to the rank-metric case in [18,20].

This affects the security level of McEliece variants that are based on interleaved codes in the Hamming and the rank metric as soon as the interleaving order s is too large (i.e. $s \geq t$ for error weight t). Cryptosystems based on interleaved codes with small interleaving order are not affected. Their security level can be evaluated based on information-set-decoding (ISD) algorithms (see e.g. [16] for an adaptation of Prange's algorithm to interleaved Hamming-metric codes).

Contribution. We present a Metzner–Kapturowski-like decoding algorithm for high-order interleaved sum-rank-metric codes with an arbitrary linear constituent code. This gives valuable insights for the design of McEliece-like cryptosystems based on interleaved codes in the sum-rank metric. The proposed algorithm is purely linear-algebraic and can guarantee to correct errors of sum-rank weight $t \leq d-2$ if the error matrix has full $\mathbb{F}_{q^m}$-rank t, where d is the minimum distance of the code. The computational complexity of the algorithm s in the order of $O(\max\{n^3, n^2 s\})$ operations over $\mathbb{F}_{q^m}$, where $s \geq t$ is the inter-eaving order and n denotes the length of the linear constituent code. Note, that he decoding complexity is independent of the code structure of the constituent ode since the proposed algorithm exploits properties of high-order interleaving nly. Since the sum-rank metric generalizes both the Hamming and the rank etric, the original Metzner–Kapturowski decoder [14] as well as its rank-metric nalog [18,20] can be recovered from our proposal.

Preliminaries

et q be a power of a prime and let $\mathbb{F}_q$ denote the finite field of order q and $_m$ an extension field of degree m. We use $\mathbb{F}_q^{a \times b}$ to denote the set of all $a \times b$ atrices over $\mathbb{F}_q$ and $\mathbb{F}_{q^m}^b$ for the set of all row vectors of length b over $\mathbb{F}_{q^m}$.

Let $\boldsymbol{b} = (b_1, \ldots, b_m) \in \mathbb{F}_{q^m}^m$ be a fixed (ordered) basis of $\mathbb{F}_{q^m}$ over $\mathbb{F}_q$. We note by $\text{ext}(\alpha)$ the column-wise expansion of an element $\alpha \in \mathbb{F}_{q^m}$ over $\mathbb{F}_q$ ith respect to $\boldsymbol{b}$), i.e.

$$\text{ext} : \mathbb{F}_{q^m} \mapsto \mathbb{F}_q^m$$

such that $\alpha = \boldsymbol{b} \cdot \text{ext}(\alpha)$. This notation is extended to vectors and matrices by applying ext($\cdot$) in an element-wise manner.

By $[a : b]$ we denote the set of integers $[a : b] := \{i : a \leq i \leq b\}$. For a matrix $\boldsymbol{A}$ of size $a \times b$ and entries $A_{i,j}$ for $i \in [1 : a]$ and $j \in [1 : b]$, we define the submatrix notation

$$\boldsymbol{A}_{[c:d],[e:f]} := \begin{pmatrix} A_{c,e} & \dots & A_{c,f} \\ \vdots & \ddots & \vdots \\ A_{d,e} & \dots & A_{d,f} \end{pmatrix}.$$

The $\mathbb{F}_{q^m}$-linear row space of a matrix $\boldsymbol{A}$ over $\mathbb{F}_{q^m}$ is denoted by $\mathcal{R}_{q^m}(\boldsymbol{A})$. Its $\mathbb{F}_q$-linear row space is defined as $\mathcal{R}_q(\boldsymbol{A}) := \mathcal{R}_q(\text{ext}(\boldsymbol{A}))$. We denote the row-echelon form and the (right) kernel of $\boldsymbol{A}$ as $\text{REF}(\boldsymbol{A})$ and $\ker_r(\boldsymbol{A})$, respectively.

2.1 Sum-Rank-Metric Codes

Let $\boldsymbol{n} = (n_1, \dots, n_\ell) \in \mathbb{N}^\ell$ with $n_i > 0$ for all $i \in [1 : \ell]$ be a length partition[1] of n, i.e. $n = \sum_{i=1}^{\ell} n_i$. Further let $\boldsymbol{x} = (\boldsymbol{x}^{(1)} \mid \boldsymbol{x}^{(2)} \mid \dots \mid \boldsymbol{x}^{(\ell)}) \in \mathbb{F}_{q^m}^n$ be a vector over a finite field $\mathbb{F}_{q^m}$ with $\boldsymbol{x}^{(i)} \in \mathbb{F}_{q^m}^{n_i}$. For each $\boldsymbol{x}^{(i)}$ define the rank $\text{rk}_\text{q}(\boldsymbol{x}^{(i)}) := \text{rk}_\text{q}(\text{ext}(\boldsymbol{x}^{(i)}))$ where $\text{ext}(\boldsymbol{x}^{(i)})$ is a matrix in $\mathbb{F}_q^{m \times n_i}$ for all $i \in [1 : \ell]$. The *sum-rank weight* of $\boldsymbol{x}$ with respect to the length partition $\boldsymbol{n}$ is defined as

$$\text{wt}_{\Sigma R}(\boldsymbol{x}) := \sum_{i=1}^{\ell} \text{rk}_q(\boldsymbol{x}^{(i)})$$

and the *sum-rank distance* of two vectors $\boldsymbol{x}, \boldsymbol{y} \in \mathbb{F}_{q^m}^n$ is defined as $d_{\Sigma R}(\boldsymbol{x}, \boldsymbol{y}) := \text{wt}_{\Sigma R}(\boldsymbol{x} - \boldsymbol{y})$. Note that the sum-rank metric equals the Hamming metric for $\ell = n$ and is equal to the rank metric for $\ell = 1$.

An $\mathbb{F}_{q^m}$*-linear sum-rank-metric code* $\mathcal{C}$ is an $\mathbb{F}_{q^m}$-subspace of $\mathbb{F}_{q^m}^n$. It has length n (with respect to a length partition $\boldsymbol{n}$), dimension $k := \dim_{q^m}(\mathcal{C})$ and minimum (sum-rank) distance $d := \min\{d_{\Sigma R}(\boldsymbol{x}, \boldsymbol{y}) : \boldsymbol{x}, \boldsymbol{y} \in \mathcal{C}\}$. To emphasize its parameters, we write $\mathcal{C}[\boldsymbol{n}, k, d]$ in the following.

2.2 Interleaved Sum-Rank-Metric Codes and Channel Model

A (vertically) s-interleaved code is a direct sum of s codes of the same length n. In this paper we consider *homogeneous* interleaved codes, i.e. codes obtained by interleaving codewords of *a single* constituent code.

Definition 1 (Interleaved Sum-Rank-Metric Code). *Let $\mathcal{C}[\boldsymbol{n}, k, d] \subseteq \mathbb{F}_{q^m}^n$ be an $\mathbb{F}_{q^m}$-linear sum-rank-metric code of length n with length partition $\boldsymbol{n} = (n_1, n_2, \dots, n_\ell) \in \mathbb{N}^\ell$ and minimum sum-rank distance d. Then the corresponding (homogeneous) s-interleaved code is defined as*

$$\mathcal{IC}[s; \boldsymbol{n}, k, d] := \left\{ \begin{pmatrix} \boldsymbol{c}_1 \\ \vdots \\ \boldsymbol{c}_s \end{pmatrix} : \boldsymbol{c}_j = (\boldsymbol{c}_j^{(1)} \mid \dots \mid \boldsymbol{c}_j^{(\ell)}) \in \mathcal{C}[\boldsymbol{n}, k, d] \right\} \subseteq \mathbb{F}_{q^m}^{s \times n}.$$

[1] Note that this is also known as (integer) composition into exactly ℓ parts in combinatorics.

Each codeword $\boldsymbol{C} \in \mathcal{IC}[s; \boldsymbol{n}, k, d]$ can be written as

$$\boldsymbol{C} = \left(\begin{array}{c|c|c|c} \boldsymbol{c}_1^{(1)} & \boldsymbol{c}_1^{(2)} & \dots & \boldsymbol{c}_1^{(\ell)} \\ \vdots & \vdots & \ddots & \vdots \\ \boldsymbol{c}_s^{(1)} & \boldsymbol{c}_s^{(2)} & \dots & \boldsymbol{c}_s^{(\ell)} \end{array}\right) \in \mathbb{F}_{q^m}^{s \times n}$$

or equivalently as

$$\boldsymbol{C} = (\boldsymbol{C}^{(1)} \mid \boldsymbol{C}^{(2)} \mid \cdots \mid \boldsymbol{C}^{(\ell)})$$

where

$$\boldsymbol{C}^{(i)} := \begin{pmatrix} \boldsymbol{c}_1^{(i)} \\ \boldsymbol{c}_2^{(i)} \\ \vdots \\ \boldsymbol{c}_s^{(i)} \end{pmatrix} \in \mathbb{F}_{q^m}^{s \times n_i}$$

for all $i \in [1 : \ell]$.

As a channel model we consider the additive sum-rank channel

$$\boldsymbol{Y} = \boldsymbol{C} + \boldsymbol{E}$$

where

$$\boldsymbol{E} = (\boldsymbol{E}^{(1)} \mid \boldsymbol{E}^{(2)} \mid \dots \mid \boldsymbol{E}^{(\ell)}) \in \mathbb{F}_{q^m}^{s \times n}$$

with $\boldsymbol{E}^{(i)} \in \mathbb{F}_{q^m}^{s \times n_i}$ and $\mathrm{rk}_q(\boldsymbol{E}^{(i)}) = t_i$ for all $i \in [1 : \ell]$ is an error matrix with $\mathrm{wt}_{\Sigma R}(\boldsymbol{E}) = \sum_{i=1}^{\ell} t_i = t$.

3 Decoding of High-Order Interleaved Sum-Rank-Metric Codes

In this section, we propose a Metzner–Kapturowski-like decoder for the sum-rank metric, that is a generalization of the decoders proposed in [14,18,20]. Similar to the Hamming- and the rank-metric case, the proposed decoder works for errors of sum-rank weight t up to $d - 2$ that satisfy the following conditions:

- *High-order condition:* The interleaving order $s \geq t$,
- *Full-rank condition:* Full $\mathbb{F}_{q^m}$-rank error matrices, i.e., $\mathrm{rk}_{q^m}(\boldsymbol{E}) = t$.

Note that the full-rank condition implies the high-order condition since the $\mathbb{F}_{q^m}$-rank of a matrix $\boldsymbol{E} \in \mathbb{F}_{q^m}^{s \times n}$ is at most s.

Throughout this section we consider a homogeneous s-interleaved sum-rank-metric code $\mathcal{IC}[s; \boldsymbol{n}, k, d]$ over a field $\mathbb{F}_{q^m}$ with a constituent code $\mathcal{C}[\boldsymbol{n}, k, d]$ defined by a parity-check matrix

$$\boldsymbol{H} = (\boldsymbol{H}^{(1)} \mid \boldsymbol{H}^{(2)} \mid \dots \mid \boldsymbol{H}^{(\ell)}) \in \mathbb{F}_{q^m}^{(n-k) \times n}$$

with $\boldsymbol{H}^{(i)} \in \mathbb{F}_{q^m}^{(n-k)\times n_i}$. The goal is to recover a codeword $\boldsymbol{C} \in \mathcal{IC}[s;\boldsymbol{n},k,d]$ from the matrix

$$\boldsymbol{Y} = \boldsymbol{C} + \boldsymbol{E} \in \mathbb{F}_{q^m}^{s\times n}$$

that is corrupted by an error matrix $\boldsymbol{E}$ of sum-rank weight $\mathrm{wt}_{\Sigma R}(\boldsymbol{E}) = t$ assuming *high-order* and *full-rank* condition.

As the Metzner–Kapturowski algorithm and its adaptation to the rank metric, the presented decoding algorithm consists of two steps. The decoder first determines the error support from the syndrome matrix $\boldsymbol{S} = \boldsymbol{H}\boldsymbol{Y}^\top$. Secondly, erasure decoding is performed to recover the error $\boldsymbol{E}$ itself.

3.1 The Error Support

The error matrix $\boldsymbol{E}$ can be decomposed as

$$\boldsymbol{E} = \boldsymbol{A}\boldsymbol{B} \tag{1}$$

where $\boldsymbol{A} = (\boldsymbol{A}^{(1)} \mid \boldsymbol{A}^{(2)} \mid \ldots \mid \boldsymbol{A}^{(\ell)}) \in \mathbb{F}_{q^m}^{s\times t}$ with $\boldsymbol{A}^{(i)} \in \mathbb{F}_{q^m}^{s\times t_i}$ and $\mathrm{rk_q}(\boldsymbol{A}^{(i)}) = t_i$ and

$$\boldsymbol{B} = \mathrm{diag}\,(\boldsymbol{B}^{(1)}, \ldots, \boldsymbol{B}^{(\ell)}) \in \mathbb{F}_q^{t\times n} \tag{2}$$

with $\boldsymbol{B}^{(i)} \in \mathbb{F}_q^{t_i\times n_i}$ and $\mathrm{rk_q}(\boldsymbol{B}^{(i)}) = t_i$ for all $i \in [1:\ell]$ (see [17, Lemma 10]). The rank support of one block $\boldsymbol{E}^{(i)}$ is defined as

$$\mathrm{supp}_R\left(\boldsymbol{E}^{(i)}\right) := \mathcal{R}_q\left(\boldsymbol{E}^{(i)}\right) = \mathcal{R}_q\left(\boldsymbol{B}^{(i)}\right).$$

The sum-rank support for the error $\boldsymbol{E}$ with sum-rank weight t is then defined as

$$\begin{aligned}\mathrm{supp}_{\Sigma R}(\boldsymbol{E}) &:= \mathrm{supp}_R\left(\boldsymbol{E}^{(1)}\right) \times \mathrm{supp}_R\left(\boldsymbol{E}^{(2)}\right) \times \cdots \times \mathrm{supp}_R\left(\boldsymbol{E}^{(\ell)}\right) \\ &= \mathcal{R}_q\left(\boldsymbol{B}^{(1)}\right) \times \mathcal{R}_q\left(\boldsymbol{B}^{(2)}\right) \times \cdots \times \mathcal{R}_q\left(\boldsymbol{B}^{(\ell)}\right).\end{aligned} \tag{3}$$

The following result from [17] shows how the error matrix $\boldsymbol{E}$ can be reconstructed from the sum-rank support and the syndrome matrix $\boldsymbol{S}$.

Lemma 1 (Column-Erasure Decoder [17, Theorem 13]). *Let $t < d$ and $\boldsymbol{B} = \mathrm{diag}\,(\boldsymbol{B}^{(1)}, \ldots, \boldsymbol{B}^{(\ell)}) \in \mathbb{F}_q^{t\times n}$ be a basis of the row space of the error matrix $\boldsymbol{E} \in \mathbb{F}_{q^m}^{s\times n}$ and $\boldsymbol{S} = \boldsymbol{H}\boldsymbol{E}^\top \in \mathbb{F}_{q^m}^{(n-k)\times \ell}$ be the corresponding syndrome matrix. Then, the error is given by $\boldsymbol{E} = \boldsymbol{A}\boldsymbol{B}$ with $\boldsymbol{A}$ being the unique solution of the linear system*

$$\boldsymbol{S} = (\boldsymbol{H}\boldsymbol{B}^\top)\boldsymbol{A}^\top$$

and $\boldsymbol{E}$ can be computed in $O\big((n-k)^3 m^2\big)$ operations over $\mathbb{F}_q$.

3.2 Recovering the Error Support

In the following we show how to recover the sum-rank support $\mathrm{supp}_{\Sigma R}(\boldsymbol{E})$ of the error $\boldsymbol{E}$ given the syndrome matrix

$$\boldsymbol{S} = \boldsymbol{H}\boldsymbol{Y}^\top = \boldsymbol{H}\boldsymbol{E}^\top = \sum_{i=1}^{\ell} \boldsymbol{H}^{(i)}(\boldsymbol{E}^{(i)})^\top$$

and the parity-check matrix $\boldsymbol{H}$ of the sum-rank-metric code $\mathcal{IC}[s;\boldsymbol{n},k,d]$. Let $\boldsymbol{P} \in \mathbb{F}_{q^m}^{(n-k)\times(n-k)}$ with $\mathrm{rk}_{q^m}(\boldsymbol{P}) = n-k$ be such that $\boldsymbol{PS} = \mathrm{REF}(\boldsymbol{S})$. Further, let $\boldsymbol{H}_{\mathrm{sub}}$ be the rows of $\boldsymbol{PH}$ corresponding to the zero rows in $\boldsymbol{PS}$, i.e. we have

$$\boldsymbol{PS} = \begin{pmatrix} \boldsymbol{S}' \\ \boldsymbol{0} \end{pmatrix} \quad \text{and} \quad \boldsymbol{PH} = \begin{pmatrix} \boldsymbol{H}' \\ \boldsymbol{H}_{\mathrm{sub}} \end{pmatrix}$$

where $\boldsymbol{S}'$ and $\boldsymbol{H}'$ have the same number of rows. Since $\boldsymbol{P}$ performs $\mathbb{F}_{q^m}$-linear row operations on $\boldsymbol{H}$, the ℓ blocks of $\boldsymbol{PH}$ are preserved, i.e. we have that

$$\boldsymbol{H}_{\mathrm{sub}} = \left(\boldsymbol{H}_{\mathrm{sub}}^{(1)} \mid \boldsymbol{H}_{\mathrm{sub}}^{(2)} \mid \dots \mid \boldsymbol{H}_{\mathrm{sub}}^{(\ell)}\right).$$

The following lemma is a generalization of [18, Lemma 3] to the sum-rank metric.

Lemma 2. *Let* $\boldsymbol{H} = (\boldsymbol{H}^{(1)} \mid \boldsymbol{H}^{(2)} \mid \dots \mid \boldsymbol{H}^{(\ell)}) \in \mathbb{F}_{q^m}^{(n-k)\times n}$ *be a parity-check matrix of a sum-rank-metric code* $\mathcal{C}$ *and let* $\boldsymbol{S} = \boldsymbol{H}\boldsymbol{E}^\top \in \mathbb{F}_{q^m}^{(n-k)\times s}$ *be the syndrome matrix of an error*

$$\boldsymbol{E} = (\boldsymbol{E}^{(1)} \mid \boldsymbol{E}^{(2)} \mid \dots \mid \boldsymbol{E}^{(\ell)}) \in \mathbb{F}_{q^m}^{s\times n}$$

of sum-rank weight $\mathrm{wt}_{\Sigma R}(\boldsymbol{E}) = t < n-k$ *where* $\boldsymbol{E}^{(i)} \in \mathbb{F}_{q^m}^{s\times n_i}$ *with* $\mathrm{rk}_q(\boldsymbol{E}^{(i)}) = t_i$ *for all* $i \in [1:\ell]$. *Let* $\boldsymbol{P} \in \mathbb{F}_{q^m}^{(n-k)\times(n-k)}$ *be a matrix with* $\mathrm{rk}_{q^m}(\boldsymbol{P}) = n-k$ *such that* $\boldsymbol{PS}$ *is in row-echelon form. Then,* $\boldsymbol{PS}$ *has at least* $n-k-t$ *zero rows. Let* $\boldsymbol{H}_{sub}$ *be the submatrix of* $\boldsymbol{PH}$ *corresponding to the zero rows in* $\boldsymbol{PS}$. *Then we have that*

$$\mathcal{R}_{q^m}(\boldsymbol{H}_{sub}) = \ker_r(\boldsymbol{E})_{q^m} \cap \mathcal{C}^\perp \iff \mathcal{R}_{q^m}(\boldsymbol{H}_{sub}) = \ker_r(\boldsymbol{E})_{q^m} \cap \mathcal{R}_{q^m}(\boldsymbol{H}).$$

Proof. Since $\boldsymbol{E}^{(i)}$ has $\mathbb{F}_q$-rank t_i, its $\mathbb{F}_{q^m}$-rank is at most t_i for all $i \in [1:\ell]$. Since $t = \sum_{i=1}^{\ell} t_i$, $\boldsymbol{E}$ has at most $\mathbb{F}_{q^m}$-rank t as well. Hence, the $\mathbb{F}_{q^m}$-rank of $\boldsymbol{S}$ is at most t and thus at least $n-k-t$ of the $n-k$ rows of $\boldsymbol{PS}$ are zero.

The rows of $\boldsymbol{PH}$ and therefore also the rows of $\boldsymbol{H}_{\mathrm{sub}}$ are in the row space of $\boldsymbol{H}$, i.e. in the dual code $\mathcal{C}^\perp$. Since $\boldsymbol{H}_{\mathrm{sub}}\boldsymbol{E}^\top = \boldsymbol{0}$ the rows of $\boldsymbol{H}_{\mathrm{sub}}$ are in the kernel of $\boldsymbol{E}$. It is left to show that the rows of $\boldsymbol{H}_{\mathrm{sub}}$ span the entire intersection space. Write

$$\boldsymbol{PS} = \begin{pmatrix} \boldsymbol{S}' \\ \boldsymbol{0} \end{pmatrix} \quad \text{and} \quad \boldsymbol{PH} = \begin{pmatrix} \boldsymbol{H}' \\ \boldsymbol{H}_{\mathrm{sub}} \end{pmatrix}$$

where $\boldsymbol{S}'$ and $\boldsymbol{H}'$ have the same number of rows and $\boldsymbol{S}'$ has full $\mathbb{F}_{q^m}$-rank. Let $\boldsymbol{v} = (\boldsymbol{v}_1, \boldsymbol{v}_2) \in \mathbb{F}_{q^m}^{n-k}$ and let

$$\boldsymbol{h} = \boldsymbol{v} \cdot \begin{pmatrix} \boldsymbol{H}' \\ \boldsymbol{H}_{\text{sub}} \end{pmatrix}$$

be a vector in the row space of $\boldsymbol{PH}$ and in the kernel of $\boldsymbol{E}$. Since $\boldsymbol{H}_{\text{sub}}\boldsymbol{E}^\top = \boldsymbol{0}$ we have that $\boldsymbol{0} = \boldsymbol{h}\boldsymbol{E}^\top = \boldsymbol{v}_1\boldsymbol{H}'\boldsymbol{E}^\top = \boldsymbol{v}_1\boldsymbol{S}'$. This implies that $\boldsymbol{v}_1 = \boldsymbol{0}$ since the rows of $\boldsymbol{S}'$ are linearly independent and thus $\boldsymbol{h}$ is in the row space of $\boldsymbol{H}_{\text{sub}}$. □

Lemma 3 shows that the kernel $\ker_r(\boldsymbol{E})_{q^m}$ of the error $\boldsymbol{E}$ is connected with the kernel of the matrix $\boldsymbol{B}$ if the $\mathbb{F}_{q^m}$-rank of the error is t, i.e. if the full-rank condition is satisfied.

Lemma 3. *Let* $\boldsymbol{E} = (\boldsymbol{E}^{(1)} \mid \boldsymbol{E}^{(2)} \mid \ldots \mid \boldsymbol{E}^{(\ell)}) \in \mathbb{F}_{q^m}^{s\times n}$ *be an error of sum-rank weight* $\text{wt}_{\Sigma R}(\boldsymbol{E}) = t$ *where* $\boldsymbol{E}^{(i)} \in \mathbb{F}_{q^m}^{s\times n_i}$ *with* $\text{rk}_q(\boldsymbol{E}) = t_i$ *for all* $i \in [1:\ell]$. *If* $\text{rk}_{q^m}(\boldsymbol{E}) = t$ *(full-rank condition), then*

$$\ker_r(\boldsymbol{E})_{q^m} = \ker_r(\boldsymbol{B})_{q^m}$$

where $\boldsymbol{B} \in \mathbb{F}_q^{t\times n}$ *is any basis for the* $\mathbb{F}_q$*-row space of* $\boldsymbol{E}$ *of the form* (2). *Further, it holds that*

$$\ker_r(\boldsymbol{E}^{(i)})_{q^m} = \ker_r(\boldsymbol{B}^{(i)})_{q^m}, \quad \forall i \in [1:\ell].$$

Proof. Let $\boldsymbol{E}$ have $\mathbb{F}_{q^m}$-rank t and let $\boldsymbol{E} = \boldsymbol{AB}$ be a decomposition of the error as in (1) such that $\boldsymbol{E}^{(i)} = \boldsymbol{A}^{(i)}\boldsymbol{B}^{(i)}$ for all $i \in [1:\ell]$. Since $\text{rk}_{q^m}(\boldsymbol{E}) = t$ implies that $\text{rk}_{q^m}(\boldsymbol{A}) = t$, we have that $\ker_r(\boldsymbol{A})_{q^m} = \{\boldsymbol{0}\}$. Hence, for all $\boldsymbol{v} \in \mathbb{F}_{q^m}^n$, $(\boldsymbol{AB})\boldsymbol{v}^\top = \boldsymbol{0}$ if and only if $\boldsymbol{B}\boldsymbol{v}^\top = \boldsymbol{0}$ which is equivalent to

$$\ker_r(\boldsymbol{E})_{q^m} = \ker_r(\boldsymbol{AB})_{q^m} = \ker_r(\boldsymbol{B})_{q^m}. \tag{4}$$

Assume a vector $\boldsymbol{v} = (\boldsymbol{v}^{(1)} \mid \boldsymbol{v}^{(2)} \mid \ldots \mid \boldsymbol{v}^{(\ell)}) \in \mathbb{F}_{q^m}^n$ and let $\boldsymbol{v}^{(i)} \in \mathbb{F}_{q^m}^{n_i}$ be any element in $\ker_r(\boldsymbol{B}^{(i)})_{q^m}$. Due to the block-diagonal structure of $\boldsymbol{B}$ (see (2)) we have that

$$\boldsymbol{B}\boldsymbol{v}^\top = \boldsymbol{0} \iff \boldsymbol{B}^{(i)}(\boldsymbol{v}^{(i)})^\top = \boldsymbol{0}, \quad \forall i \in [1:\ell]$$

which is equivalent to

$$\boldsymbol{v} \in \ker_r(\boldsymbol{B})_{q^m} \iff \boldsymbol{v}^{(i)} \in \ker_r(\boldsymbol{B}^{(i)})_{q^m}, \quad \forall i \in [1:\ell]. \tag{5}$$

Combining (4) and (5) yields the result. □

Combining Lemma 2 and Lemma 3 finally allows us to recover the sum-rank support of $\boldsymbol{E}$.

Theorem 1. *Let* $\boldsymbol{E} = (\boldsymbol{E}^{(1)} \mid \boldsymbol{E}^{(2)} \mid \ldots \mid \boldsymbol{E}^{(\ell)}) \in \mathbb{F}_{q^m}^{s\times n}$ *be an error of sum-rank weight* $\text{wt}_{\Sigma R}(\boldsymbol{E}) = t \leq d-2$ *where* $\boldsymbol{E}^{(i)} \in \mathbb{F}_{q^m}^{s\times n_i}$ *with* $\text{rk}_q(\boldsymbol{E}^{(i)}) = t_i$ *for all* $i \in [1:\ell]$. *If* $s \geq t$ *(high-order condition) and* $\text{rk}_{q^m}(\boldsymbol{E}) = t$ *(full-rank condition), then*

$$\mathcal{R}_q\left(\boldsymbol{E}^{(i)}\right) = \ker_r\left(ext(\boldsymbol{H}_{sub}^{(i)})\right)_q, \quad \forall i \in [1:\ell]. \tag{6}$$

Proof. In the following, we prove that the $\mathbb{F}_q$-row space of the extended $\boldsymbol{H}_{\text{sub}}$ instead of the $\mathbb{F}_{q^m}$-row space of $\boldsymbol{H}_{\text{sub}}$ is equal to the $\mathbb{F}_q$-kernel of $\boldsymbol{B}$, i.e.,

$$\mathcal{R}_q(\text{ext}(\boldsymbol{H}_{\text{sub}})) = \ker_r(\boldsymbol{B})_q.$$

Recall that $\mathcal{R}_q(\boldsymbol{E}^{(i)}) = \mathcal{R}_q(\boldsymbol{B}^{(i)})$ holds for all $i \in [1:\ell]$ according to the definition of the error decomposition (1). With this in mind, the statement of the theorem is equivalent to showing $\ker_r(\boldsymbol{B}^{(i)})_q = \mathcal{R}_q\left(\text{ext}(\boldsymbol{H}_{\text{sub}}^{(i)})\right)$ for all $i \in [1:\ell]$ since $\mathcal{R}_q(\boldsymbol{B}^{(i)})^{\perp} = \ker_r(\boldsymbol{B}^{(i)})_q$ and $\ker_r\left(\text{ext}(\boldsymbol{H}_{\text{sub}}^{(i)})\right)_q^{\perp} = \mathcal{R}_q\left(\text{ext}(\boldsymbol{H}_{\text{sub}}^{(i)})\right)$ hold.

First we show that $\mathcal{R}_q(\text{ext}(\boldsymbol{H}_{\text{sub}})) \subseteq \ker_r(\boldsymbol{B})_q$ which, due to the block-diagonal structure of $\boldsymbol{B}$, implies that $\mathcal{R}_q\left(\text{ext}(\boldsymbol{H}_{\text{sub}}^{(i)})\right) \subseteq \ker_r(\boldsymbol{B}^{(i)})_q$ for all $i \in [1:\ell]$. Let $\boldsymbol{v} = (\boldsymbol{v}^{(1)} \mid \boldsymbol{v}^{(2)} \mid \ldots \mid \boldsymbol{v}^{(\ell)}) \in \mathbb{F}_{q^m}^n$ with $\boldsymbol{v}^{(i)} \in \mathbb{F}_{q^m}^{n_i}$ for all $i \in [1:\ell]$ be any element in the $\mathbb{F}_{q^m}$-linear row space of $\boldsymbol{H}_{\text{sub}}$. Then, by [18, Lemma 5] we have that each row $\boldsymbol{v}_j$ for $j \in [1:m]$ of $\text{ext}(\boldsymbol{v})$ is in $\mathcal{R}_q(\text{ext}(\boldsymbol{H}_{\text{sub}}))$ which implies that $\boldsymbol{v}_j^{(i)} \in \mathcal{R}_q\left(\text{ext}(\boldsymbol{H}_{\text{sub}}^{(i)})\right)$ for all $i \in [1:\ell]$. By Lemma 3 we have that $\boldsymbol{v} \in \ker_r(\boldsymbol{B})_{q^m}$, i.e. we have

$$\boldsymbol{B}\boldsymbol{v}^\top = \boldsymbol{0} \iff \boldsymbol{B}^{(i)}(\boldsymbol{v}^{(i)})^\top = \boldsymbol{0}, \quad \forall i \in [1:\ell]$$

where the right-hand side follows from the block-diagonal structure of $\boldsymbol{B}$. Since the entries of $\boldsymbol{B}$ are from $\mathbb{F}_q$, we have that

$$\text{ext}(\boldsymbol{B}\boldsymbol{v}^\top) = \boldsymbol{B}\text{ext}(\boldsymbol{v})^\top = \boldsymbol{0} \tag{7}$$

which implies that $\boldsymbol{v} \in \ker_r(\boldsymbol{B})_q$ and thus $\mathcal{R}_q(\text{ext}(\boldsymbol{H}_{\text{sub}})) \subseteq \ker_r(\boldsymbol{B})_q$. Due to the block-diagonal structure of $\boldsymbol{B}$ we get from (7) that

$$\text{ext}(\boldsymbol{B}^{(i)}(\boldsymbol{v}^{(i)})^\top) = \boldsymbol{B}^{(i)}\text{ext}(\boldsymbol{v}^{(i)})^\top = \boldsymbol{0}, \quad \forall i \in [1:\ell] \tag{8}$$

which implies that $\boldsymbol{v}_j^{(i)} \in \ker_r(\boldsymbol{B}^{(i)})_q$ for all $i \in [1:\ell]$ and $j \in [1:m]$. Therefore, we have that $\mathcal{R}_q\left(\text{ext}(\boldsymbol{H}_{\text{sub}}^{(i)})\right) \subseteq \ker_r(\boldsymbol{B}^{(i)})_q$, for all $i \in [1:\ell]$.

Next, we show that $\ker_r(\boldsymbol{B}^{(i)})_q = \mathcal{R}_q\left(\text{ext}(\boldsymbol{H}_{\text{sub}}^{(i)})\right)$ for all $i \in [1:\ell]$ by showing that

$$r_i := \dim\left(\mathcal{R}_q\left(\text{ext}(\boldsymbol{H}_{\text{sub}}^{(i)})\right)\right) = n_i - t_i, \quad \forall i \in [1:\ell].$$

Since $\mathcal{R}_q\left(\text{ext}(\boldsymbol{H}_{\text{sub}}^{(i)})\right) \subseteq \ker_r(\boldsymbol{B}^{(i)})_q$ we have that $r_i > n_i - t_i$ is not possible for all $i \in [1:\ell]$.

In the following we show that $r < n-t$ is not possible and therefore $r_i = n_i - t_i$ holds for all $i = [1:\ell]$. Let $\{\boldsymbol{h}_1, \ldots, \boldsymbol{h}_r\} \subseteq \mathbb{F}_q^n$ be a basis for $\mathcal{R}_q(\text{ext}(\boldsymbol{H}_{\text{sub}}))$ and define

$$\boldsymbol{H}_b = \begin{pmatrix} \boldsymbol{h}_1 \\ \boldsymbol{h}_2 \\ \vdots \\ \boldsymbol{h}_r \end{pmatrix} \in \mathbb{F}_q^{r \times n}$$

with $\boldsymbol{h}_j = (\boldsymbol{h}_j^{(1)} \mid \boldsymbol{h}_j^{(2)} \mid \ldots \mid \boldsymbol{h}_j^{(\ell)}) \in \mathbb{F}_q^n$ where $\boldsymbol{h}_j^{(i)} \in \mathcal{R}_q\left(\text{ext}(\boldsymbol{H}_{\text{sub}}^{(i)})\right)$ for $j \in [1:r]$ and $i \in [1:\ell]$. Also define

$$\boldsymbol{H}_b^{(i)} = \begin{pmatrix} \boldsymbol{h}_1^{(i)} \\ \boldsymbol{h}_2^{(i)} \\ \vdots \\ \boldsymbol{h}_r^{(i)} \end{pmatrix} \in \mathbb{F}_q^{r\times n_i}, \quad \forall i \in [1:\ell].$$

By the basis-extension theorem, there exist matrices $\boldsymbol{B}^{(i)\prime\prime} \in \mathbb{F}_q^{(n_i-t_i)\times n_i}$ such that the matrices

$$\boldsymbol{B}^{(i)\prime} := \left(\left(\boldsymbol{B}^{(i)}\right)^\top \mid \left(\boldsymbol{B}^{(i)\prime\prime}\right)^\top \right) \in \mathbb{F}_q^{n_i\times n_i}$$

have $\mathbb{F}_q$-rank n_i for all $i \in [1:\ell]$.

Next define $\check{\boldsymbol{H}}^{(i)} = \boldsymbol{H}_b^{(i)} \boldsymbol{B}^{(i)\prime} \in \mathbb{F}_q^{r\times n_i}$ for all $i \in [1:\ell]$ and

$$\check{\boldsymbol{H}} := \left(\check{\boldsymbol{H}}^{(1)} \mid \check{\boldsymbol{H}}^{(2)} \mid \ldots \mid \check{\boldsymbol{H}}^{(\ell)}\right) = \boldsymbol{H}_b \cdot \text{diag}\left(\boldsymbol{B}^{(1)\prime}, \ldots, \boldsymbol{B}^{(\ell)\prime}\right).$$

Since $\boldsymbol{h}_1^{(i)}, \boldsymbol{h}_2^{(i)}, \ldots, \boldsymbol{h}_r^{(i)}$ are in the right $\mathbb{F}_q$-kernel of $\boldsymbol{B}^{(i)}$ (see (8)) we have that

$$\check{\boldsymbol{H}}^{(i)} = \begin{pmatrix} 0 \ldots 0 & \check{h}_{1,t_i+1}^{(i)} & \cdots & \check{h}_{1,n_i}^{(i)} \\ \vdots \;\ddots\; \vdots & \vdots & \ddots & \vdots \\ 0 \ldots 0 & \check{h}_{r,t_i+1}^{(i)} & \cdots & \check{h}_{r,n_i}^{(i)} \end{pmatrix}$$

for all $i \in [1:\ell]$ and thus $\check{\boldsymbol{H}}$ has at least $t = \sum_{i=1}^{\ell} t_i$ all-zero columns.

By the assumption that $r < n - t$ it follows that $r_i < n_i - t_i$ holds for at least one block. Without loss of generality assume that this holds for the ℓ-th block, i.e. we have $r_\ell < n_\ell - t_\ell$. Then there exists a full-rank matrix

$$\boldsymbol{J} = \left(\begin{array}{c|c} \boldsymbol{I}_{t_\ell} & \boldsymbol{0} \\ \hline \boldsymbol{0} & \widetilde{\boldsymbol{J}} \end{array}\right) \in \mathbb{F}_q^{n_\ell \times n_\ell}$$

with $\widetilde{\boldsymbol{J}} \in \mathbb{F}_q^{(n_\ell-t_\ell)\times(n_\ell-t_\ell)}$ such that the matrix

$$\widetilde{\boldsymbol{H}} = \check{\boldsymbol{H}} \cdot \text{diag}\left(\boldsymbol{I}_{n_1}, \ldots, \boldsymbol{I}_{n_{\ell-1}}, \boldsymbol{J}\right) \quad (9$$

has at least $t+1$ all-zero columns.

Define $\boldsymbol{D} := \text{diag}\left(\boldsymbol{B}^{(1)\prime}, \ldots, \boldsymbol{B}^{(\ell-1)\prime}, \boldsymbol{B}^{(\ell)\prime}\boldsymbol{J}\right) \in \mathbb{F}_q^{n\times n}$ which has full $\mathbb{F}_q$-ran n. Then we have that $\widetilde{\boldsymbol{H}} = \boldsymbol{H}_b \cdot \boldsymbol{D}$. Since $\boldsymbol{D}$ has full $\mathbb{F}_q$-rank n, the submatr $\boldsymbol{D}' := \boldsymbol{D}_{[1:n],\mathcal{I}} \in \mathbb{F}_q^{n\times(t+1)}$ has $\mathbb{F}_q$-rank $t+1$, where

$$\mathcal{I} = [1:t_1] \cup [n_1+1:n_1+t_2] \cup [n_{\ell-2}+1:n_{\ell-2}+t_{\ell-1}] \cup [n_{\ell-1}+1:n_{\ell-1}+t_\ell+$$

By (9) it follows that

$$\boldsymbol{h}_j \cdot \boldsymbol{D}' = \boldsymbol{0} \in \mathbb{F}_q^{t+1} \tag{10}$$

for all $j \in [1:r]$. Since $\boldsymbol{H} \in \mathbb{F}_{q^m}^{(n-k)\times n}$ is a parity-check matrix of an $[\boldsymbol{n}, k, d]$ code it has at most $d-1$ $\mathbb{F}_{q^m}$-linearly dependent columns (see [17, Lemma 12]). Since by assumption $t+1 \leq d-1$ and $\mathrm{rk}_{\mathrm{q}}(\boldsymbol{D}') = t+1$ we have that $\mathrm{rk}_{\mathrm{q^m}}(\boldsymbol{H}\boldsymbol{D}') = t+1$. Thus, there exists a vector $\boldsymbol{g} \in \mathcal{R}_{q^m}(\boldsymbol{H})$ such that

$$\boldsymbol{g}\boldsymbol{D}' = (\boldsymbol{0}, g'_{t+1}) \in \mathbb{F}_{q^m}^{t+1}$$

with $g'_{t+1} \neq 0$. Since the first t positions of $\boldsymbol{g}\boldsymbol{D}'$ are equal to zero we have that $\boldsymbol{g} \in \mathcal{R}_{q^m}(\boldsymbol{H}_{\mathrm{sub}})$. Expanding the vector $\boldsymbol{g}\boldsymbol{D}'$ over $\mathbb{F}_q$ gives

$$\mathrm{ext}(\boldsymbol{g})\boldsymbol{D}' = \begin{pmatrix} \boldsymbol{0} & g'_{1,t+1} \\ \boldsymbol{0} & g'_{2,t+1} \\ \vdots & \vdots \\ \boldsymbol{0} & g'_{m,t+1} \end{pmatrix} \in \mathbb{F}_q^{m\times(t+1)}$$

where $\mathrm{ext}(g'_{t+1}) = (g'_{1,t+1}, g'_{2,t+1}, \ldots, g'_{m,t+1})^\top \in \mathbb{F}_q^{m\times 1}$. Since $g'_{t+1} \neq 0$ there exists at least one row with index ι in $\mathrm{ext}(g'_{t+1})$ such that $g'_{\iota,t+1} \neq 0$. Let $\boldsymbol{g}_\iota$ be the row in $\mathrm{ext}(\boldsymbol{g})$ for which $\boldsymbol{g}_\iota\boldsymbol{D}'$ is not all-zero. This leads to a contradiction according to (10). Thus $r < n-t$ is not possible and leaves $r = n-t$ and therefore also $r_i = n_i - t_i$ for all $i \in [1:\ell]$ as the only valid option. □

3.3 A Metzner–Kapturowski-Like Decoding Algorithm

Using Theorem 1 we can formulate an efficient decoding algorithm for high-order interleaved sum-rank-metric codes. The algorithm is given in Algorithm 1 and proceeds similar to the Metzner–Kapturowski(-like) decoding algorithms for Hamming- or rank-metric codes. As soon as $\boldsymbol{H}_{\mathrm{sub}}$ is computed from the syndrome natrix $\boldsymbol{S}$, the rank support of each block can be recovered independently using he results from Theorem 1. This corresponds to finding a matrix $\boldsymbol{B}^{(i)}$ with $\mathrm{k}_q(\boldsymbol{B}^{(i)}) = t_i$ such that $\mathrm{ext}(\boldsymbol{H}_{\mathrm{sub}}^{(i)})(\boldsymbol{B}^{(i)})^\top = \boldsymbol{0}$ for all $i \in [1:\ell]$ (see (6)).

heorem 2. *Let $\boldsymbol{C}$ be a codeword of a homogeneous s-interleaved sum-rank-etric code $\mathcal{IC}[s; \boldsymbol{n}, k, d]$ of minimum sum-rank distance d. Furthermore, let $\boldsymbol{E} \in$ $_{q^m}^{s\times n}$ be an error matrix of sum-rank weight $\mathrm{wt}_{\Sigma R}(\boldsymbol{E}) = t \leq d-2$ that fulfills $\leq s$ (*high-order condition*) and $\mathrm{rk}_{\mathrm{q^m}}(\boldsymbol{E}) = t$ (*full-rank condition*). Then $\boldsymbol{C}$ an be uniquely recovered from the received word $\boldsymbol{Y} = \boldsymbol{C} + \boldsymbol{E}$ using Algorithm 1 a time complexity equivalent to*

$$O(\max\{n^3, n^2 s\})$$

erations in $\mathbb{F}_{q^m}$.

Algorithm 1: Decoding High-Order Interleaved Sum-Rank-Metric Codes

Input : Parity-check matrix $\boldsymbol{H}$, Received word $\boldsymbol{Y}$

Output: Transmitted codeword $\boldsymbol{C}$

1 $\boldsymbol{S} \leftarrow \boldsymbol{H}\boldsymbol{Y}^\top \in \mathbb{F}_{q^m}^{(n-k)\times s}$

2 Compute $\boldsymbol{P} \in \mathbb{F}_{q^m}^{(n-k)\times(n-k)}$ s.t. $\boldsymbol{PS} = \mathrm{REF}(\boldsymbol{S})$

3 $\boldsymbol{H}_{\text{sub}} = \left(\boldsymbol{H}_{\text{sub}}^{(1)} \mid \boldsymbol{H}_{\text{sub}}^{(2)} \mid \ldots \mid \boldsymbol{H}_{\text{sub}}^{(\ell)}\right) \leftarrow (\boldsymbol{PH})_{[t+1:n-k],[1:n]} \in \mathbb{F}_{q^m}^{(n-t-k)\times n}$

4 **for** $i = 1, \ldots, \ell$ **do**

5 Compute $\boldsymbol{B}^{(i)} \in \mathbb{F}_q^{t_i \times n_i}$ s.t. $\mathrm{ext}(\boldsymbol{H}_{\text{sub}}^{(i)})(\boldsymbol{B}^{(i)})^\top = \boldsymbol{0}$ and $\mathrm{rk}_q(\boldsymbol{B}^{(i)}) = t_i$

6 $\boldsymbol{B} \leftarrow \mathrm{diag}(\boldsymbol{B}^{(1)}, \boldsymbol{B}^{(2)}, \ldots, \boldsymbol{B}^{(\ell)}) \in \mathbb{F}_q^{t\times n}$

7 Compute $\boldsymbol{A} \in \mathbb{F}_{q^m}^{s\times t}$ s.t. $(\boldsymbol{H}\boldsymbol{B}^\top)\boldsymbol{A}^\top = \boldsymbol{S}$

8 $\boldsymbol{C} \leftarrow \boldsymbol{Y} - \boldsymbol{AB} \in \mathbb{F}_{q^m}^{s\times n}$

9 **return** $\boldsymbol{C}$

Proof. By Lemma 1 the error matrix $\boldsymbol{E}$ can be decomposed into $\boldsymbol{E} = \boldsymbol{AB}$. Algorithm 1 first determines a basis of the error support $\mathrm{supp}_{\Sigma R}(\boldsymbol{E})$ and then performs erasure decoding to obtain $\boldsymbol{A}$. The matrix $\boldsymbol{B}$ is computed by transforming $\boldsymbol{S}$ into row-echelon form using a transformation matrix $\boldsymbol{P}$ (see Line 2). In Line 3, $\boldsymbol{H}_{\text{sub}}$ is obtained by choosing the last $n-k-t$ rows of $\boldsymbol{PH}$. Then using Theorem 1 for each block (see Line 5) we find a matrix $\boldsymbol{B}^{(i)}$ whose rows form a basis for $\ker_r\left(\mathrm{ext}(\boldsymbol{H}_{\text{sub}}^{(i)})\right)_q$ and therefore a basis for $\mathrm{supp}_R(\boldsymbol{E}^{(i)})$ for all $i \in [1:\ell]$. The matrix $\boldsymbol{B}$ is the block-diagonal matrix formed by $\boldsymbol{B}^{(i)}$ (cf. (2) and see Line 6). Finally, $\boldsymbol{A}$ can be computed from $\boldsymbol{B}$ and $\boldsymbol{H}$ using Lemma 1 in Line 7. Hence, Algorithm 1 returns the transmitted codeword in Line 9. The complexities of the lines in the algorithm are as follows:

- Line 1: The syndrome matrix $\boldsymbol{S} = \boldsymbol{H}\boldsymbol{Y}^\top$ can be computed in at most $O(n^2 s)$ operations in $\mathbb{F}_{q^m}$.
- Line 2: The transformation of $[\boldsymbol{S} \mid \boldsymbol{I}]$ into row-echelon form requires
$$O((n-k)^2(s+n-k)) \subseteq O(\max\{n^3, n^2 s\})$$
operations in $\mathbb{F}_{q^m}$.
- Line 3: The product $(\boldsymbol{PH})_{[t+1:n-k],[1:n]}$ can be computed requiring at mos $O(n(n-k-t)(n-k)) \subseteq O(n^3)$ operations in $\mathbb{F}_{q^m}$.
- Line 5: The transformation of $[\mathrm{ext}(\boldsymbol{H}_{\text{sub}}^{(i)})^\top \mid \boldsymbol{I}^\top]^\top$ into column-echelon for requires $O(n_i^2((n-k-t)m + n_i))$ operations in $\mathbb{F}_q$ per block. Overall we g $O\left(\sum_{i=1}^{\ell} n_i^2((n-k-t)m + n_i)\right) \subseteq O(n^3 m)$ operations in $\mathbb{F}_q$ since we ha that $O\left(\sum_{i=1}^{\ell} n_i^2\right) \subseteq O(n^2)$.

- Line 7: According to Lemma 1, this step can be done in $O\big((n-k)^3m^2\big)$ operations over $\mathbb{F}_q$.
- Line 8: The product $\boldsymbol{AB} = (\boldsymbol{A}^{(1)}\boldsymbol{B}^{(1)} \mid \boldsymbol{A}^{(2)}\boldsymbol{B}^{(2)} \mid \dots \mid \boldsymbol{A}^{(\ell)}\boldsymbol{B}^{(\ell)})$ can be computed in $\sum_{i=1}^{\ell} O(st_in_i) \subseteq O\big(sn^2\big)$ and the difference of $\boldsymbol{Y} - \boldsymbol{AB}$ can be computed in $O(sn)$ operations in $\mathbb{F}_{q^m}$.

The complexities for Line 5 and Line 7 are given for operations in $\mathbb{F}_q$. The number of $\mathbb{F}_q$-operations of both steps together is in $O\big(n^3m^2\big)$ and their execution complexity can be bounded by $O\big(n^3\big)$ operations in $\mathbb{F}_{q^m}$ (see [3]).

Thus, Algorithm 1 requires $O\big(\max\{n^3, n^2s\}\big)$ operations in $\mathbb{F}_{q^m}$ and $O\big(n^3m^2\big)$ operations in $\mathbb{F}_q$. □

Note that the complexity of Algorithm 1 is not affected by the decoding complexity of the underlying constituent code since a generic code with no structure is assumed.

Example 1. Let $\mathbb{F}_{q^m} = \mathbb{F}_{5^2}$ with the primitive polynomial $x^2 + 4x + 2$ and the primitive element α be given. Further let $\mathcal{IC}[s; \boldsymbol{n}, k, d]$ be an interleaved sum-rank-metric code of length n with $\boldsymbol{n} = (2, 2, 2)$, $k = 2$, $d = 5$, $\ell = 3$ and $s = 3$, defined by a generator matrix

$$\boldsymbol{G} = \left(\begin{array}{cc|cc|cc} \alpha^4 & \alpha^7 & \alpha^{21} & \alpha^4 & \alpha^3 & \alpha^5 \\ \alpha^{20} & \alpha^{11} & \alpha^{10} & \alpha^{21} & \alpha^{17} & \alpha^3 \end{array}\right)$$

and a parity-check matrix

$$\boldsymbol{H} = \left(\begin{array}{cc|cc|cc} 1 & 0 & 0 & 0 & \alpha^8 & \alpha^{19} \\ 0 & 1 & 0 & 0 & \alpha^5 & \alpha^{12} \\ 0 & 0 & 1 & 0 & \alpha^{17} & \alpha \\ 0 & 0 & 0 & 1 & \alpha^{22} & \alpha^{18} \end{array}\right).$$

Suppose that the codeword

$$\boldsymbol{C} = \left(\begin{array}{cc|cc|cc} \alpha^{20} & \alpha^{22} & 1 & \alpha^6 & \alpha^{11} & \alpha^{10} \\ \alpha^{23} & \alpha^7 & \alpha^4 & 0 & \alpha^{17} & \alpha^9 \\ \alpha^{15} & 1 & \alpha^{22} & \alpha^{12} & \alpha^{22} & \alpha^{10} \end{array}\right) \in \mathcal{IC}[s; \boldsymbol{n}, k, d]$$

is corrupted by the error

$$\boldsymbol{E} = \left(\begin{array}{cc|cc|cc} \alpha^{19} & \alpha & \alpha^6 & \alpha^9 & 0 & 0 \\ \alpha^{17} & \alpha^{23} & \alpha^{10} & \alpha^7 & 0 & 0 \\ \alpha^2 & \alpha^8 & \alpha^{15} & \alpha^6 & 0 & 0 \end{array}\right)$$

with $\mathrm{wt}_{\Sigma R}(\boldsymbol{E}) = \mathrm{rk}_{q^m}(\boldsymbol{E}) = t = 3$ and $t_1 = 1, t_2 = 2$ and $t_3 = 0$. The resulting received matrix is

$$\boldsymbol{Y} = \left(\begin{array}{cc|cc|cc} \alpha^{17} & \alpha^8 & \alpha^{18} & \alpha^{16} & \alpha^{11} & \alpha^{10} \\ \alpha^{11} & \alpha^3 & \alpha^{22} & \alpha^7 & \alpha^{17} & \alpha^9 \\ \alpha^7 & \alpha^4 & \alpha^{23} & 1 & \alpha^{22} & \alpha^{10} \end{array}\right).$$

First the syndrome matrix is computed as

$$S = HY^\top = \begin{pmatrix} \alpha^{19} & \alpha^{17} & \alpha^2 \\ \alpha & \alpha^{23} & \alpha^8 \\ \alpha^6 & \alpha^{10} & \alpha^{15} \\ \alpha^9 & \alpha^7 & \alpha^6 \end{pmatrix}$$

and then $\boldsymbol{P}$

$$P = \begin{pmatrix} 0 & \alpha^2 & \alpha^6 & \alpha^8 \\ 0 & \alpha^4 & \alpha^{20} & \alpha^{15} \\ 0 & \alpha^{23} & 0 & \alpha^3 \\ 1 & \alpha^6 & 0 & 0 \end{pmatrix} \Longrightarrow PS = \begin{pmatrix} 1 & 0 & 0 \\ 0 & 1 & 0 \\ 0 & 0 & 1 \\ 0 & 0 & 0 \end{pmatrix}$$

with $\mathrm{rk}_{q^m}(P) = 4$. The last $n - k - t = 1$ rows of

$$PH = \left(\begin{array}{cc|cc|cc} 0 & \alpha^2 & \alpha^6 & \alpha^8 & \alpha^{13} & \alpha^7 \\ 0 & \alpha^4 & \alpha^{20} & \alpha^{15} & \alpha^{22} & \alpha^{16} \\ 0 & \alpha^{23} & 0 & \alpha^3 & \alpha^{11} & 1 \\ 1 & \alpha^6 & 0 & 0 & \alpha^{18} & \alpha^{16} \end{array}\right)$$

gives us $H_{\mathrm{sub}} = (1\ \alpha^6 \,|\, 0\ 0 \,|\, \alpha^{18}\ \alpha^{16})$. We expand every block of H_{sub} over $\mathbb{F}_5$ and get

$$\mathrm{ext}(H_{\mathrm{sub}}^{(1)}) = \begin{pmatrix} 1 & 2 \\ 0 & 0 \end{pmatrix}, \quad \mathrm{ext}(H_{\mathrm{sub}}^{(2)}) = \begin{pmatrix} 0 & 0 \\ 0 & 0 \end{pmatrix} \quad \text{and} \quad \mathrm{ext}(H_{\mathrm{sub}}^{(3)}) = \begin{pmatrix} 3 & 3 \\ 0 & 3 \end{pmatrix}.$$

We observe that the second block $H_{\mathrm{sub}}^{(2)}$ is zero which corresponds to a full-rank error. Next we compute a basis for each of the right kernels of $\mathrm{ext}(H_{\mathrm{sub}}^{(1)})$, $\mathrm{ext}(H_{\mathrm{sub}}^{(2)})$, and $\mathrm{ext}(H_{\mathrm{sub}}^{(3)})$ which gives us

$$B^{(1)} = \begin{pmatrix} 1 & 2 \end{pmatrix}, \quad B^{(2)} = \begin{pmatrix} 1 & 0 \\ 0 & 1 \end{pmatrix}, \quad B^{(3)} = (),$$

where $B^{(3)}$ is empty since $\mathrm{ext}(H_{\mathrm{sub}}^{(3)})$ has full rank. The matrix $\boldsymbol{B}$ is then given by

$$B = \mathrm{diag}(B^{(1)}, B^{(2)}, B^{(3)}) = \left(\begin{array}{cc|cc|cc} 1 & 2 & 0 & 0 & 0 & 0 \\ \hline 0 & 0 & 1 & 0 & 0 & 0 \\ 0 & 0 & 0 & 1 & 0 & 0 \end{array}\right).$$

Solving for $\boldsymbol{A}$

$$HB^\top A^\top = S$$

$$\begin{pmatrix} 1 & 0 & 0 \\ \alpha^6 & 0 & 0 \\ 0 & 1 & 0 \\ 0 & 0 & 1 \end{pmatrix} A^\top = \begin{pmatrix} \alpha^{19} & \alpha^{17} & \alpha^2 \\ \alpha & \alpha^{23} & \alpha^8 \\ \alpha^6 & \alpha^{10} & \alpha^{15} \\ \alpha^9 & \alpha^7 & \alpha^6 \end{pmatrix}$$

gives

$$\boldsymbol{A}^\top = \begin{pmatrix} \alpha^{19} & \alpha^{17} & \alpha^{2} \\ \alpha^{6} & \alpha^{10} & \alpha^{15} \\ \alpha^{9} & \alpha^{7} & \alpha^{6} \end{pmatrix} \Rightarrow \hat{\boldsymbol{E}} = \boldsymbol{AB} = \left(\begin{array}{cc|cc|cc} \alpha^{19} & \alpha & \alpha^{6} & \alpha^{9} & 0 & 0 \\ \alpha^{17} & \alpha^{23} & \alpha^{10} & \alpha^{7} & 0 & 0 \\ \alpha^{2} & \alpha^{8} & \alpha^{15} & \alpha^{6} & 0 & 0 \end{array}\right)$$

and $\hat{\boldsymbol{E}} = \boldsymbol{E}$. Finally, the codeword $\boldsymbol{C}$ can be recovered as $\boldsymbol{C} = \boldsymbol{Y} - \hat{\boldsymbol{E}}$.

4 Implications for Decoding High-Order Interleaved Skew-Metric Codes

The *skew metric* is closely related to the sum-rank metric and was first considered in [10]. In particular, there exists an isometry between the sum-rank metric and the skew metric for most code parameters (see [10, Theorem 3]).

We show in this section how an interleaved skew-metric code can be constructed from a high-order interleaved sum-rank-metric code. This enables us to apply the presented decoder to the obtained high-order interleaved skew-metric codes and correct errors of a fixed skew weight.

The mentioned isometry can be described and applied to the interleaved context as follows: Let us consider vectors from $\mathbb{F}_{q^m}^n$, where n satisfies the constraints in [10, Theorem 2]. By [10, Theorem 3], there exists an invertible diagonal matrix $\boldsymbol{D} \in \mathbb{F}_{q^m}^{n \times n}$ such that

$$\mathrm{wt}_{\Sigma R}(\boldsymbol{xD}) = \mathrm{wt}_{skew}(\boldsymbol{x}), \qquad \forall \boldsymbol{x} \in \mathbb{F}_{q^m}^n, \tag{11}$$

where for the definition of the skew weight $\mathrm{wt}_{skew}(\cdot)$ see [10, Definition 9]. The skew metric for interleaved matrices has been considered in [2]. Namely, the extension of (11) to $\mathbb{F}_{q^m}^{s \times n}$, we get (see [2])

$$\mathrm{wt}_{\Sigma R}(\boldsymbol{XD}) = \mathrm{wt}_{skew}(\boldsymbol{X}), \qquad \forall \boldsymbol{X} \in \mathbb{F}_{q^m}^{s \times n}. \tag{12}$$

Now consider a linear s-interleaved sum-rank-metric code $\mathcal{IC}[s; \boldsymbol{n}, k, d]$ with parity-check matrix $\boldsymbol{H}$. Then by (12) the code

$$\mathcal{IC}_{skew}[s; n, k, d] := \left\{\boldsymbol{C}\boldsymbol{D}^{-1} : \boldsymbol{C} \in \mathcal{IC}[s; \boldsymbol{n}, k, d]\right\}$$

is an s-interleaved skew-metric code with minimum skew distance d. Observe that the parity-check matrix of the constituent skew-metric code $\mathcal{C}_{skew}[n, k, d]$ of $\mathcal{IC}_{skew}[s; n, k, d]$ is given by $\boldsymbol{H}_{skew} = \boldsymbol{HD}$.

Let us now study a decoding problem related to the obtained skew-metric code. Consider a matrix $\boldsymbol{Y} = \boldsymbol{C} + \boldsymbol{E}$ where $\boldsymbol{C} \in \mathcal{IC}_{skew}[s; n, k, d]$ and $\boldsymbol{E}$ is an error matrix with $\mathrm{wt}_{skew}(\boldsymbol{E}) = t$. Then (12) implies that we have

$$\widetilde{\boldsymbol{Y}} := (\boldsymbol{C} + \boldsymbol{E})\boldsymbol{D} = \widetilde{\boldsymbol{C}} + \widetilde{\boldsymbol{E}}$$

where $\widetilde{\boldsymbol{C}} \in \mathcal{IC}[s; \boldsymbol{n}, k, d]$ and $\mathrm{wt}_{\Sigma R}(\boldsymbol{E}) = t$. Hence, using the isometry from [10, Theorem 3] we can map the decoding problem in the skew metric to the sum-rank metric and vice versa (see also [2]).

In particular, this allows us to use Algorithm 1 to solve the posed decoding problem in the skew metric. The steps to decode a high-order interleaved skew-metric code $\mathcal{IC}_{skew}[s;n,k,d]$ with parity-check matrix $\boldsymbol{H}_{skew}$ (whose parameters comply with [10, Theorem 2]) can be summarized as follows:

1. Compute the transformed received matrix $\widetilde{\boldsymbol{Y}} := (\boldsymbol{C}+\boldsymbol{E})\boldsymbol{D} = \widetilde{\boldsymbol{C}} + \widetilde{\boldsymbol{E}}$ where $\boldsymbol{C} \in \mathcal{IC}_{skew}[s;n,k,d]$ and $\mathrm{wt}_{skew}(\boldsymbol{E}) = t$.
2. Apply Algorithm 1 to $\widetilde{\boldsymbol{Y}}$. If $\mathrm{rk}_{q^m}(\widetilde{\boldsymbol{E}}) = t$, which is equivalent to $\mathrm{rk}_{q^m}(\boldsymbol{E}) = t$, the algorithm recovers $\widetilde{\boldsymbol{C}} \in \mathcal{IC}[s;\boldsymbol{n},k,d]$.
3. Recover $\boldsymbol{C} \in \mathcal{IC}_{skew}[s;n,k,d]$ as $\boldsymbol{C} = \widetilde{\boldsymbol{C}}\boldsymbol{D}^{-1}$.

Since the first and the third step both require $O(sn)$ operations in $\mathbb{F}_{q^m}$, the overall complexity is dominated by the complexity of Algorithm 1, that is $O(\max\{n^3, n^2 s\})$ operations in $\mathbb{F}_{q^m}$.

5 Comparison of Metzner-Kapturowski-Like Decoders in the Hamming, Rank and Sum-Rank Metric

The decoder presented in Algorithm 1 is a generalization of the Metzner–Kapturowski decoder for the Hamming metric [14] and the Metzner–Kapturowski-like decoder for the rank metric [18]. In this section we illustrate how the proposed decoder works in three different metrics: 1.) Hamming metric, 2.) Rank metric and 3.) Sum-rank metric. Note that the Hamming and the rank metric are both special cases of the sum-rank metric. We also show the analogy of the different definitions of the error support for all three cases.

The support for the Hamming-metric case is defined as

$$\mathrm{supp}_H(\boldsymbol{E}) := \{j : j\text{-th column of } \boldsymbol{E} \text{ is non-zero}\}.$$

In the Hamming metric an error matrix $\boldsymbol{E}$ with t_H errors can be decomposed into $\boldsymbol{E} = \boldsymbol{A}\boldsymbol{B}$, where the rows of $\boldsymbol{B}$ are the unit vectors corresponding to the t_H error positions. This means the support of the error matrix is given by the union of the supports of the rows $\boldsymbol{B}_i$ of $\boldsymbol{B}$ ($\forall i \in [1 : t_H]$), hence

$$\mathrm{supp}_H(\boldsymbol{E}) = \bigcup_{i=1}^{t_H} \mathrm{supp}_H(\boldsymbol{B}_i).$$

If the condition for the Metzner–Kapturowski decoder is fulfilled (*full-rank condition*), then the zero columns in $\boldsymbol{H}_{\mathrm{sub}}$ indicate the error positions and thus give rise to the error support, i.e. we have that

$$\mathrm{supp}_H(\boldsymbol{E}) = [1 : n] \setminus \bigcup_{i=1}^{n-k-t_H} \mathrm{supp}_H(\boldsymbol{H}_{\mathrm{sub},i})$$

where $\boldsymbol{H}_{\mathrm{sub},i}$ is the i-th row of $\boldsymbol{H}_{\mathrm{sub}}$. Figure 1 illustrates how the error support $\mathrm{supp}_H(\boldsymbol{E})$ can be recovered from $\boldsymbol{H}_{\mathrm{sub}}$.

The rank-metric case is similar, except for a different notion for the error support. Again, the error $\boldsymbol{E}$ with $\text{rk}_q(\boldsymbol{E}) = t_R$ can be decomposed as $\boldsymbol{E} = \boldsymbol{A}\boldsymbol{B}$. Then the rank support $\text{supp}_R(\boldsymbol{E})$ of $\boldsymbol{E}$ equals the row space of $\text{ext}(\boldsymbol{B})$, which is spanned by the union of all rows of $\text{ext}(\boldsymbol{B}_i)$ with $\boldsymbol{B}_i$ being the i-th row of $\boldsymbol{B}$. This means the support of $\boldsymbol{E}$ is given by

$$\text{supp}_R(\boldsymbol{E}) = \bigoplus_{i=1}^{t_R} \text{supp}_R(\boldsymbol{B}_i)$$

with $\bigoplus$ being the addition of vector spaces, which means the span of the union of the considered spaces. If the condition on the error matrix (*full-rank condition*) is fulfilled, the rank support of $\boldsymbol{E}$ is given by the kernel of $\text{ext}(\boldsymbol{H}_{\text{sub}})$ [20]. As illustrated in Fig. 2 the row space of $\text{ext}(\boldsymbol{H}_{\text{sub}})$ can be computed by obtaining the span of the union of spaces $\text{supp}_R(\boldsymbol{H}_{\text{sub},i})$, where $\boldsymbol{H}_{\text{sub},i}$ is the i-th row of $\boldsymbol{H}_{\text{sub}}$. Finally, the support of $\boldsymbol{E}$ is given by

$$\text{supp}_R(\boldsymbol{E}) = \left(\bigoplus_{i=1}^{n-k-t_R} \text{supp}_R(\boldsymbol{H}_{\text{sub},i})\right)^{\perp}.$$

For the sum-rank metric we get from (3) that

$$\begin{aligned}\text{supp}_{\Sigma R}(\boldsymbol{E}) &= \text{supp}_R\left(\boldsymbol{B}^{(1)}\right) \times \text{supp}_R\left(\boldsymbol{B}^{(2)}\right) \times \cdots \times \text{supp}_R\left(\boldsymbol{B}^{(\ell)}\right) \\ &= \left(\bigoplus_{i=1}^{n-k-t_1} \text{supp}_R(\boldsymbol{B}_1^{(1)})\right) \times \cdots \times \left(\bigoplus_{i=1}^{n-k-t_\ell} \text{supp}_R(\boldsymbol{B}_\ell^{(\ell)})\right).\end{aligned}$$

According to Theorem 1 we have that

$$\begin{aligned}\text{supp}_{\Sigma R}(\boldsymbol{E}) = &\left(\bigoplus_{i=1}^{n-k-t_1} \text{supp}_R(\boldsymbol{H}_{\text{sub},1}^{(1)})\right)^{\perp} \times \dots \\ &\dots \times \left(\bigoplus_{i=1}^{n-k-t_\ell} \text{supp}_R(\boldsymbol{H}_{\text{sub},\ell}^{(\ell)})\right)^{\perp}.\end{aligned}$$

The relation between the error matrix $\boldsymbol{E}$, the matrix $\boldsymbol{H}_{\text{sub}}$ and the error supports for the Hamming metric, rank metric and sum-rank metric are illustrated in Fig. 1, Fig. 2 and Fig. 3, respectively.

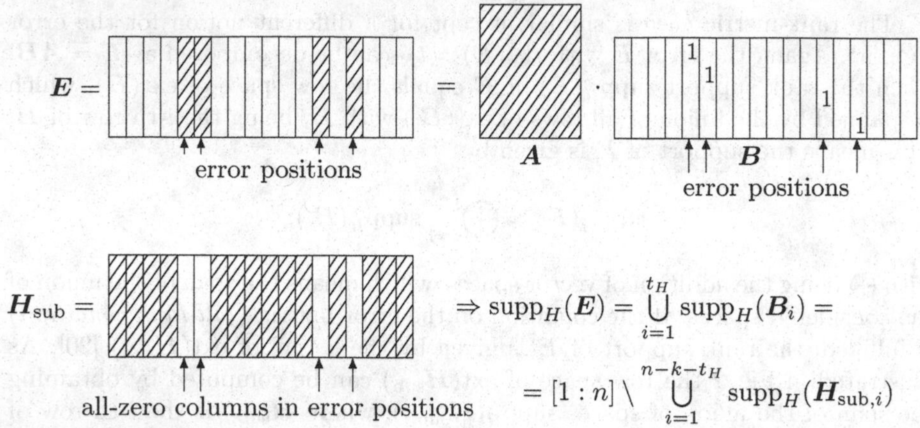

Fig. 1. Illustration of the error support for the Hamming-metric case with $\boldsymbol{E} \in \mathbb{F}_{q^m}^{s \times n}$, $\boldsymbol{A} \in \mathbb{F}_{q^m}^{s \times t_H}$, $\boldsymbol{B} \in \mathbb{F}_{q}^{t_H \times n}$ and $\boldsymbol{H}_{\text{sub}} \in \mathbb{F}_{q^m}^{(n-k-t_H) \times n}$. $\boldsymbol{B}_i$ is the i-th row of $\boldsymbol{B}$ and $\boldsymbol{H}_{\text{sub},i}$ the i-th row of $\boldsymbol{H}_{\text{sub}}$.

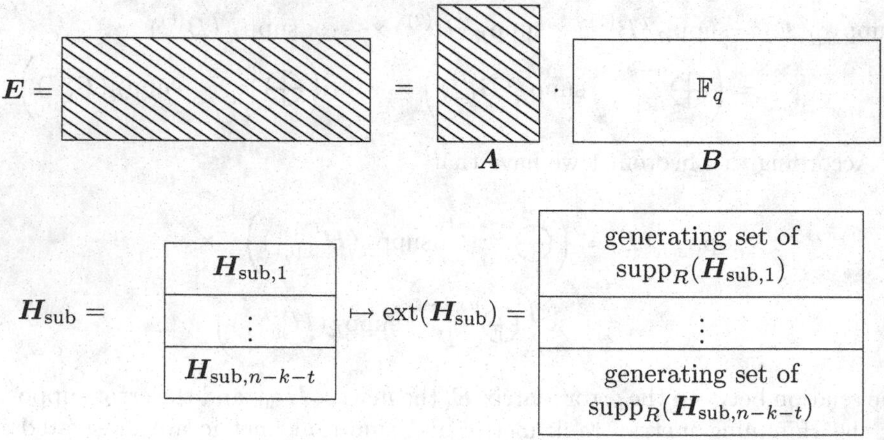

Fig. 2. Illustration of the error support for the rank-metric case with $\boldsymbol{E} \in \mathbb{F}_{q^m}^{s \times n}$ $\boldsymbol{A} \in \mathbb{F}_{q^m}^{s \times t_R}$, $\boldsymbol{B} \in \mathbb{F}_{q}^{t_R \times n}$ and $\boldsymbol{H}_{\text{sub}} \in \mathbb{F}_{q^m}^{(n-k-t_R) \times n}$. $\boldsymbol{B}_i$ is the i-th row of $\boldsymbol{B}$ and $\boldsymbol{H}_{\text{sub},}$ the i-th row of $\boldsymbol{H}_{\text{sub}}$.

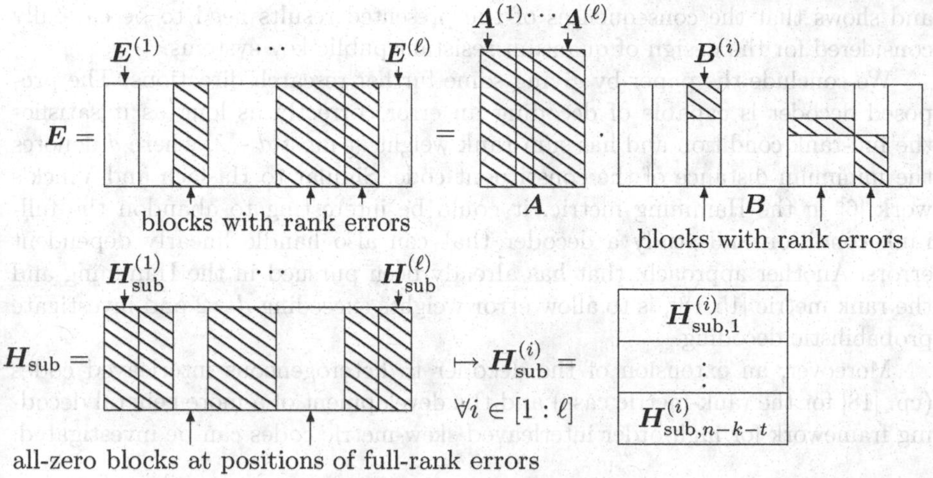

Fig. 3. Illustration of the error support for the sum-rank-metric case with $\boldsymbol{E} \in \mathbb{F}_{q^m}^{s \times n}$, $\boldsymbol{A} \in \mathbb{F}_{q^m}^{s \times t_{\Sigma R}}$, $\boldsymbol{B} \in \mathbb{F}_q^{t_{\Sigma R} \times n}$ and $\boldsymbol{H}_{\text{sub}} \in \mathbb{F}_{q^m}^{(n-k-t_{\Sigma R}) \times n}$. $\boldsymbol{B}_i$ is the i-th row of $\boldsymbol{B}$ and $\boldsymbol{H}_{\text{sub},i}$ the i-th row of $\boldsymbol{H}_{\text{sub}}$.

6 Conclusion

We studied the decoding of homogeneous s-interleaved sum-rank-metric codes that are obtained by vertically stacking s codewords of the same arbitrary linear constituent code $\mathcal{C}$ over $\mathbb{F}_{q^m}$. The proposed Metzner–Kapturowski-like decoder for the sum-rank metric relies on linear-algebraic operations only and has a complexity of $O(\max\{n^3, n^2 s\})$ operations in $\mathbb{F}_{q^m}$, where n denotes the length of ;. The decoder works for any linear constituent code and therefore the decoding omplexity is not affected by the decoding complexity of the constituent code. The proposed Metzner–Kapturowski-like decoder can guarantee to correct error natrices $\boldsymbol{E} \in \mathbb{F}_{q^m}^{s \times n}$ of sum-rank weight $t \leq d-2$, where d is the minimum istance of $\mathcal{C}$, if $\boldsymbol{E}$ has full $\mathbb{F}_{q^m}$-rank t, which implies the high-order condition $\geq t$.

As the sum-rank metric generalizes both, the Hamming metric and the rank etric, Metzner and Kapturowski's decoder in the Hamming metric and its nalog in the rank metric are both recovered as special cases from our proposal. oreover, we showed how the presented algorithm can be used to solve the coding problem of some high-order interleaved skew-metric codes.

Since the decoding process is independent of any structural knowledge about e constituent code, this result has a high impact on the design and the security-vel estimation of new code-based cryptosystems in the sum-rank metric. In fact, igh-order interleaved codes are e.g. used in a classical McEliece-like scheme, error of sum-rank weight $t \leq d-2$ with full $\mathbb{F}_{q^m}$-rank t can be decoded with- knowledge of the private key. This directly renders this approach insecure and shows that the consequences of the presented results need to be carefully considered for the design of quantum-resistant public-key systems.

We conclude the paper by giving some further research directions: The proposed decoder is capable of decoding an error correctly as long as it satisfies the full-rank condition and has sum-rank weight at most $d-2$, where d denotes the minimum distance of the constituent code. Similar to Haslach and Vinck's work [6] in the Hamming metric, it could be interesting to abandon the full-rank condition and study a decoder that can also handle linearly dependent errors. Another approach, that has already been pursued in the Hamming and the rank metric [15,18], is to allow error weights exceeding $d-2$ and investigate probabilistic decoding.

Moreover, an extension of the decoder to heterogeneous interleaved codes (cp. [18] for the rank-metric case) and the development of a more general decoding framework for high-order interleaved skew-metric codes can be investigated.

References

1. Alagic, G., et al.: Status report on the third round of the NIST post-quantum cryptography standardization process (2022)
2. Bartz, H., Puchinger, S.: Fast decoding of interleaved linearized Reed-Solomon codes and variants. IEEE Trans. Inf. Theory. arXiv preprint arXiv:2201.01339 (2022)
3. Couveignes, J.M., Lercier, R.: Elliptic periods for finite fields. Finite Fields Appl. **15**(1), 1–22 (2009). https://doi.org/10.1016/j.ffa.2008.07.004
4. Elleuch, M., Wachter-Zeh, A., Zeh, A.: A public-key cryptosystem from interleaved Goppa codes. arXiv preprint arXiv:1809.03024 (2018)
5. Haslach, C., Vinck, A.H.: A decoding algorithm with restrictions for array codes. IEEE Trans. Inf. Theory **45**(7), 2339–2344 (1999)
6. Haslach, C., Vinck, A.H.: Efficient decoding of interleaved linear block codes. In: 2000 IEEE International Symposium on Information Theory (Cat. No. 00CH37060), p. 149. IEEE (2000)
7. Holzbaur, L., Liu, H., Puchinger, S., Wachter-Zeh, A.: On decoding and applications of interleaved Goppa codes. In: 2019 IEEE International Symposium on Information Theory (ISIT), pp. 1887–1891 (2019)
8. Krachkovsky, V.Y., Lee, Y.X.: Decoding for iterative Reed-Solomon coding schemes. IEEE Trans. Magn. **33**(5), 2740–2742 (1997)
9. Loidreau, P., Overbeck, R.: Decoding rank errors beyond the error correcting capability. In: International Workshop on Algebraic and Combinatorial Coding Theory (ACCT), pp. 186–190 (2006)
10. Martínez-Peñas, U.: Skew and linearized Reed-Solomon codes and maximum sum rank distance codes over any division ring. J. Algebra **504**, 587–612 (2018)
11. McEliece, R.J.: A public-key cryptosystem based on algebraic coding theory. Coding THV **4244**, 114–116 (1978)
12. Metzner, J.J.: Vector symbol decoding with erasures, errors and symbol list decisions. In: Proceedings IEEE International Symposium on Information Theory, 34. IEEE (2002)
13. Metzner, J.J.: Vector symbol decoding with list inner symbol decisions. IEEE Trans. Commun. **51**(3), 371–380 (2003)

14. Metzner, J.J., Kapturowski, E.J.: A general decoding technique applicable to replicated file disagreement location and concatenated code decoding. IEEE Trans. Inf. Theory **36**(4), 911–917 (1990)
15. Oh, K.T., Metzner, J.J.: Performance of a general decoding technique over the class of randomly chosen parity check codes. IEEE Trans. Inf. Theory **40**(1), 160–166 (1994)
16. Porwal, A., Holzbaur, L., Liu, H., Renner, J., Wachter-Zeh, A., Weger, V.: Interleaved Prange: a new generic decoder for interleaved codes. In: Cheon, J.H., Johansson, T. (eds.) Post-Quantum Cryptography (PQCrypto 2022). LNCS, vol. 13512, pp. 69–88. Springer, Cham (2022). https://doi.org/10.1007/978-3-031-17234-2_4
17. Puchinger, S., Renner, J., Rosenkilde, J.: Generic decoding in the sum-rank metric. In: 2020 IEEE International Symposium on Information Theory (ISIT), pp. 54–59. IEEE (2020)
18. Puchinger, S., Renner, J., Wachter-Zeh, A.: Decoding high-order interleaved rank-metric codes. arXiv preprint arXiv:1904.08774 (2019)
19. Renner, J., Puchinger, S., Wachter-Zeh, A.: Interleaving Loidreau's rank-metric cryptosystem. In: 2019 XVI International Symposium "Problems of Redundancy in Information and Control Systems" (REDUNDANCY), pp. 127–132. IEEE (2019)
20. Renner, J., Puchinger, S., Wachter-Zeh, A.: Decoding high-order interleaved rank-metric codes. In: 2021 IEEE International Symposium on Information Theory (ISIT), pp. 19–24. IEEE (2021)
21. Roth, R.M., Vontobel, P.O.: Coding for combined block-symbol error correction. IEEE Trans. Inf. Theory **60**(5), 2697–2713 (2014)

Information Set Decoding for Lee-Metric Codes Using Restricted Balls

Jessica Bariffi[1,2(✉)], Karan Khathuria[3], and Violetta Weger[4]

[1] Institute of Communication and Navigation, German Aerospace Center, Oberpfaffenhofen-Wessling, Germany
jessica.bariffi@dlr.de

[2] Institute of Mathematics, University of Zurich, Zürich, Switzerland

[3] Institute of Computer Science, University of Tartu, Tartu, Estonia
karan.khathuria@ut.ee

[4] Department of Electrical and Computer Engineering, Technical University of Munich, Munich, Germany
violetta.weger@tum.de

Abstract. The Lee metric syndrome decoding problem is an NP-hard problem and several generic decoders have been proposed. The observation that such decoders come with a larger cost than their Hamming metric counterparts make the Lee metric a promising alternative for classical code-based cryptography. Unlike in the Hamming metric, an error vector that is chosen uniformly at random of a given Lee weight is expected to have only few entries with large Lee weight. Using this expected distribution of entries, we are able to drastically decrease the cost of generic decoders in the Lee metric, by reducing the original problem to a smaller instance, whose solution lives in restricted balls.

Keywords: Information Set Decoding · Lee Metric · Code-Based Cryptography

1 Introduction

The original syndrome decoding problem (SDP) asks to decode a random linea code over a finite field endowed with the Hamming metric. This problem has been long studied and is well understood. The SDP is an NP-hard problem [5,8] and lays the foundation of code-based cryptography, which is a promising candidate for post-quantum cryptography.

The fastest algorithms to solve the syndrome decoding problem are calle information set decoding (ISD) algorithms and started with the work of Prang [19] in 1962. Although the literature on ISD algorithms in this classical case vast (see [18] for an overview), the cost of generic decoding has only decrease little and is considered stable. One of fastest algorithms over the binary field called BJMM algorithm [7]. Note that BJMM is a generalization of MMT [1 and has also been generalized to the ternary case [9].

Due to new challenges in code-based cryptography, such as the search efficient signature schemes, other metrics are now investigated. For example t

J.-C. Deneuville (Ed.): CBCrypto 2022, LNCS 13839, pp. 110–136, 2023.
https://doi.org/10.1007/978-3-031-29689-5_7

rank metric has gained a lot of attention due to the NIST submission ROLLO [1] and RQC [2]. While the understanding of the hardness of the rank-metric SDP is rapidly developing, it is still unknown whether the rank-metric SDP is an NP-hard problem.

The situation for the Lee metric is quite different. The Lee-metric SDP was first studied for codes over $\mathbb{Z}/4\mathbb{Z}$ in [13]. Later, in [22] the problem was shown to be NP-hard over any $\mathbb{Z}/p^s\mathbb{Z}$ and several generic decoding algorithms to solve the problem have been provided. Also the paper [11] confirmed the cost regimes of [22] and more importantly the observation, that Lee-metric ISD algorithms cost more than their Hamming metric counterparts for fixed input parameters. Thus, the Lee metric has a great potential to reduce the key sizes or signature sizes in code-based cryptosystems. For example, Lee-metric codes can be used to develop Stern-like authentication and signature schemes. This could be of special interest, since NIST recently launched a second call for post-quantum signature schemes.

Furthermore, modern code-based cryptography is moving away from the classical idea of McEliece [17], where the distinguishability of the secret code obstructs a security reduction to the random instance of SDP, and moving towards ideas from lattice-based cryptography such as the ring learning with error (RLWE) problem, which dates back to Alekhnovich's code-based cryptosystem [3]. The Lee metric is the closest metric in coding theory to the Euclidean metric used in lattice-based cryptography, in the sense that both metrics take into consideration the magnitude of the entries. Note that the Lee metric can be thought of as the L_1-norm in $\mathbb{Z}/m\mathbb{Z}$, for any positive integer m. In fact, to consider the Lee metric in code-based cryptography is a very natural choice, for this new direction: in [20] it was shown that a lattice-based problem in the Euclidean metric can be reduced to solving the problem in the L_1-norm, while a reduction in the other direction is not known yet. Moreover, the reduction in [20] blows-up the dimension only by a constant factor. Hence, an algorithm to solve problems in the L_1-norm can be applied to solve problems in the L_2-norm.

In this paper, we improve existing Lee-metric ISD algorithms using the new results from [6] on the marginal distribution of vectors of given Lee weight. Thus, the paper contributes to the recent advances in understanding the hardness of this problem, with the final goal of deeming this setting secure for applications.

For the Lee-metric SDP we assume that the instance is given by a randomly chosen parity-check matrix and an error vector of fixed Lee weight which was also chosen uniformly at random. The results from [6] now provide us with new and central information on the sought-after error vector $\mathbf{e}$. In fact, using the marginal distribution we are able to determine the expected number of entries of $\mathbf{e}$, which have a fixed Lee weight. The main idea of the novel algorithm is that we expect only very few entries of $\mathbf{e}$ to have a large Lee weight (which is defined through a threshold r) if the relative Lee weight is lower than a fixed constant depending on the size p^s of the residue ring $\mathbb{Z}/p^s\mathbb{Z}$. Thus, using the partial Gaussian elimination (PGE) approaches, like in BJMM [7], we are able to reduce the original instance to a smaller instance, where the sought-after smaller error vector now only has entries of Lee weight up to r and thus lives in smaller Lee-metric balls. This will clearly help reducing the cost of ISD algorithms. This paper thus reduces the cost of the algorithms from [22] and [11], which were the fastest known Lee-metric ISD algorithms up to now.

This paper is organized as follows. In Sect. 2 we introduce the required notions on ring-linear codes and results for Lee-metric codes, such as the restricted spheres. In Sect. 3 we recall the results of [6] on the marginal distribution and introduce the necessary values for our algorithm. The main part, the new Lee-metric ISD algorithm, is presented in Sect. 4 together with an asymptotic cost analysis. Finally, in Sect. 5 we compare the new algorithm to the previously fastest Lee-metric ISD algorithms.

2 Preliminaries

Notation: Let p be a prime and s be a positive integer and let us consider the integer residue ring $\mathbb{Z}/p^s\mathbb{Z}$. The cardinality of a set V is denoted as $|V|$ and its complement by V^C. We use bold lower case (respectively, upper case) letters to denote vectors (respectively, matrices). By abuse of notation, a tuple in a module over a ring will still be denoted by a vector. The $n \times n$ identity matrix will be denoted by Id_n. Let $S \subseteq \{1, \dots, n\}$. For a vector $\mathbf{x} \in (\mathbb{Z}/p^s\mathbb{Z})^n$, we denote by $\mathbf{x}_S$ the vector consisting of the entries of $\mathbf{x}$ indexed by S. Similarly, for a matrix $\mathbf{A} \in (\mathbb{Z}/p^s\mathbb{Z})^{k\times n}$, we denote by $\mathbf{A}_S$ the matrix consisting of the columns of $\mathbf{A}$ indexed by S.

Definition 1. *A* ***linear code*** $\mathcal{C} \subseteq (\mathbb{Z}/p^s\mathbb{Z})^n$ *is a* $\mathbb{Z}/p^s\mathbb{Z}$*-submodule of* $(\mathbb{Z}/p^s\mathbb{Z})^n$.

Since we are over a ring, our code does not possess a dimension, instead we denote by the $\mathbb{Z}/p^s\mathbb{Z}$**-dimension** of the code $\mathcal{C} \subseteq (\mathbb{Z}/p^s\mathbb{Z})^n$ the following

$$k := \log_{p^s}(|\mathcal{C}|).$$

The **rate** of the code is given by $R = \frac{k}{n}$. In addition to the $\mathbb{Z}/p^s\mathbb{Z}$-dimension, the code $\mathcal{C} \subseteq (\mathbb{Z}/p^s\mathbb{Z})^n$ also possesses a **rank** K, which is defined as the minimal number of generators of $\mathcal{C}$ as a $\mathbb{Z}/p^s\mathbb{Z}$-module. In the case of a non-free code note that $k < K$. As for classical codes, we still have the notion of generator matrix and parity-check matrix.

Definition 2. *Let* $\mathcal{C} \subseteq (\mathbb{Z}/p^s\mathbb{Z})^n$ *be a linear code, then a matrix* $\mathbf{G}$ *over* $\mathbb{Z}/p^s\mathbb{Z}$ *is called a* ***generator matrix*** *for* $\mathcal{C}$*, if it has the code as row span and a matrix* $\mathbf{H}$ *is called a* ***parity-check matrix*** *for* $\mathcal{C}$ *if it has the code as kernel.*

For a code $\mathcal{C} \subseteq (\mathbb{Z}/p^s\mathbb{Z})^n$, we denote by $\mathcal{C}_S$ the code consisting of all codewords $\mathbf{c}_S$, where $\mathbf{c} \in \mathcal{C}$. The notion of information set remains as in the classical case.

Definition 3. *Let* $\mathcal{C} \subseteq (\mathbb{Z}/p^s\mathbb{Z})^n$ *be a linear code of rank* K*, then a set* $I \subseteq \{1, \dots, n\}$ *of size* K *is called an* ***information set*** *of* $\mathcal{C}$ *if* $|\mathcal{C}_I| = |\mathcal{C}|$.

In this paper we are interested in the Lee metric, which can be thought of as the L_1 norm modulo p^s.

Definition 4. *Let $x \in \mathbb{Z}/p^s\mathbb{Z}$. The* ***Lee weight*** *of x is given by*

$$wt_L(x) = \min\{x, |p^s - x|\}.$$

The Lee weight of a vector is defined additively, i.e., for $\mathbf{x} \in (\mathbb{Z}/p^s\mathbb{Z})^n$, we have

$$wt_L(\mathbf{x}) = \sum_{i=1}^{n} wt_L(x_i).$$

Finally, this weight induces a distance, that is, for $\mathbf{x}, \mathbf{y} \in (\mathbb{Z}/p^s\mathbb{Z})^n$ the ***Lee distance*** *between $\mathbf{x}$ and $\mathbf{y}$ is given by $d_L(\mathbf{x}, \mathbf{y}) = wt_L(\mathbf{x} - \mathbf{y})$.*

Let us denote by $M := \lfloor \frac{p^s}{2} \rfloor$, then one can easily see that for $x \in \mathbb{Z}/p^s\mathbb{Z}$ we have $0 \leq \text{wt}_L(x) \leq M$. The Lee-metric ball, respectively the Lee-metric sphere, of radius r around $\mathbf{x} \in (\mathbb{Z}/p^s\mathbb{Z})^n$ are defined as

$$B(\mathbf{x}, r, n, p^s) := \{\mathbf{y} \in (\mathbb{Z}/p^s\mathbb{Z})^n \mid d_L(\mathbf{x} - \mathbf{y}) \leq r\},$$
$$S(\mathbf{x}, r, n, p^s) := \{\mathbf{y} \in (\mathbb{Z}/p^s\mathbb{Z})^n \mid d_L(\mathbf{x} - \mathbf{y}) = r\}.$$

Since the size of a Lee-metric ball or a Lee-metric sphere is independent of the center, we will denote their cardinalities by

$$V(r, n, p^s) := |B(0, r, n, p^s)|, \qquad F(r, n, p^s) := |S(0, r, n, p^s)|.$$

Definition 5. *Let $\mathcal{C} \subseteq (\mathbb{Z}/p^s\mathbb{Z})^n$ be a linear code endowed with the Lee-metric, then the* ***minimum Lee distance*** *of $\mathcal{C}$ is given by*

$$d_L(\mathcal{C}) = \min\{d_L(\mathbf{x}, \mathbf{y}) \mid \mathbf{x} \neq \mathbf{y} \in \mathcal{C}\}.$$

In this paper we are interested in algorithms that have as input a code generated by a matrix chosen uniformly at random. Due to the result in [10, Proposition 6], we therefore assume that our code is free, i.e., $k = K$ and a generator matrix nd a parity-check matrix having the following form (up to permutation):

$$\mathbf{G} = \begin{pmatrix} \text{Id}_k & \mathbf{A} \end{pmatrix}, \quad \mathbf{H} = \begin{pmatrix} \text{Id}_{n-k} & \mathbf{B} \end{pmatrix},$$

here $\mathbf{A} \in (\mathbb{Z}/p^s\mathbb{Z})^{k \times (n-k)}$ and $\mathbf{B} \in (\mathbb{Z}/p^s\mathbb{Z})^{(n-k) \times k}$.

In addition, in [10, Theorem 20] it was shown that such a random code also tains the Gilbert-Varshamov bound with high probability. Let $AL(n, d, p^s)$ enote the maximal cardinality of a code $\mathcal{C} \subseteq (\mathbb{Z}/p^s\mathbb{Z})^n$ of minimum Lee distance and let us consider the maximal information rate

$$R(n, d, p^s) := \frac{1}{n} \log_{p^s}(AL(n, d, p^s)),$$

$0 \leq d \leq nM$. We define the relative minimum distance to be $\delta := \frac{d}{nM}$.

eorem 1 (Asymptotic Gilbert-Varshamov Bound [4]). *It holds that*

$$\liminf_{n \to \infty} R(n, \delta M n, p^s) \geq \lim_{n \to \infty} \left(1 - \frac{1}{n} \log_{p^s}(V(\delta M n, n, p^s))\right).$$

Let $\mathcal{C} \subseteq (\mathbb{Z}/p^s\mathbb{Z})^n$ be a linear code with parity-check matrix $\mathbf{H}$, then for an $\mathbf{x} \in (\mathbb{Z}/p^s\mathbb{Z})^n$ we say that $\mathbf{s} = \mathbf{x}\mathbf{H}^\top$ is a **syndrome**. In this paper we give an algorithm that solves the following problem, called Lee syndrome decoding problem (LSDP), which was shown to be NP-complete in [22]:

Problem 1. Let $\mathbf{H} \in (\mathbb{Z}/p^s\mathbb{Z})^{(n-k)\times n}$, $\mathbf{s} \in (\mathbb{Z}/p^s\mathbb{Z})^{n-k}$ and $t \in \mathbb{N}$. Find $\mathbf{e} \in (\mathbb{Z}/p^s\mathbb{Z})^n$ such that $\mathbf{s} = \mathbf{e}\mathbf{H}^\top$ and $\mathrm{wt}_L(\mathbf{e}) = t$.

To this end, we assume that the input parity-check matrix $\mathbf{H}$ is chosen uniformly at random in $(\mathbb{Z}/p^s\mathbb{Z})^{(n-k)\times n}$ and that there exists a solution $\mathbf{e} \in (\mathbb{Z}/p^s\mathbb{Z})^n$, which was chosen uniformly at random in $S(0, t, n, p^s)$ and set $\mathbf{s}$ to be its syndrome $\mathbf{s} = \mathbf{e}\mathbf{H}^\top$. We provide two new algorithms, taking care of two different scenarios. The main idea of these new algorithms is to use the results of [6], which provide us with additional information on the unique solution $\mathbf{e} \in (\mathbb{Z}/p^s\mathbb{Z})^n$. For example, the expected number of entries of $\mathbf{e}$ having a fixed Lee weight.

In the first scenario, we want to decode up to the minimum distance of the code having $\mathbf{H}$ as parity-check matrix. For this, we let d_L be the minimum distance from the Gilbert-Varshamov bound. Hence, even if we assume full distance decoding, i.e., $t = d_L$, we expect to have a unique solution $\mathbf{e}$ to Problem 1. In fact, the expected number of solutions to the LSDP is given by

$$N = \frac{F(t, n, p^s)}{p^{s(n-k)}} = \frac{F(d_L, n, p^s)}{p^{s(n-k)}} \leq 1.$$

In the second scenario, we consider a Lee weight t larger than the minimum distance, and solve this new problem by reversing the idea of the first algorithm.

Similar to the size of the Lee sphere $F(t, n, p^s)$, we define the size of the restricted Lee spheres, where each entry has the Lee weight at most r, respectively at least r, for some $r \in \{0, \ldots, M\}$, as

$$F_{(r)}(t, n, p^s) = |\{\mathbf{x} \in \{0, \pm 1, \ldots, \pm r\}^n \mid \mathrm{wt}_L(\mathbf{x}) = t \text{ in } \mathbb{Z}/p^s\mathbb{Z}\}|,$$
$$F^{(r)}(t, n, p^s) = |\{\mathbf{x} \in \{\pm r, \ldots, \pm M\}^n \mid \mathrm{wt}_L(\mathbf{x}) = t \text{ in } \mathbb{Z}/p^s\mathbb{Z}\}|.$$

Let us consider t as a function in n and define $T := \lim_{n\to\infty} t(n)/n$. We denote their asymptotic sizes as

$$A_{(r)}(T, p^s) := \lim_{n\to\infty} \frac{1}{n} \log_{p^s}\left(F_{(r)}(t(n), n, p^s)\right),$$
$$A^{(r)}(T, p^s) := \lim_{n\to\infty} \frac{1}{n} \log_{p^s}\left(F^{(r)}(t(n), n, p^s)\right).$$

We provide the formula for the asymptotic sizes of the restricted Lee spheres in Appendix A. The derivation of the asymptotic formulas follows the saddle point technique used in [12].

Lastly, we need a notion of restricted compositions of a number. Recall that for a given integer t, a **weak integer composition** of t into n parts is an n-tuple $\lambda = (\lambda_1, \ldots, \lambda_n)$ of non-negative integers satisfying $\lambda_1 + \cdots + \lambda_n = t$. A weak composition π of a positive integer v into n parts is said to **fit** into a we composition λ of a positive integer t of the same number of parts n, if the part sizes of π are upper bounded by the part sizes of λ, i.e., for every $i \in \{1, \ldots, n\}$ it holds $\pi_i \leq \lambda_i$. Let λ be a (weak) composition of t of n parts. We denote by $C(v, t, \lambda, n, p^s)$ the number of weak compositions π of v which fit into λ. If we assume that v, t are functions of n and λ is the expected composition of t in n parts, then the asymptotic size of $C(v, t, \lambda, n, p^s)$ can be computes as

$$\gamma(V, T) := \lim_{n \to \infty} \frac{1}{n} \log_{p^s} \left(C(v, t, \lambda, n, p^s) \right), \tag{2.1}$$

where $V := \lim_{n \to \infty} \frac{v}{n}$. The formula and its derivation can be found in Appendix A.

3 Distribution of a Random Lee Vector

In this section, we analyze the error vector $\mathbf{e}$ that is chosen uniformly at random from $S(0, t, n, p^s)$. We first recall the results from [6] that studies the distribution of the entries of a random vector having a fixed Lee weight.

Let E denote a random variable corresponding to the realization of an entry of $\mathbf{e}$. As n tends to infinity we have the following result on the distribution of the elements in $\mathbf{e}$.

Lemma 1 ([6, Lemma 1]). *For any $j \in \mathbb{Z}/p^s\mathbb{Z}$,*

$$\mathbb{P}(E = j) = \frac{1}{Z(\beta)} \exp(-\beta \mathrm{wt}_L(j)), \tag{3.1}$$

where Z denotes the normalization constant and β is the unique solution to $T = \sum_{i=0}^{p^s-1} \mathrm{wt}_L(i)\, \mathbb{P}(E = i)$.

Note, that if $\beta = 0$, the entries of $\mathbf{e}$ are uniformly distributed over $\mathbb{Z}/p^s\mathbb{Z}$. In that case, the relative weight of a randomly chosen entry is equal to $\frac{p^{2s}-1}{4p^s}$ if p is odd, respectively $p^s/4$ if $p = 2$. Furthermore, if $\beta > 0$ the relative weight becomes smaller. In addition, since the marginal distribution (3.1) is an exponential function with negative exponent, it is decreasing in the weight. This means that for $\beta > 0$ the elements of smallest Lee weight, i.e., 0, are the most probable, then elements of weight 1 until the least probable Lee weight M. Let us emphasize here that, by Remark 2, if we are in scenario 1, where we decode up to the minimum distance given by the Gilbert-Varshamov bound, we will always have $t/n \leq M/2$, which is roughly the threshold $\frac{p^{2s}-1}{4p^s}$ for p odd, respectively $p^s/4$ for $p = 2$, and hence elements of small weight will always be more probable. In the other case, where $\beta < 0$, the elements of largest Lee weight, i.e., M, are the most probable, followed by the elements of weight $M - 1$, and so on, until the least probable of Lee weight 0. This is the case for the second scenario, where we decode beyond the minimum distance, i.e., $t/n \geq M/2$. As a direct consequence of Lemma 1, we can give the probability of a random entry E having some given Lee weight $j \in \{0, \ldots, M\}$ (Fig. 1).

$$\mathbb{P}(\mathrm{wt}_L(E) = j) = \begin{cases} \mathbb{P}(E = j) & \text{if } (j = 0) \text{ or } (j = M \text{ and } p \text{ is even}), \\ 2\mathbb{P}(E = j) & \text{else.} \end{cases} \tag{3.2}$$

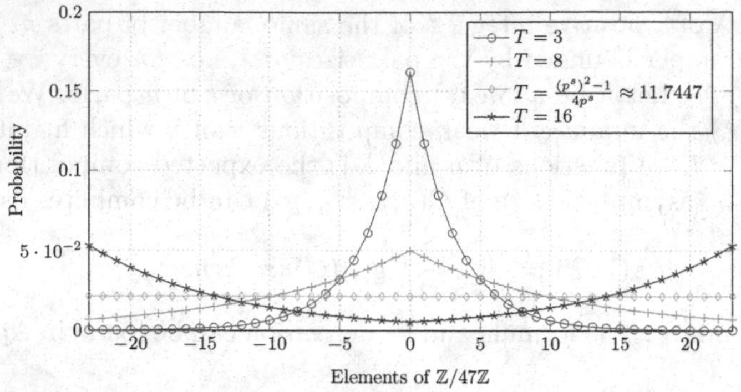

Fig. 1. Marginal distribution for the elements in $\mathbb{Z}/47\mathbb{Z}$ for different values of $T = \lim_{n\to\infty} t(n)/n$.

In this work, we are interested in the expected number of entries that have 'large' Lee weight, i.e., entries having Lee weight larger than some threshold $r \in \{0,\dots,M\}$. Let $\psi(r,t,n,p^s)$ denote the expected number of entries of $\mathbf{e}$ which have a larger Lee weight than r and let $\varphi(r,t,n,p^s)$ denote the expected Lee weight of $\mathbf{e}$ without the entries of larger Lee weight than r. In addition, for some randomly chosen set $S \subseteq \{1,\dots,n\}$ of size $0 \le \ell \le n$, let us denote by $\sigma(\ell,t,n,p^s)$ the expected support size of $\mathbf{e}_S$.

Lemma 2. *Let* $\mathbf{e}$ *be chosen uniformly at random in* $S(0,t,n,p^s)$, $r \in \{0,\dots,M\}$ *and* $0 \le \ell \le n$. *Then*

$$\psi(r,t,n,p^s) = n \sum_{i=r+1}^{M} \mathbb{P}(\mathrm{wt}_L(E) = i),$$

$$\varphi(r,t,n,p^s) = n \sum_{i=0}^{r} i \cdot \mathbb{P}(\mathrm{wt}_L(E) = i),$$

$$\sigma(\ell,t,n,p^s) = \ell \sum_{i=1}^{M} \mathbb{P}(\mathrm{wt}_L(E) = i).$$

Proof. The proof easily follows from (3.2) and using the assumption that eac
entry of $\mathbf{e}$ is independent. [

4 Restricted-Balls Algorithm

The idea of the new information set decoding algorithms is to use the informatic on the uniformly chosen $\mathbf{e} \in S(0,t,n,p^s)$. We start with the algorithm for t first scenario, where we only decode up to the minimum distance given by t Gilbert-Varshamov bound and later adapt this algorithm to the second scenar where we decode beyond the minimum distance.

4.1 Decoding up to the Minimum Lee Distance

The high level idea lies in the following observation: for $t/n < M/2$, which is given by the Gilbert-Varshamov bound, we know, as n grows large, that 0 is the most likely entry of $\mathbf{e}$, the second most likely is ± 1 and so on, until the least likely entry is $\pm M$. Hence, if we define a threshold Lee weight $0 \leq r \leq M$, with a high probability (depending on the choice of r) we have that all entries of $\mathbf{e}$ of Lee weight larger than r can be found outside an information set. Thus, using the partial Gaussian elimination (PGE) algorithms, we are left with finding a smaller error vector which only takes values in $\{0, \pm 1, \ldots, \pm r\}$. This will make a huge difference for algorithms such as the Lee-metric BJMM [22], where the list sizes are the main factor in the cost.

General Framework: In general, this idea can be considered as a framework, where we can apply any algorithm that solves the smaller instance, but now in a smaller space. The framework takes as input $(\mathbf{H}, \mathbf{s}, t, r, \mathcal{S})$, where $\mathcal{S}$ denotes a solver for the smaller instance in the space $\{0, \pm 1, \ldots, \pm r\}$ which, instead of outputting a list of possible solutions for the smaller instance, immediately checks whether the smaller solution at hand leads to a solution of the original instance. Let us consider a random instance of the LSDP given by

$$\mathbf{H} \in (\mathbb{Z}/p^s\mathbb{Z})^{(n-k)\times n}, \ \mathbf{s} \in (\mathbb{Z}/p^s\mathbb{Z})^{n-k} \ \text{ and } \ t \in \mathbb{N} \text{ with } t/n < M/2.$$

The framework on $(\mathbf{H}, \mathbf{s}, t, r, \mathcal{S})$ works as follows:

Step 1: For some $0 \leq \ell \leq n-k$, we will bring the parity-check matrix into partial ystematic form by multiplying $\mathbf{H}$ with some invertible $\mathbf{U} \in (\mathbb{Z}/p^s\mathbb{Z})^{(n-k)\times(n-k)}$ nd adapting the syndrome accordingly to $\mathbf{s}\mathbf{U}^\top$. For simplicity, assume that we ave an information set in the last k positions. Thus, the LSDP becomes

$$(\mathbf{e}_1 \ \mathbf{e}_2) \begin{pmatrix} \mathrm{Id}_{n-k-\ell} & 0 \\ \mathbf{A}^\top & \mathbf{B}^\top \end{pmatrix} = (\mathbf{s}_1 \ \mathbf{s}_2),$$

ith $\mathbf{A} \in (\mathbb{Z}/p^s\mathbb{Z})^{(n-k-\ell)\times(k+\ell)}$, $\mathbf{B} \in (\mathbb{Z}/p^s\mathbb{Z})^{\ell\times(k+\ell)}$, $\mathbf{s}_1 \in (\mathbb{Z}/p^s\mathbb{Z})^{n-k-\ell}$ and $\in (\mathbb{Z}/p^s\mathbb{Z})^{\ell}$. Hence, we have to solve two parity-check equations:

$$\mathbf{e}_1 + \mathbf{e}_2\mathbf{A}^\top = \mathbf{s}_1, \ \mathbf{e}_2\mathbf{B}^\top = \mathbf{s}_2, \tag{4.1}$$

re, we assume that $\mathbf{e}_2$ has Lee weight v and $\mathbf{e}_1$ has Lee weight $t - v$, for some sitive integer $0 \leq v \leq t$.

ep 2: We solve the smaller instance of the LSDP given by the second equality Eq. (4.1) using algorithm $\mathcal{S}$. In particular, we find an error vector $\mathbf{e}_2$ such t $\mathbf{e}_2\mathbf{B}^\top = \mathbf{s}_2$, $\mathrm{wt}_L(\mathbf{e}_2) = v$, and it has entries in $\{0, \pm 1, \ldots, \pm r\}$. Instead of ring a list of solutions $\mathbf{e}_2$, $\mathcal{S}$ will immediately check whether $\mathbf{e}_1 = \mathbf{s}_1 - \mathbf{e}_2\mathbf{A}^\top$ the remaining Lee weight $t - v$. Clearly, v also depends on the choice of r.

Solving the smaller instance can be achieved using various techniques, for example via Wagner's approach used in [11,22] or via the representation technique used in [22]. We adapt these techniques to make use of the assumption that the entries are restricted to $\{0, \pm 1, \dots, \pm r\}$. Let $S_{(r)}(0, v, n, p^s)$ denote the Lee sphere of weight v centered at the origin with entries restricted to $\{0, \pm 1, \dots, \pm r\}$, i.e.,

$$S_{(r)}(0, v, n, p^s) := \{\mathbf{x} \in \{0, \pm 1, \dots, \pm r\}^n \mid \mathrm{wt}_L(\mathbf{x}) = v\}.$$

In the following lemma, we show that if $\mathbf{e}$ is a random vector of length n and Lee weight t which splits as $(\mathbf{e}_1, \mathbf{e}_2)$ with $\mathbf{e}_2 \in S_{(r)}(0, v, k+\ell, p^s)$, then $\mathbf{e}_2$ has a uniform distribution in $S_{(r)}(0, v, k+\ell, p^s)$.

Lemma 3. *Let* $\mathbf{e}$ *be chosen uniformly at random in* $S(0, t, n, p^s)$ *such that* $\mathbf{e} = (\mathbf{e}_1, \mathbf{e}_2)$ *with* $\mathbf{e}_2 \in S_{(r)}(0, v, k+\ell, p^s)$. *Then* $\mathbf{e}_2$ *follows a uniform distribution in* $S_{(r)}(0, v, k+\ell, p^s)$, *and henceforth* $\mathbf{e}_1$ *follows a uniform distribution in* $S(0, t-v, n-k-\ell, p^s)$.

Proof. We note that for an arbitrary $\mathbf{e}_2 \in S_{(r)}(0, v, k+\ell, p^s)$, there are exactly $|S(0, t-v, n-k-\ell, p^s)|$ possible vectors $\mathbf{e}$ that restrict to $\mathbf{e}_2$ in their last $k+\ell$ coordinates. Therefore, if $\mathbf{e}$ is chosen uniformly at random, then each $\mathbf{e}_2$ has an equal chance of being chosen in $S_{(r)}(0, v, k+\ell, p^s)$. □

As a corollary, we see that this splitting of $\mathbf{e}$ comes with a probability of

$$P = F_{(r)}(v, k+\ell, p^s) F(t-v, n-k-\ell, p^s) F(t, n, p^s)^{-1}. \tag{4.2}$$

Now, it is easy to see that the average time complexity of the generic ISD algorithm is P^{-1} times the cost of one iteration.

Solving Smaller SDP Using the BJMM-Approach: The BJMM algorithm belongs to a class of ISD algorithms that finds a desired vector $\mathbf{e}_2$ in a multi-level approach. For an a-level algorithm, we split $\mathbf{e}_2$ into 2^a parts in a certain way. At each level, we merge all the adjacent parts together to satisfy the syndrome equations partially or completely. This merging can be performed in several ways, for example, using generalized birthday algorithm introduced in [21], or using the representation technique introduced in [14]. In this section, we consider the Lee-BJMM algorithm from [22] which is a two-level Lee metric adaptation of the original BJMM algorithm. The BJMM algorithm uses representation technique where a vector $\mathbf{e}_2$ is built from the sum of two vectors $\mathbf{y}_1 + \mathbf{y}_2$ and the merging forces some fixed number of positions to overlap and cancel out. Although the smaller error vector $\mathbf{e}_2$ now only has entries in $\{0, \pm 1, \dots, \pm r\}$, to enable representation technique, we will assume that ε positions cancel out and thus are allowed to live in the whole ring $\mathbb{Z}/p^s\mathbb{Z}$.

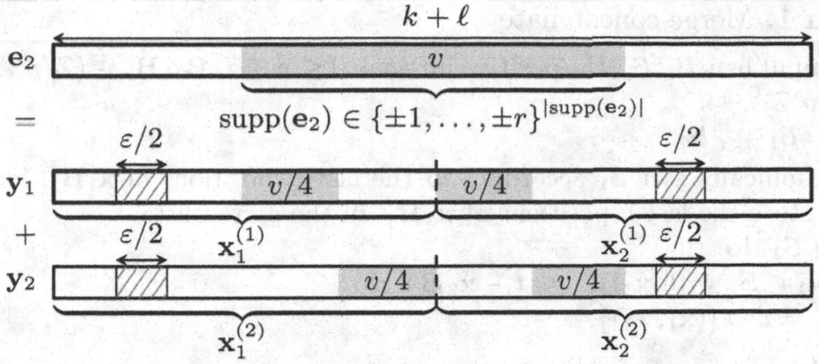

Fig. 2. Two levels decomposition of the vector $\mathbf{e}_2$ into $\mathbf{y}_1$ and $\mathbf{y}_2$, where $\mathbf{y}_i = (\mathbf{x}_1^{(i)}, \mathbf{x}_2^{(i)})$ for $i = 1, 2$. with corresponding Lee weights in the support (gray areas).

Description of the Algorithm: The high level idea of BJMM on two levels is as follows: we split $\mathbf{e}_2$ as

$$\mathbf{e}_2 = \mathbf{y}_1 + \mathbf{y}_2 = \left(\mathbf{x}_1^{(1)}, \mathbf{x}_2^{(1)}\right) + \left(\mathbf{x}_1^{(2)}, \mathbf{x}_2^{(2)}\right),$$

where $\mathbf{x}_j^{(i)} \in (\mathbb{Z}/p^s\mathbb{Z})^{(k+\ell)/2}$ for $i, j \in \{1, 2\}$. Thus, for the syndrome equation to be satisfied, we want that

$$\mathbf{s}_2 = \mathbf{e}_2\mathbf{B}^\top = \mathbf{y}_1\mathbf{B}^\top + \mathbf{y}_2\mathbf{B}^\top.$$

Let us also split $\mathbf{B} \in (\mathbb{Z}/p^s\mathbb{Z})^{\ell\times(k+\ell)}$ into two matrices $\mathbf{B} = (\mathbf{B}_1\ \mathbf{B}_2)$, where $\mathbf{B}_i \in (\mathbb{Z}/p^s\mathbb{Z})^{\ell\times(k+\ell)/2}$, for $i \in \{1, 2\}$. In order to obtain syndrome equations containing $\mathbf{x}_j^{(i)}$, we assume that $\mathbf{y}_1\mathbf{B}^\top = \mathbf{0}$ and $\mathbf{y}_2\mathbf{B}^\top = \mathbf{s}_2$ in the last u positions, where $0 \le u \le \ell$ is a fixed parameter. To ease the notation, we write $\mathbf{x} =_u \mathbf{y}$ to denote that $\mathbf{x} = \mathbf{y}$ in the last u positions. Hence, in the first merge we get $\mathbf{y}_i = (\mathbf{x}_1^{(i)}, \mathbf{x}_2^{(i)})$ for $i \in \{1, 2\}$ satisfying the following syndrome equations

$$\mathbf{x}_1^{(1)}\mathbf{B}_1^\top =_u -\mathbf{x}_2^{(1)}\mathbf{B}_2^\top,$$
$$\mathbf{x}_1^{(2)}\mathbf{B}_1^\top =_u \mathbf{s}_2 - \mathbf{x}_2^{(2)}\mathbf{B}_2^\top.$$

We also split the ε overlapping positions evenly into two parts such that $\varepsilon/2$ positions overlap within $\{1, \dots, \frac{k+\ell}{2}\}$ and $\varepsilon/2$ overlap within $\{\frac{k+\ell}{2} + 1, \dots, k+\ell\}$. Therefore, the weight distribution of $\mathbf{e}_2$ is as follows: each $\mathbf{y}_i$ has Lee weight $v/2$ on some $k + \ell - \varepsilon$ positions, and each $\mathbf{x}_j^{(i)}$ has Lee weight $v/4$ on some $\frac{k+\ell-\varepsilon}{2}$ positions. See Fig. 2 for an illustration of the weight distribution.

The algorithm starts with building the base list $\mathcal{B}$ defined as follows:

$$\mathcal{B} = \left\{\mathbf{x} \mid \mathbf{x}_{\mathcal{E}^C} \in S_{(r)}\left(0, \tfrac{v}{4}, \tfrac{k+\ell-\varepsilon}{2}, p^s\right) \text{ for some } \mathcal{E} \subseteq \left\{1, \dots, \tfrac{k+\ell}{2}\right\} \text{ with } |\mathcal{E}| = \tfrac{\varepsilon}{2}\right\},$$

which corresponds to all the possible vectors for $\mathbf{x}_j^{(i)}$. Next, we apply the first merging algorithm, (Algorithm 1), two times: first to obtain a list $\mathcal{L}_1$ using the

Algorithm 1. Merge-concatenate

Input: The input lists $\mathcal{B}_1, \mathcal{B}_2$, the positive integers $0 \leq u \leq \ell$, $\mathbf{B}_1, \mathbf{B}_2 \in (\mathbb{Z}/p^s\mathbb{Z})^{\ell \times (k+\ell)/2}$ and $\mathbf{t} \in (\mathbb{Z}/p^s\mathbb{Z})^{\ell}$.
Output: $\mathcal{L} = \mathcal{B}_1 +\!\!+_{\mathbf{t}} \mathcal{B}_2$.

Lexicographically sort $\mathcal{B}_1$ according to the last u positions of $\mathbf{x}_1\mathbf{B}_1^\top$ for $\mathbf{x}_1 \in \mathcal{B}_1$. We also store the last u positions of $\mathbf{x}_1\mathbf{B}_1^\top$ in the sorted list.
for $\mathbf{x}_2 \in \mathcal{B}_2$ **do**
  for $\mathbf{x}_1 \in \mathcal{B}_1$ with $\mathbf{x}_1\mathbf{B}_1^\top =_u \mathbf{t} - \mathbf{x}_2\mathbf{B}_2^\top$ **do**
    $\mathcal{L} = \mathcal{L} \cup \{(\mathbf{x}_1, \mathbf{x}_2)\}$.
Return $\mathcal{L}$.

Algorithm 2. Last Merge

Input: The input lists $\mathcal{L}_1, \mathcal{L}_2$, the positive integers $0 \leq v \leq t, 0 \leq u \leq \ell$, $\mathbf{B} \in (\mathbb{Z}/p^s\mathbb{Z})^{\ell \times (k+\ell)}$, $\mathbf{s}_2 \in (\mathbb{Z}/p^s\mathbb{Z})^{\ell}$ and $\mathbf{s}_1 \in (\mathbb{Z}/p^s\mathbb{Z})^{n-k-\ell}$, $\mathbf{A} \in (\mathbb{Z}/p^s\mathbb{Z})^{(n-k-\ell)\times(k+\ell)}$.
Output: $\mathbf{e} \in \mathcal{L}_1 \bowtie \mathcal{L}_2$.

Lexicographically sort $\mathcal{L}_1$ according to $\mathbf{y}_1\mathbf{B}^\top$ for $\mathbf{y}_1 \in \mathcal{L}_1$. We also store $\mathbf{y}_1\mathbf{B}^\top$ in the sorted list.
for $\mathbf{y}_2 \in \mathcal{L}_2$ **do**
  for $\mathbf{y}_1 \in \mathcal{L}_1$ with $\mathbf{y}_1\mathbf{B}^\top = \mathbf{s}_2 - \mathbf{y}_2\mathbf{B}^\top$ **do**
    if $\mathrm{wt}_L(\mathbf{y}_1 + \mathbf{y}_2) = v$ and $\mathrm{wt}_L\left(\mathbf{s}_1 - (\mathbf{y}_1 + \mathbf{y}_2)\mathbf{A}^\top\right) = t - v$ **then**
      Return $(\mathbf{s}_1 - (\mathbf{y}_1 + \mathbf{y}_2)\mathbf{A}^\top, \mathbf{y}_1 + \mathbf{y}_2)$.

input $\mathcal{B}_1 = \mathcal{B}_2 = \mathcal{B}$ and $\mathbf{t} = \mathbf{0}$, and second to obtain a list $\mathcal{L}_2$ using the input $\mathcal{B}_1 = \mathcal{B}_2 = \mathcal{B}$ and $\mathbf{t} = \mathbf{s}_2$. The lists $\mathcal{L}_i$ contain all the possible vectors $\mathbf{y}_i$ and can be written as:

$$\mathcal{L}_1 = \{\mathbf{y} \mid \mathbf{y}\mathbf{B}^\top =_u \mathbf{0}, \mathbf{y}_{\mathcal{E}^C} \in S_{(r)}\left(0, \tfrac{v}{2}, k+\ell-\varepsilon, p^s\right) \text{ for some } \mathcal{E} \subseteq \{1,\dots,k+\ell\} \text{ with } |\mathcal{E}| = \varepsilon\}$$
$$\mathcal{L}_2 = \{\mathbf{y} \mid \mathbf{y}\mathbf{B}^\top =_u \mathbf{s}_2, \mathbf{y}_{\mathcal{E}^C} \in S_{(r)}\left(0, \tfrac{v}{2}, k+\ell-\varepsilon, p^s\right) \text{ for some } \mathcal{E} \subseteq \{1,\dots,k+\ell\} \text{ with } |\mathcal{E}| = \varepsilon\}.$$

We then merge $\mathcal{L}_1 \bowtie \mathcal{L}_2$ on the syndrome $\mathbf{s}_2$ and ℓ positions using Algo- rithm 2. As a result, we get $\mathbf{e}_2 = \mathbf{y}_1 + \mathbf{y}_2$, for $(\mathbf{y}_1, \mathbf{y}_2) \in \mathcal{L}_1 \times \mathcal{L}_2$ such tha $\mathrm{wt}_L(\mathbf{e}_2) = v$ and that satisfies the original syndrome Eq. (4.1). The complet Lee-BJMM algorithm using restricted weights is given in Algorithm 3.

Remark 1. Note that, it might happen that $\mathbf{y}_1 + \mathbf{y}_2$ results in a vector of Le weight v, but the $\mathcal{E}$ positions did not cancel out, or the positions of low L weight are going above the threshold r. This will not be a problem for us, this only results in a larger final list, which does not need to be stored and t success probability of the algorithm would then even be larger than P given (4.2). As a result, the final cost of the algorithm we get will be an upper bou on the actual cost.

In order for the algorithm to succeed, we must ensure that there exists at le one representative $\mathbf{y}_1 \in \mathcal{L}_1$ of the solution $\mathbf{e}_2$, i.e., such that there exists $\mathbf{y}_2 \in$

Algorithm 3. Lee-BJMM with Restricted Balls

Input: $\mathbf{H} \in (\mathbb{Z}/p^s\mathbb{Z})^{(n-k)\times n}, \mathbf{s} \in (\mathbb{Z}/p^s\mathbb{Z})^{n-k}, t \in \mathbb{N}$, given the positive integers $0 \leq \ell \leq n-k, 0 \leq v \leq t, 0 \leq \varepsilon \leq k+\ell$.

Output: $\mathbf{e} \in (\mathbb{Z}/p^s\mathbb{Z})^n$ with $\mathbf{s} = \mathbf{e}\mathbf{H}^\top$ and $\mathrm{wt}_L(\mathbf{e}) = t$.

1: Choose an $n \times n$ permutation matrix $\mathbf{P}$ and find an invertible matrix $\mathbf{U} \in (\mathbb{Z}/p^s\mathbb{Z})^{(n-k)\times(n-k)}$ such that

$$\mathbf{UHP} = \begin{pmatrix} \mathrm{Id}_{n-k-\ell} & \mathbf{A} \\ 0 & \mathbf{B} \end{pmatrix},$$

where $\mathbf{A} \in (\mathbb{Z}/p^s\mathbb{Z})^{(n-k-\ell)\times(k+\ell)}, \mathbf{B} \in (\mathbb{Z}/p^s\mathbb{Z})^{\ell\times(k+\ell)}$.

2: Compute

$$\mathbf{s}\mathbf{U}^\top = (\mathbf{s}_1 \; \mathbf{s}_2),$$

where $\mathbf{s}_1 \in (\mathbb{Z}/p^s\mathbb{Z})^{n-k-\ell}, \mathbf{s}_2 \in (\mathbb{Z}/p^s\mathbb{Z})^{\ell}$.

3: Build the list $\mathcal{B}$ as

$$\mathcal{B} = \left\{\mathbf{x} \mid \mathbf{x}_{\mathcal{E}^C} \in S_{(r)}\left(0, \tfrac{v}{4}, \tfrac{k+\ell-\varepsilon}{2}, p^s\right) \text{ for some } \mathcal{E} \subseteq \left\{1, \ldots, \tfrac{k+\ell}{2}\right\} \text{ with } |\mathcal{E}| = \varepsilon/2\right\}$$

4: Compute $\mathcal{L}_1 = \mathcal{B}_1 +\!\!\!+_{\mathbf{0}} \mathcal{B}_2$ and $\mathcal{L}_2 = \mathcal{B}_1 +\!\!\!+_{\mathbf{s}_2} \mathcal{B}_2$ using Algorithm 1.

5: Compute $\mathbf{e} \in \mathcal{L}_1 \bowtie \mathcal{L}_2$ using Algorithm 2.

6: If this fails, return to Step 1.

7: Return $\mathbf{P}^\top\mathbf{e}$.

with $\mathbf{y}_1 + \mathbf{y}_2 = \mathbf{e}_2$. This is achieved by a correct choice of the parameter u. We first compute the expected total number of such representatives for a fixed $\mathbf{e}_2$. From Lemma 3, we know that $\mathbf{e}_2$ follows a uniform distribution in $S_{(r)}(0, v, k+l, p^s)$. Using the marginal distribution in (3.1) and (3.2), we can compute the expected Lee weight distribution for $\mathbf{e}_2$. Let λ be the expected Lee weight composition of $\mathbf{e}_2$, and σ be the expected support size of $\mathbf{e}_2$. Also recall that for a weak composition λ of v, we denote by $C(v/2, v, \lambda, k+\ell, p^s)$ the number of weak compositions π of $v/2$ which fit into a composition λ of length $k+\ell$, i.e., the maximal part sizes are given by λ.

Lemma 4. *The expected number of representatives* $(\mathbf{y}_1, \mathbf{y}_2) \in \mathcal{L}_1 \times \mathcal{L}_2$ *for a fixed solution* $\mathbf{e}_2$ *is at least given by*

$$R_U = C(v/2, v, \lambda, k+\ell, p^s)\binom{k+\ell-\sigma}{\varepsilon}(p^s-1)^{\varepsilon},$$

where λ *is the expected Lee weight composition of* $\mathbf{e}_2$*, and* σ *is the expected support size of* $\mathbf{e}_2$.

The proof of Lemma 4 can be found in Appendix B. In order to expect the existence of at least one representative $\mathbf{y}_1 \in \mathcal{L}_1$ of $\mathbf{e}_2$, we choose $u = \lfloor \log_{p^s}(R_U) \rfloor$.

Asymptotic Cost of the Algorithm: We now present an upper bound on the asymptotic costs of the algorithm. For this, let R be the rate of the code and $M = \lfloor p^s/2 \rfloor$. We assume that the internal algorithm parameters $t, v, \ell, \varepsilon, u$ are some functions depending on n. We define the real numbers $T := \lim_{n\to\infty} \frac{t(n)}{n}$, $V := \lim_{n\to\infty} \frac{v(n)}{n}$, $L := \lim_{n\to\infty} \frac{\ell(n)}{n}$, $E := \lim_{n\to\infty} \frac{\varepsilon(n)}{n}$ and $U := \lim_{n\to\infty} \frac{u(n)}{n}$. Note that these real numbers satisfy the following inequalities:

$$0 \leq V \leq \min\{T, \varphi(r,t,n,p^s)/n\},\ \ 0 \leq L \leq 1-R,\ \ 0 < E < R+L$$
$$0 \leq T - 2V \leq M(1-R-L) \ \text{ and } \ 0 < U < L.$$

We first provide the asymptotic cost of Algorithm 1 and Algorithm 2. In the following results, we compute the asymptotic exponent e of the cost of an algorithm, which means that the cost is given by $(p^s)^{(e+o(1))n}$.

Lemma 5 ([22, **Lemma 4.3**]). *The asymptotic exponent of the average cost of Algorithm 1 is*

$$\lim_{n\to\infty} \frac{1}{n} \max\left\{\log_{p^s}(|\mathcal{B}_1|), \log_{p^s}(|\mathcal{B}_2|), \log_{p^s}(|\mathcal{B}_1|) + \log_{p^s}(|\mathcal{B}_2|) - U\right\}.$$

Lemma 6 ([22, **Corollary 2**]). *The asymptotic exponent of the average cost of the last merge (Algorithm 2) is given by*

$$\lim_{n\to\infty} \frac{1}{n} \max\left\{\log_{p^s}(|\mathcal{L}_1|), \log_{p^s}(|\mathcal{L}_2|), \left(\log_{p^s}(|\mathcal{L}_1|) + \log_{p^s}(|\mathcal{L}_2|)\right) - (L-U)\right\}.$$

Note that the $L - U$ comes from the fact that the vectors already merge to $\mathbf{s}_2$ on U positions due to the first merge.

Let us denote the asymptotics of the binomial coefficient by

$$\begin{aligned} H(F,G) &:= \lim_{n\to\infty} \frac{1}{n} \log_{p^s}\left(\binom{f(n)}{g(n)}\right) \\ &= F\log_{p^s}(F) - G\log_{p^s}(G) - (F-G)\log_{p^s}(F-G), \end{aligned}$$

where $f(n), g(n)$ are integer-valued functions such that $\lim_{n\to\infty} \frac{f(n)}{n} = F$ and $\lim_{n\to\infty} \frac{g(n)}{n} = G$. Recall, from (2.1), that

$$\gamma(V/2, V) = \lim_{n'\to\infty} \frac{1}{n'} \log_{p^s}\left(C(v/2, v, \lambda, n', p^s)\right).$$

For us $n' = k + \ell$, which also tends to infinity for n going to infinity. Thus,

$$\lim_{n\to\infty} \frac{k+\ell}{n} \lim_{k+\ell\to\infty} \frac{1}{k+\ell} \log_{p^s}\left(C(v/2, v, \lambda, k+\ell, p^s)\right) = (R+L)\gamma(V/2, V).$$

Let $S = \lim_{n\to\infty} \sigma(n)/n$. By Lemma 4 we choose U as

$$U = (R+L)\gamma(V/2, V) + H(R+L-S, E) + E.$$

Theorem 2. *The asymptotic exponent of the average time complexity of the Lee-metric BJMM algorithm on two levels is at most given by* $I+C$, *where*

$$I = A_{(M)}(T,p^s) - A_{(r)}\left(\tfrac{V}{R+L},p^s\right) - A_{(M)}\left(\tfrac{T-V}{1-R-L},p^s\right),$$

is the exponent of the expected number of iterations and $C = \max\{B, 2D-L+U, D\}$ *is the exponent of the expected cost of one iteration with*

$$B = A_{(r)}\left(\tfrac{V}{4},\tfrac{R+L-E}{2},p^s\right) + H\left(\tfrac{R+L}{2},\tfrac{E}{2}\right) + E/2,$$
$$D = A_{(r)}\left(\tfrac{V}{2},R+L-E,p^s\right) + H(R+L,E) + E - U.$$

Proof. For our base lists $\mathcal{B}_i$, we have that

$$|\mathcal{B}| = F_{(r)}\left(\tfrac{v}{4},\tfrac{k+\ell-\varepsilon}{2},p^s\right)\binom{(k+\ell)/2}{\varepsilon/2}(p^s)^{\varepsilon/2}.$$

Due to Lemma 5 and Corollary 2, the asymptotic exponent of the average cost of the first merge is then given by

$$B = A_{(r)}\left(\tfrac{V}{4},\tfrac{R+L-E}{2},p^s\right) + H\left(\tfrac{R+L}{2},\tfrac{E}{2}\right) + E/2.$$

For the second merge we also need to compute the asymptotic sizes of $\mathcal{L}_i$. First, we note that the expected size of $\mathcal{L}_i$ is given by

$$|\mathcal{L}_i| = \left(F_{(r)}\left(\tfrac{v}{2},k+\ell-\varepsilon,p^s\right)\binom{k+\ell}{\varepsilon}(p^s)^{\varepsilon}\right)/p^{su}.$$

Thus,

$$D = \lim_{n\to\infty}\frac{1}{n}\log_{p^s}(|\mathcal{L}_i|) = A_{(r)}\left(\tfrac{V}{2},R+L-E,p^s\right) + H(R+L,E) + E - U.$$

sing Lemma 6, the asymptotic exponent of the average cost of the last merge then given by

$$2D - L + U = 2A_{(r)}(V/2, R+L-E, p^s) + 2H(R+L,E) + 2E - U - L.$$

e recall from Eq. (4.2) that the success probability of the algorithm is given P, hence, we get the asymptotic number of iterations I. □

bserve that ℓ, v, r, ε are internal parameters, which can be chosen optimal, i.e., ch that the algorithm achieves the minimal cost. Clearly, the choice for the eshold r will influence the possible choices for v.

e Amortized Case: If we only consider p^{su} many vectors from the base lists we can potentially reduce the cost. The algorithm is going to work exactly same way, with the only difference that the base lists $\mathcal{B}'$ have size p^{su}. Thus, r using the merging Algorithm 1 on u positions we get lists $\mathcal{L}_i'$ of size p^{su} as well. Finally, we merge these lists using Algorithm 2 on ℓ positions. Note that the condition on $U = \lim_{n\to\infty} u(n)/n$ now is

$$L/3 \leq U \leq \min\{(R+L)\gamma(V/2, V) + H(R+L-S, E) + E, B, L\},$$

where B denotes the asymptotic size of the original base lists, i.e.,

$$B = A_{(r)}(V/4, (R+L-E)/2, p^s) + H((R+L)/2, E/2) + E/2.$$

The condition $L/3 \leq U$, comes from the size of the final list, i.e., the number of solutions for the smaller instance, which is $\frac{p^{s2u}}{p^{s(\ell-u)}} = p^{s(3u-\ell)}$. In order to have at least one solution, we require $3u \geq \ell$. The other conditions are as before. Note that in the amortized case, the success probability of splitting $\mathbf{e} = (\mathbf{e}_1, \mathbf{e}_2)$ is not simply given by

$$P = F_{(r)}(v, k+\ell, p^s)F(t-v, n-k-\ell, p^s)F(t, n, p^s)^{-1}$$

as in the non-amortized case, since our list of $\mathbf{e}_2$ is by construction smaller. That is: instead of all solutions to the smaller problem $F_{(r)}(v, k+\ell, p^s)p^{-s\ell}$, we only consider Z many solutions to the smaller problem. In other words, Z is the number of distinct $\mathbf{e}_2$ in our last list. Similar to the approach of [11], we have a success probability of

$$P' = Zp^{s\ell}F(t-v, n-k-\ell, p^s)F(t, n, p^s)^{-1}.$$

In order to compute Z, let us denote by X the maximal amount of collisions of the last merge which would lead to an $\mathbf{e}_2$ (i.e., with possible repetitions), by Y the total number of solutions to $\mathbf{e}_2\mathbf{B}^\top = \mathbf{s}_2$ with $\mathbf{e}_2 \in S_{(r)}(0, v, k+\ell, p^s)$, namely

$$Y = F_{(r)}(v, k+\ell, p^s)p^{-s\ell},$$

and finally by W the number of collisions that we are considering, that is

$$W = p^{s(3u-\ell)} = p^{s2u}p^{-s(\ell-u)}.$$

This leaves us with a combinatorial problem: given a basket with X balls having Y colors, if we pick W balls at random, how many colors are we going to see on average? This will determine the number of distinct tuples $\mathbf{e}_2$ in the final list. This number is on average

$$Y\left(1 - \binom{X - X/Y}{W}\binom{X}{W}^{-1}\right),$$

which can be lower bounded by W. In fact,

$$1 - \binom{X - X/Y}{W}\binom{X}{W}^{-1} \geq 1 - (1 - W/X)^{X/Y} \sim W/Y.$$

Hence, $Z \geq p^{s(3u-\ell)}$ and we get a success probability of at least

$$p^{s3u}F(t-v, n-k-\ell, p^s)F(t, n, p^s)^{-1}.$$

The asymptotic exponent of the average cost of the amortized version of Algorithm 3 is then given by $I' + \max\{U, 3U - L\}$, where I' corresponds to the expected number of iterations, i.e.,

$$I' \leq A_{(M)}(T, p^s) - 3U - A_{(M)}((T - V)/(1 - R - L), p^s).$$

Hence, we can see that the restriction to the smaller balls does not influence the amortized version of BJMM, as the idea of amortizing is already to restrict the balls. The restriction only influences the conditions and thus the choice of U.

4.2 Decoding Beyond the Minimum Distance

There could be scenarios where one wants to decode more errors than the minimum Lee distance of the code at hand.

In a scenario where we have $t > Mn/2$, the marginal distribution of $\mathbf{e} \in (\mathbb{Z}/p^s\mathbb{Z})^n$ implies that $\pm M$ is the most likely entry of $\mathbf{e}$, then the second most likely is $\pm(M-1)$ and so on, until the least likely entry is 0. In this case, we will reverse the previous algorithm and for some threshold Lee weight $0 \leq r \leq M$, we want the vector $\mathbf{e}_2$ of Lee weight $t - \varphi(r-1, t, n, p^s) \leq v \leq t$ to live in $\{\pm r, \ldots, \pm M\}^{k+\ell}$. In order to construct such a vector, we will use a similar construction as before, where we exchange the set $\{0, \pm 1, \ldots, \pm r\}$ with $\{\pm r, \ldots, \pm M\}$. Note that the success probability of such splitting is given by

$$P = F^{(r)}(v, k+\ell, p^s) F(t - v, n - k - \ell, p^s) F(t, n, p^s)^{-1}.$$

Furthermore, there are two main differences to the previous algorithm: firstly, he ε overlapping positions now sum up to $\pm M$, since M is the most likely Lee veight. Secondly, we require to partition the weights in order to guarantee that he large weight entries of $\mathbf{y}_1$ will not be decreased after adding $\mathbf{y}_2$. Therefore, he weight distribution of $\mathbf{e}_2$ is as follows: on some $(k+\ell-\varepsilon)/2$ positions $\mathbf{y}_1$ has ee weight $(v - \varepsilon M)/2$ and $\mathbf{y}_2$ is zero, and on some other $(k+\ell-\varepsilon)/2$ positions $_2$ has Lee weight $(v - \varepsilon M)/2$ and $\mathbf{y}_1$ is zero. The vectors $\mathbf{x}_j^{(i)}$ follow a similar artition as before. See Fig. 3 for an illustration. The base list $\mathcal{B}$ is then

$$= \Big\{ \mathbf{x} \mid \mathbf{x}_Z = \mathbf{0}, \mathbf{x}_W \in S^{(r)}\left(0, \tfrac{v - \varepsilon M}{4}, \tfrac{k+\ell-\varepsilon}{4}, p^s\right), \mathbf{x}_{\mathcal{E}} \in (\mathbb{Z}/p^s\mathbb{Z})^{\varepsilon/2} \text{ for a partition } Z \cup W \cup \mathcal{E} \text{ of } \left\{1, \ldots, \tfrac{k+\ell}{2}\right\} \text{ with } |Z| = |W| = \tfrac{k+\ell-\varepsilon}{4}, |\mathcal{E}| = \tfrac{\varepsilon}{2} \Big\}.$$

l of the base lists have the same size, which is given by

$$\binom{(k+\ell)/2}{\varepsilon/2} p^{s\varepsilon/2} \binom{(k+\ell-\varepsilon)/2}{(k+\ell-\varepsilon)/4} F^{(r)}((v - \varepsilon M)/4, (k+\ell-\varepsilon)/4, p^s).$$

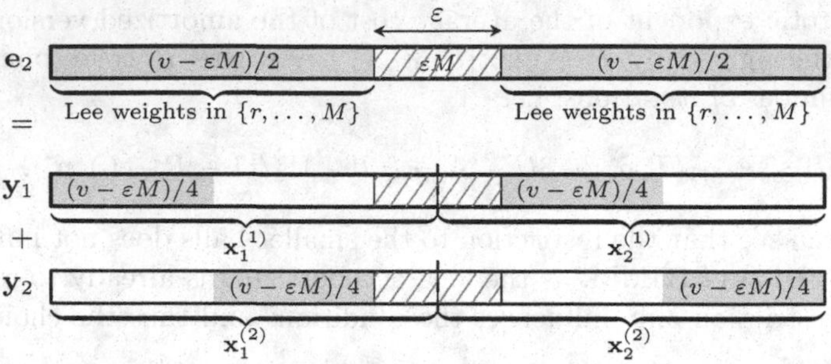

Fig. 3. Two levels decomposition of the vector $\mathbf{e}_2$ into $\mathbf{y}_1$ and $\mathbf{y}_2$, where $\mathbf{y}_i = (\mathbf{x}_1^{(i)}, \mathbf{x}_2^{(i)})$ for $i = 1, 2$ with corresponding Lee weights in the support (gray areas). For $(\mathbf{y}_1)_i$ and $(\mathbf{y}_2)_i$ with $i \in \mathcal{E}$, we require $\mathrm{wt}_L\left((\mathbf{y}_1)_i + (\mathbf{y}_2)_i\right) = M$.

Performing the concatenation merge of Algorithm 1 on $\mathcal{B}_1 = \mathcal{B}_2 = \mathcal{B}$, we obtain the lists $\mathcal{L}_1$ and $\mathcal{L}_2$ for $\mathbf{y}_1$ and $\mathbf{y}_2$, respectively, as follows

$$\mathcal{L}_1 = \Big\{ \mathbf{y} \mid \mathbf{y}\mathbf{B}^\top =_u \mathbf{0}, \mathbf{y}_Z = \mathbf{0}, \mathbf{y}_{\mathcal{E}} \in (\mathbb{Z}/p^s\mathbb{Z})^{\varepsilon}, \mathbf{y}_W \in S^{(r)}\left(0, \tfrac{v-\varepsilon M}{2}, \tfrac{k+\ell-\varepsilon}{2}, p^s\right), \text{for a partition } Z \cup W \cup \mathcal{E} \text{ of } \{1, \dots, k+\ell\} \text{ with } |Z| = |W| = \tfrac{k+\ell-\varepsilon}{2}, |\mathcal{E}| = \varepsilon \Big\},$$

$$\mathcal{L}_2 = \Big\{ \mathbf{y} \mid \mathbf{y}\mathbf{B}^\top =_u \mathbf{s}_2, \mathbf{y}_Z = \mathbf{0}, \mathbf{y}_{\mathcal{E}} \in (\mathbb{Z}/p^s\mathbb{Z})^{\varepsilon}, \mathbf{y}_W \in S^{(r)}\left(0, \tfrac{v-\varepsilon M}{2}, \tfrac{k+\ell-\varepsilon}{2}, p^s\right), \text{for a partition } Z \cup W \cup \mathcal{E} \text{ of } \{1, \dots, k+\ell\} \text{ with } |Z| = |W| = \tfrac{k+\ell-\varepsilon}{2}, |\mathcal{E}| = \varepsilon \Big\}.$$

Both lists are of size

$$\binom{k+\ell}{\varepsilon} p^{s(\varepsilon-u)} \binom{k+\ell-\varepsilon}{(k+\ell-\varepsilon)/2} F^{(r)}\left((v-\varepsilon M)/2, (k+\ell-\varepsilon)/2, p^s\right).$$

For this procedure to work, we also need the additional condition on v, r and ε, that $v \geq \varepsilon(M-r) + r(k+\ell)$. Then, a final merge using Algorithm 2 produces a final list of all solutions of the smaller instance which does not need to be stored

Lemma 7. *The number of representations* $\mathbf{e}_2 = \mathbf{y}_1 + \mathbf{y}_2$ *for* $(\mathbf{y}_1, \mathbf{y}_2) \in \mathcal{L}_1 \times \mathcal{L}_2$ *for* $\varepsilon' = k + \ell - \varepsilon$*, is then given by at least*

$$R_B = \binom{k+\ell}{\varepsilon} \left(\sum_{i=0}^{\varepsilon} \binom{\varepsilon}{i} (M-r+1)^i r^{\varepsilon-i} \binom{\varepsilon'}{i} (M-r+1)^i \binom{\varepsilon'-i}{(\varepsilon'-i)/2} \right).$$

The proof of this Lemma can be found in Appendix B. Thus, we will need th additional condition $\varepsilon \leq (k+\ell)/2$ and we choose $u = \left\lfloor \log_{p^s}(R_B) \right\rfloor$. Since w cannot take the asymptotic of an infinite sum, we need to bound this quantit In fact, setting $i = \varepsilon$ gives such lower bound.

$$R_B \geq \binom{k+\ell}{\varepsilon} (M-r+1)^{2\varepsilon} \binom{k+\ell-\varepsilon}{\varepsilon} \binom{k+\ell-2\varepsilon}{(k+\ell-2\varepsilon)/2}.$$

Thus, we choose $U = \lim_{n\to\infty} u(n)/n$ as

$$H(R+L, E)+2E\log_{p^s}(M-r+1)+H(R+L-E, E)+H(R+L-2E, (R+L-2E)/2).$$

In addition, since we decode beyond the minimum distance, the LSDP has several solutions. Since the inputs have been chosen uniformly at random, we can assume that these solutions are independent from each other. Thus, to find just one of all the expected $N = F(t, n, p^s)p^{-s(n-k)}$ solutions we have an expected number of iterations given by $(NP)^{-1}$, instead of P^{-1}. Note that asymptotically this value is bounded by R, as

$$X := \lim_{n\to\infty} \frac{1}{n}\log_{p^s}\left(F(t, n, p^s)p^{-s(n-k)}\right) = A_{(M)}(T, p^s) - 1 + R \leq R.$$

Corollary 1. *The asymptotic exponent of the average time complexity of the Lee-metric BJMM algorithm on two levels for $t > Mn/2$ is given by at most $I + C$, where*

$$I = (1-R) - A^{(r)}\left(\tfrac{V}{R+L}, p^s\right) - A_{(M)}\left(\tfrac{T-V}{1-R-L}, p^s\right)$$

is the expected number of iterations and $C = \max\{B, D, 2D-L+U\}$ is the cost of one iteration, where

$$B = \tfrac{E}{2} + H\left(\tfrac{R+L}{2}, \tfrac{E}{2}\right) + H\left(\tfrac{R+L-E}{2}, \tfrac{R+L-E}{4}\right) + A^{(r)}\left(\tfrac{V-EM}{R+L-E}, p^s\right),$$
$$D = E - U + H(R+L, E) + H\left(R+L-E, \tfrac{R+L-E}{2}\right) + A^{(r)}\left(\tfrac{V-EM}{R+L-E}, p^s\right).$$

The Amortized Case: We consider again the amortized version of this algorithm, .e., we only take p^{su} many vectors from the base lists $\mathcal{B}$. The algorithm is going o work exactly the same way, similar to the amortized version for the first cenario. The asymptotic cost of the amortized version of Algorithm 3 is then iven by $I' + \max\{U, 3U - L\}$, where I' is as before the expected number of erations, i.e.,

$$I' \leq (1-R) - 3U - A_{(M)}((T-V)/(1-R-L), p^s).$$

Comparison

this section we compare the new Lee-metric BJMM algorithm to the e-metric BJMM algorithm from [22] and to the Lee-metric Wagner algohm [11]. For this we denote by $e(R, p^s)$ the exponent of the asymptotic st, i.e., the asymptotic cost is given by $(p^s)^{(e(R,p^s)+o(1))n}$. We compare worst case cost exponent $e(R^*, p^s)$ for $R^* = \text{argmax}_{0\leq R\leq 1}(e(R, p^s))$. computations made in this section are based on Mathematica [15] proms available at https://git.math.uzh.ch/isd/lee-isd/lee-isd-algorithm-comple es/-/blob/master/Lee-ISD-restricted.nb.

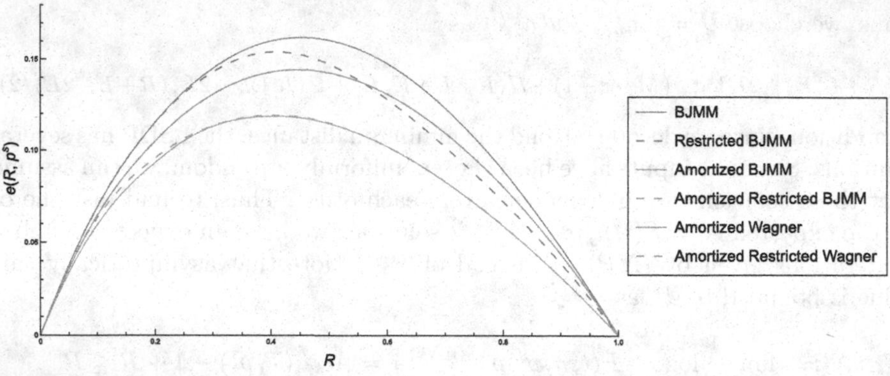

Fig. 4. Comparison of asymptotic costs $(p^s)^{(e(R,p^s)+o(1))n}$ of various Lee ISD algorithms for full-distance decoding for $p^s = 47$.

Table 1. Comparison of asymptotic costs $(p^s)^{(e(R,p^s)+o(1))n}$ of various Lee ISD algorithms for full-distance decoding for $p^s = 47$.

Algorithm	$e(R^*, p^s)$	R^*	Optimal internal parameters	Memory
Lee-BJMM	0.1620	0.4514	$T = 1.4680, V = 0.0692$ $L = 0.0405, E = 0.0017$	0.0376
Restricted Lee-BJMM for $r = 5$	0.1541	0.4081	$T = 1.7516, V = 0.2502$ $L = 0.1007, E = 0$	0.0791
Amortized Lee-BJMM	0.1190	0.4056	$T = 1.7691, V = 0.5868$ $L = 0.1787, E = 0.1331$	0.0894
Amortized Restricted Lee-BJMM for $r = 6$	0.1191	0.4046	$T = 1.7765, V = 0.6195$ $L = 0.1838, E = 0.0200$	0.0919
Amortized Lee-Wagner	0.1441	0.4454	$T = 1.5048, V = 0.3245$ $L = 0.0939$	0.0470
Amortized Restricted Lee-Wagner for $r = 7$	0.1441	0.4451	$T = 1.5063, V = 0.3248$ $L = 0.0940$	0.0470

In the first scenario, we only decode up to the Gilbert-Varshamov bound that is $V(d(n), n, p^s) = 1 - R$, thus giving an immediate relation between T and R, where T is $\lim_{n\to\infty} d(n)/n$, i.e., we are considering full-distance decoding.

In the second scenario, where we have $N > 1$ solutions, one possible analysis technique, proposed in [11], is to fix a rate R and go through all $M/2 \leq T \leq M$ to see at which T the largest cost is attained for this fixed rate. However, this approach gives for the algorithm in [11] as well as for our algorithm always either $T = M$ or T very close to M (see [11, Figure 1-2, Table 1]). This is a very high weight, where $\mathbf{e}$ will mostly have entries $\pm M$. Hence, this approach is not suitable for the comparison of different ISD algorithms for all rates.

In order to compare ISD algorithms for all rates, we adapt the full distance decoding approach that fixes a relation between R and T. Note that for a rando

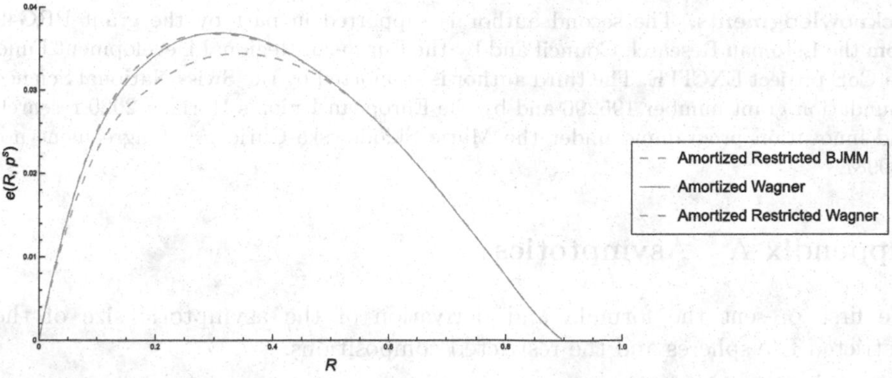

Fig. 5. Comparison of asymptotic costs $(p^s)^{(e(R,p^s)+o(1))n}$ of various Lee ISD algorithms for decoding beyond the minimum distance for $p^s = 47$.

Table 2. Comparison of asymptotic costs $(p^s)^{(e(R,p^s)+o(1))n}$ of various Lee ISD algorithms for decoding beyond the minimum distance for $p^s = 47$.

Algorithm	$e(R^*, p^s)$	R^*	Optimal internal parameters	Memory
Amortized Restricted Lee-BJMM for $r = 20$	0.0346	0.3424	$T = 18.9921, V = 9.4574$ $L = 0.0692, E = 0.2145$	0.0346
Amortized Lee-Wagner	0.0370	0.3118	$T = 18.7093, V = 8.6930$ $L = 0.0717$	0.0359
Amortized Restricted Lee-Wagner for $r = 20$	0.0369	0.2912	$T = 18.5065, V = 8.2049$ $L = 0.0718$	0.0359

nstance of LSDP, the asymptotic value for the number of solutions N is given y

$$X = A_{(M)}(T, p^s) - 1 + R \leq R,$$

ius we can fix X to be a function in R, e.g. $X = R/2$. This will also directly ad to a $T = \lim_{n\to\infty} t(n)/n$, for which $A_{(M)}(T, p^s) = 1 - R/2$. If we would have ked X to be a constant independent of R instead, this would have obstructed e comparison for all rates smaller than this constant. Since there is no other n-amortized algorithm which considers the second case, we will only compare r amortized version with the algorithm provided in [11].

We can observe in Table 1 and 2 and Fig. 4 and 5 that the restricted algohms using the information from the distribution are indeed improving the t of the known ISD algorithms. Since amortized ISD algorithms are already tricting the sizes of the balls, we get little to no improvement to these algoıms.

Acknowledgments. The second author is supported in part by the grant PRG49 from the Estonian Research Council and by the European Regional Development Fund via CoE project EXCITE. The third author is supported by the Swiss National Science Foundation grant number 195290 and by the European Union's Horizon 2020 research and innovation programme under the Marie Skłodowska-Curie grant agreement no. 899987.

Appendix A Asymptotics

We first present the formula and derivation of the asymptotic size of the restricted Lee spheres and the restricted compositions.

Appendix A.1 Asymptotics of Lee Spheres

In the complexity analysis of our algorithm, we are interested in the asymptotic size of Lee spheres, Lee balls, and some types of restricted Lee spheres. All these quantities can be described using generating functions, and their limit for n going to infinity can be computed using the saddle point technique used in [12].

Generally, we consider two functions $f(x)$ and $g(x)$ both not depending on n and define a generating function

$$\Phi(x) = f(x)^n g(x).$$

We are usually interested in the coefficients of generating functions. Therefore, for some positive integer k we denote the coefficient of x^k in $\Phi(x)$ by

$$[x^t]\Phi(x).$$

In the course of the paper, for a given length-n vector of Lee weight t we are mainly focusing on the relative Lee weight per entry. Let us therefore denote the relative Lee weight by $T := t/n$. The goal now is to estimate the coefficient $[x^{Tn}]\Phi(x)$, for some fixed $T \in (0, 1)$. The following gives an asymptotic result on the growth rate of this coefficient.

Lemma 8 ([12, **Corollary** 1]). *Let $\Phi(x) = f(x)^n g(x)$ with $f(0) \neq 0$, and $t(n$ be a function in n. Set $T := \lim_{n\to\infty} t(n)/n$ and set ρ to be the solution to*

$$\Delta(x) := \frac{xf'(x)}{f(x)} = T.$$

If $\Delta'(\rho) > 0$, and the modulus of any singularity of $g(x)$ is larger than ρ, the for large n

$$\frac{1}{n}\log_{p^s}([x^{t(n)}]\Phi(x)) \approx \log_{p^s}(f(\rho)) - T\log_{p^s}(\rho) + o(1).$$

(Restricted) Lee Spheres. We consider now the function

$$f(x) := \begin{cases} 1 + 2\sum_{i=1}^{M} x^i & \text{if } p \neq 2, \\ 1 + 2\sum_{i=1}^{M-1} x^i + x^M & \text{if } p = 2. \end{cases}$$

The generating functions of the sizes of n-dimensional Lee spheres and Lee balls are known to be $\Phi(x) = f(x)^n$ and $\Phi'(x) = \frac{f(x)^n}{1-x}$, respectively. The asymptotics of these sizes have been computed in [12,22].

The generating function of the size of the restricted Lee sphere $F_{(r)}(t, n, p^s)$ is given by $\Phi_{(r)}(x) = f_{(r)}(x)^n$, where

$$f_{(r)}(x) := \begin{cases} 1 + 2\sum_{i=1}^{M-1} x^i + x^M & \text{if } p = 2 \text{ and } r = M, \\ 1 + 2\sum_{i=1}^{r} x^i & \text{otherwise.} \end{cases}$$

whereas, for $F^{(r)}(t, n, p^s)$ the generating function is given by $\Phi^{(r)}(x) = f^{(r)}(x)^n$, where

$$f^{(r)}(x) = \begin{cases} f_{(M)}(x) & \text{if } r = 0, \\ 2\sum_{i=r}^{M-1} x^i + x^M & \text{if } p = 2 \text{ and } r > 0, \\ 2\sum_{i=r}^{M} x^i & \text{if } p \neq 2 \text{ and } r > 0. \end{cases}$$

Note that the coefficient of x^t in $\Phi^{(r)}(x)$ is equal to the coefficient of x^{t-rn} in $\Psi^{(r)}(x) = g^{(r)}(x)^n$, where

$$g^{(r)}(x) := \begin{cases} f_{(M)}(x) & \text{if } r = 0, \\ 2\sum_{i=0}^{M-1-r} x^i + x^{M-r} & \text{if } p = 2 \text{ and } r > 0, \\ 2\sum_{i=0}^{M-r} x^i & \text{if } p \neq 2 \text{ and } r > 0. \end{cases}$$

n particular, we have that $F_{(r)}(t, n, p^s) = [x^t]\Phi_{(r)}(x)$ and $F^{(r)}(t, n, p^s) =$ $x^{t-rn}]\Psi^{(r)}(x)$. Note that $F_{(M)}(t, n, p^s) = F^{(0)}(t, n, p^s) = F(t, n, p^s)$. Using emma 8, we get the following asymptotic behavior of restricted Lee spheres.

orollary 2. *Let $T \in [0, M)$ and $t = t(n)$ be a function of n such that $t(n) :=$ n for large n. Then,*

for $p \neq 2$ or $r < M$, we get

$$\lim_{n\to\infty} \frac{1}{n} \log_{p^s}(F_{(r)}(t(n), n, p^s)) = \log_{p^s}(f_{(r)}(\rho)) - T\log_{p^s}(\rho),$$

where ρ is the unique real positive solution of $2\sum_{i=1}^{r}(i - T)x^i = T$.
for $p = 2$ and $r = M$, respectively $r' = 0$, we get

$$\lim_{n\to\infty} \frac{1}{n} \log_{p^s}(F_{(r)}(t(n), n, p^s)) = \log_{p^s}(f_{(r)}(\rho)) - T\log_{p^s}(\rho),$$

where ρ is the unique real positive solution of $2\sum_{i=1}^{M-1}(i - T)x^i + (M - T)$ $x^M = T$.

3. for $p = 2$ *and* $0 < r \leq T$*, we get*

$$\lim_{n\to\infty} \frac{1}{n} \log_{p^s}(F^{(r)}(t(n), n, p^s)) = \log_{p^s}(g^{(r)}(\rho)) - (T-r)\log_{p^s}(\rho),$$

where ρ *is the unique real positive solution of*

$$2\sum_{i=1}^{M-1-r}(i-T+r)x^i + (M-T)x^{M-r} = 2(T-r).$$

4. for $p \neq 2$ *and* $0 < r \leq T$*, we get*

$$\lim_{n\to\infty} \frac{1}{n} \log_{p^s}(F^{(r)}(t(n), n, p^s)) = \log_{p^s}(g^{(r)}(\rho)) - (T-r)\log_{p^s}(\rho),$$

where ρ *is the unique real positive solution of* $2\sum_{i=1}^{M-r}(i-T+r)x^i = 2(T-r)$.

Proof. For the parts 1 and 2, we apply Lemma 8 to the generating function $\Phi_{(r)}(x)$ and obtain the mentioned results, similar to $r = M$ for $f_{(r)}$ case proved in [22, Lemma 2.6]. For the parts 3 and 4, we apply Lemma 8 to the generating function $\Psi^{(r)}(x)$ and obtain the mentioned results. □

Remark 2. Note that, for p odd (respectively, even), we get $T \geq M(M+1)/(2M+1)$ (respectively, $T \geq M/2$) if and only if

$$\lim_{n\to\infty} \frac{1}{n} \log_{p^s}(V(Tn, n, p^s)) = 1.$$

Hence, if $0 < R$, then a code that attains the asymptotic Gilbert-Varshamov bound has

$$\lim_{n\to\infty} \frac{1}{n} \log_{p^s}(V(Tn, n, p^s)) = 1 - R < 1,$$

and we get that $T < M(M+1)/(2M+1)$ if p is odd, or $T < M/2$ if p is even.

Restricted Compositions. Recall that we denote by $C(v, t, \lambda, n, p^s)$ the number of weak compositions π of v, which fit into the composition λ of t both having n part sizes, i.e., for all $i \in \{1, \dots, n\}$ we have $\pi_i \leq \lambda_i$. The reason we are interested in this number is that we can think of the Lee weight composition of a vector $\mathbf{e} \in (\mathbb{Z}/p^s\mathbb{Z})^n$ as $\lambda = (\lambda_1, \dots, \lambda_n)$, which is such that $\lambda_i = \mathrm{wt}_L((\mathbf{e})_i$

For a given composition λ of t, let m denote the maximal part size, i.e.,

$$m = \max\{\lambda_i \mid i \in \{1, \dots, n\}\}.$$

Then, the generating function of $C(v, t, \lambda, n, p^s)$ is given by

$$\Phi(z) = \prod_{i=1}^{n}\left(\sum_{j=0}^{\lambda_i} z^j\right) = \prod_{i=1}^{m}\left(\sum_{j=0}^{i} z^j\right)^{c_i n},$$

where c_i corresponds to the multiplicity of i in the composition λ, i.e., there are $c_i n$ entries of $\mathbf{e} \in (\mathbb{Z}/p^s\mathbb{Z})^n$ which have Lee weight i. Thus, $\Phi(z) = f(z)^n$, for

$$f(z) = \prod_{i=1}^{m} \left(\sum_{j=0}^{i} z^j \right)^{c_i}.$$

To get the asymptotics of $C(v, t, \lambda, n, p^s)$ we are interested in the coefficient of z^v in $\Phi(z)$. For this, let v be a function of n and $V = \lim_{n\to\infty} v(n)/n$. Now using the saddle point technique of [12] we define $\Delta(f(z)) = \frac{zf'(z)}{f(z)}$. Let ρ be the unique positive real solution to $\Delta(f(z)) = V$. Then

$$\lim_{n\to\infty} \frac{1}{n} \log_{p^s} (C(v, t, \lambda, n, p^s)) = \log_{p^s}(f(\rho)) - V \log_{p^s}(\rho).$$

Let us summarize this discussion in the following lemma.

Lemma 9. *Let us consider a weak composition $\lambda = (\lambda_1, \ldots, \lambda_n)$ of t and asymptotic relative Lee weight $T := \lim_{n\to\infty} t(n)/n$. In addition, let us consider a positive integer $v \leq t$ with $V := \lim_{n\to\infty} v(n)/n$. Let $m = \max\{\lambda_i \mid i \in \{1, \ldots, n\}\}$. If $0 \leq V < M$, then*

$$\lim_{n\to\infty} \frac{1}{n} \log_{p^s} (C(v, t, \lambda, n, p^s)) = \log_{p^s}(f(\rho)) - V \log_{p^s}(\rho),$$

where ρ is the unique real positive solution of $\sum_{i=1}^{m} c_i \frac{z + 2z^2 + \cdots + iz^i}{1 + z + \cdots + z^i} = V.$

Appendix B Proofs of Lemma 4 and 7

Lemma 4. *The expected number of representatives $(\mathbf{y}_1, \mathbf{y}_2) \in \mathcal{L}_1 \times \mathcal{L}_2$ for a fixed solution $\mathbf{e}_2$ is at least given by*

$$R_U = C(v/2, v, \lambda, k + \ell, p^s) \binom{k + \ell - \sigma}{\varepsilon} (p^s - 1)^{\varepsilon},$$

where λ is the expected Lee weight composition of $\mathbf{e}_2$, and σ is the expected support size of $\mathbf{e}_2$.

Proof. Consider the Lee weight composition of $\mathbf{e}_2$ to be $\lambda = (\lambda_1, \ldots, \lambda_{k+\ell})$, which is such that $\lambda_i = \mathrm{wt}_L((\mathbf{e}_2)_i)$. Thus, $\mathbf{e}_2 = (s_1\lambda_1, \ldots, s_{k+\ell}\lambda_{k+\ell})$, for $s_i \in \{1, -1\}$. Then, to get all possible representatives $\mathbf{y}_1$, we need the number of weak compositions π of $v/2$ fitting into λ. In fact, for any $\pi = (\pi_1, \ldots, \pi_{k+\ell})$ fitting into λ, there will exist exactly one eligible $\mathbf{y}_1$ with $\mathrm{wt}_L((\mathbf{y}_1)_i) = \pi_i$ and $(\mathbf{y}_1)_i = s_i\pi_i$. Note that the Lee weight composition of $\mathbf{y}_2 \in \mathcal{L}_2$ is then $|\lambda - \pi| = (|\lambda_1 - \pi_1|, \ldots, |\lambda_{k+\ell} - \pi_{k+\ell}|)$.

On the other hand, for any representative $\mathbf{y}_1$, we cannot have $\pi_i = \mathrm{wt}_L((\mathbf{y}_1)_i) > \mathrm{wt}_L((\mathbf{e}_2)_i)$ and $(\mathbf{y}_1)_i = -s_i\pi_i$ for any $i \in \{1, \ldots, \sigma\}$. In fact, let us assume we have A many positions in $\mathbf{y}_1$ which are such that $\pi_i = \mathrm{wt}_L((\mathbf{y}_1)_i) > \mathrm{wt}_L((\mathbf{e}_2)_i) = \lambda_i$. Due to the entry-wise additivity of the Lee weight, we have that $\mathbf{y}_2$, with composition $|\lambda - \pi|$, has $\mathrm{wt}_L(\mathbf{y}_2) > v/2$: in the considered A positions we have that $\mathrm{wt}_L((\mathbf{y}_2)_j) = \pi_j - \lambda_j$ and the Lee weight of the remaining $\sigma - A$ positions is given by $\mathrm{wt}_L((\mathbf{y}_2)_j) = \lambda_j - \pi_j$, which if we sum over all positions gives

$$\begin{aligned}\mathrm{wt}_L(\mathbf{y}_2) &= \sum_{j=1}^{A}(\pi_j - \lambda_j) + \sum_{j=A+1}^{k+\ell}(\lambda_j - \pi_j)\\ &= \sum_{j=1}^{A}(\pi_j - \lambda_j) + v - \sum_{j=1}^{A}\lambda_j - \left(v/2 - \sum_{j=1}^{A} -\pi_j\right)\\ &= v/2 + 2\left(\sum_{j=1}^{A}\pi_j - \lambda_j\right) \neq v/2.\end{aligned}$$

It is easy to see, that for each fixed π, there exists only one representative $\mathbf{y}_1$, which has in each position the same sign as $\mathbf{e}_2$.

Recall that $C(v/2, v, \lambda, k+\ell, p^s)$ denotes the number of weak compositions π of $v/2$ which fit into λ. Now, since $\mathbf{y}_1$ can take any non-zero value on the ε positions outside of the support of $\mathbf{e}_2$, we get the claim. Finally, the exact number of representations might even be larger than this, since a solution $\mathbf{e}_2$ might also be formed from positions $\mathcal{E}$ which will not cancel out, as assumed for this computation. □

Lemma 7. *The number of representations $\mathbf{e}_2 = \mathbf{y}_1 + \mathbf{y}_2$ for $(\mathbf{y}_1, \mathbf{y}_2) \in \mathcal{L}_1 \times \mathcal{L}_2$, for $\varepsilon' = k + \ell - \varepsilon$, is then given by at least*

$$R_B = \binom{k+\ell}{\varepsilon}\left(\sum_{i=0}^{\varepsilon}\binom{\varepsilon}{i}(M-r+1)^i r^{\varepsilon-i}\binom{\varepsilon'}{i}(M-r+1)^i\binom{\varepsilon'-i}{(\varepsilon'-i)/2}\right).$$

Proof. To give a lower bound on the number of representations it is enoug to give one construction. The overall idea of this construction is to split the positions of $\mathbf{y}_1$ (denoted by set $\mathcal{E}_1$) and ε positions of $\mathbf{y}_2$ (denoted by set $\mathcal{E}_2$) int those parts where they overlap and those parts where they do not overlap. I the parts where $\mathcal{E}_1$ does not overlap with $\mathcal{E}_2$, we can only allow small Lee weight in $\mathbf{y}_1$ such that, by adding large Lee weight entries of $\mathbf{y}_2$, we can still reach th large Lee weight entries of $\mathbf{e}_2$.

So let us consider a fixed $\mathbf{e}_2 \in F^{(r)}(v, k+\ell, p^s)$. As a first step we fix the $\mathcal{E}$ positions which gives $\binom{k+\ell}{\varepsilon}$. Then, within the $\mathcal{E}_1$ position we fix those of sma Lee weight. This means for a fixed position we can assume that the entry in $\mathbf{e}_2$ a with $r \leq \mathrm{wt}_L(a) \leq M$. Small Lee weights of $\mathbf{y}_1$ now refer to the possible valu of $\mathbf{y}_1$ in this position such that a can be reached through large Lee weight entri of $\mathbf{y}_2$. That is, for example if $a = r$, we allow in $\mathbf{y}_1$ the entries $\{0, -1, \ldots, r-M$ or if $a = M$ we allow in $\mathbf{y}_1$ the entries $\{M-r, \ldots, 0\}$. These allowed sets of sm

Lee weight always have size $M - r + 1$, independently of the value a. Thus, in $\mathcal{E}_1$ of size ε we choose i entries of small Lee weight, which give $\binom{\varepsilon}{i}(M - r + 1)^i$ many choices. For the remaining $\varepsilon - i$ positions in $\mathcal{E}_1$ we have large Lee weights in $\mathbf{y}_1$, which cannot reach the large Lee weight entries of $\mathbf{e}_2$ through large Lee weight entries in $\mathbf{y}_2$. Thus, they must come for the $\mathcal{E}_2$ positions. In these entries we have $r^{\varepsilon-i}$ possible choices. Note that out of the ε many positions of $\mathcal{E}_2$ we have only assigned $\varepsilon - i$ many. Hence, as a next step we choose of the remaining $k + \ell - \varepsilon$ positions the remaining i positions to have small Lee weight in $\mathbf{y}_2$. Thus, the fixed large Lee weight entries of $\mathbf{e}_2$ can be reached by adding these positions to large Lee weight entries of $\mathbf{y}_1$. For this we have $\binom{k+\ell-\varepsilon-i}{i}(M-r+1)^i$ possibilities. As a final step we then partition the remaining positions to either be 0 or of large Lee weight, i.e., $\binom{k+\ell-\varepsilon-i}{(k+\ell-\varepsilon-i)/2}$. □

References

1. Aguilar Melchor, C., et al.: ROLLO-Rank-Ouroboros, LAKE & LOCKER. NIST PQC Call for Proposals (2020)
2. Aguilar Melchor, C., et al.: Rank Quasi-Cyclic (RQC). NIST PQC Call for Proposals (2020)
3. Alekhnovich, M.: More on average case vs approximation complexity. In: Proceedings of the 44th Annual IEEE Symposium on Foundations of Computer Science, pp. 298–307. IEEE (2003)
4. Astola, J.: On the asymptotic behaviour of Lee-codes. Discret. Appl. Math. **8**(1), 13–23 (1984)
5. Barg, A.: Some new NP-complete coding problems. Problemy Peredachi Informatsii **30**(3), 23–28 (1994)
6. Bariffi, J., Bartz, H., Liva, G., Rosenthal, J.: On the properties of error patterns in the constant Lee weight channel. In: International Zurich Seminar on Information and Communication (IZS), pp. 44–48 (2022)
7. Becker, A., Joux, A., May, A., Meurer, A.: Decoding random binary linear codes in $2^{n/20}$: how $1 + 1 = 0$ improves information set decoding. In: Pointcheval, D., Johansson, T. (eds.) EUROCRYPT 2012. LNCS, vol. 7237, pp. 520–536. Springer, Heidelberg (2012). https://doi.org/10.1007/978-3-642-29011-4_31
8. Berlekamp, E., McEliece, R., Van Tilborg, H.: On the inherent intractability of certain coding problems. IEEE Trans. Inf. Theory **24**(3), 384–386 (1978)
9. Bricout, R., Chailloux, A., Debris-Alazard, T., Lequesne, M.: Ternary syndrome decoding with large weight. In: Paterson, K.G., Stebila, D. (eds.) SAC 2019. LNCS, vol. 11959, pp. 437–466. Springer, Cham (2020). https://doi.org/10.1007/978-3-030-38471-5_18
10. Byrne, E., Horlemann, A.-L., Khathuria, K., Weger, V.: Density of free modules over finite chain rings. arXiv preprint arXiv:2106.09403 (2021)
11. Chailloux, A., Debris-Alazard, T., Etinski, S.: Classical and quantum algorithms for generic syndrome decoding problems and applications to the Lee metric. In: Cheon, J.H., Tillich, J.-P. (eds.) PQCrypto 2021 2021. LNCS, vol. 12841, pp. 44–62. Springer, Cham (2021). https://doi.org/10.1007/978-3-030-81293-5_3
12. Gardy, D., Solé, P.: Saddle point techniques in asymptotic coding theory. In: Cohen, G., Lobstein, A., Zémor, G., Litsyn, S. (eds.) Algebraic Coding 1991. LNCS, vol. 573, pp. 75–81. Springer, Heidelberg (1992). https://doi.org/10.1007/BFb0034343

13. Horlemann-Trautmann, A.-L., Weger, V.: Information set decoding in the Lee metric with applications to cryptography. Adv. Math. Commun. **15**(4), 677–699 (2021)
14. Howgrave-Graham, N., Joux, A.: New generic algorithms for hard knapsacks. In: Gilbert, H. (ed.) EUROCRYPT 2010. LNCS, vol. 6110, pp. 235–256. Springer, Heidelberg (2010). https://doi.org/10.1007/978-3-642-13190-5_12
15. Wolfram Research, Inc., Mathematica, Version 12.3.1. Champaign, IL (2021)
16. May, A., Meurer, A., Thomae, E.: Decoding random linear codes in $\tilde{\mathcal{O}}(2^{0.054n})$. In: Lee, D.H., Wang, X. (eds.) ASIACRYPT 2011. LNCS, vol. 7073, pp. 107–124. Springer, Heidelberg (2011). https://doi.org/10.1007/978-3-642-25385-0_6
17. McEliece, R.J.: A public-key cryptosystem based on algebraic coding theory. Deep Space Netw. Progress Rep. **44**, 114–116 (1978)
18. Meurer, A.: A coding-theoretic approach to cryptanalysis. Ph.D. thesis, Ruhr Universität Bochum (2013)
19. Prange, E.: The use of information sets in decoding cyclic codes. IRE Trans. Inf. Theory **8**(5), 5–9 (1962)
20. Regev, O., Rosen, R.: Lattice problems and norm embeddings. In: Proceedings of the Thirty-Eighth Annual ACM Symposium on Theory of Computing, pp. 447–456 (2006)
21. Wagner, D.: A generalized birthday problem. In: Yung, M. (ed.) CRYPTO 2002. LNCS, vol. 2442, pp. 288–304. Springer, Heidelberg (2002). https://doi.org/10.1007/3-540-45708-9_19
22. Weger, V., Khathuria, K., Horlemann-Trautmann, A.-L., Battaglioni, M., Santini, P., Persichetti, E.: On the hardness of the Lee syndrome decoding problem. In: Advances in Mathematics of Communications (2022)

Cryptanalysis of Ivanov–Krouk–Zyablov Cryptosystem

Kirill Vedenev(✉) and Yury Kosolapov

Southern Federal University, Rostov-on-Don, Russia
vedenevk@gmail.com

Abstract. Recently, F. Ivanov, E. Krouk and V. Zyablov proposed new cryptosystem based of Generalized Reed–Solomon (GRS) codes over field extensions. In their approach, the subfield images of GRS codes are masked by a special transform, so that the resulting public codes are not equivalent to subfield images of GRS code but burst errors still can be decoded. In this paper, we show that the complexity of message–recovery attack on this cryptosystem can be reduced due to using burst errors, and the secret key of Ivanov–Krouk–Zyablov cryptosystem can successfully recovered in polynomial time with a linear–algebra based attack and a square–based attack.

Keywords: Code–based cryptography · GRS codes · Field extensions · Subspace subcodes · Projected codes · Information–set decoding · Key–recovery attack

1 Introduction

)ue to the development of quantum computing and the vulnerability of tradi-ional asymmetric cryptosystems to attacks using quantum computers, there is need to create new secure cryptosystems. Code–based cryptography is con-idered as one of the most promising and mature candidates for post–quantum ryptography. The first code–based cryptosystem based on binary Goppa codes as proposed by R. J. McEliece in 1978 [19] and in its modern version *ClassicM-Eliece* [7] submitted to NIST–PQC competition is still believed to be secure. owever due to large public key sizes, the McEliece cryptosystem is limited in me practical applications. In order to get smaller key sizes, there were attempts replace binary Goppa codes by other classes of efficient algebraic codes, such Generalized Reed–Solomon (GRS) codes [22], Reed–Muller codes [26], AG–des [16], concatenated codes [25], rank–metric Gabidulin codes [13]. However, st of this modifications were proven unsecure [8,11,21,24,25,27]. With gen-l McEliece framework being masking a fast–decodable code by using a hid-permutation, there were also attempts to employ more sophisticated hiding chanisms (e.g. [3,6,26,28,29]). However most of this modifications were also cessfully attacked [10,12,29]. Another approach to reduce public key size is ıg random group–structured codes, which was successfully implemented in

Deneuville (Ed.): CBCrypto 2022, LNCS 13839, pp. 137–153, 2023.
s://doi.org/10.1007/978-3-031-29689-5_8

BIKE [1,2] and HQC [20] cryptosystems, however this introduces some decryption failure rate (DFR) making it harder to prove CCA security.

Recently, several protocols based on subfield images of algebraic codes over field extensions were proposed. Namely, in [5] T. Berger, C. Gueye, J. Klamti introduced the notion of generalized subspace (GS) subcodes, which are intermediate level between subfield subcodes and subfield images of codes over field extensions $\mathbb{F}_{q^m}$, and proposed using such codes in cryptography. In addition, it was shown in [5] that a McEliece–like cryptosystem based on subfield images of GRS codes can be attacked by a modification of the Sidelnikov–Shestakov attack, and quasi–cyclic variant of this cryptosystem can be attacked by using approach of [23]. In [17], K. Khathuria, J. Rosenthal and V. Weger proposed using the punctured subfield images of GRS codes in the Niederreiter–like cryptosystem (XGRS cryptosystem). However, in [9], a cryptosystem based on generalized subspace subcodes of GRS codes (SSRS cryptosystem), which generalizes XGRS cryptosystem, was successfully attacked using a modification of Schur–Hadamard product in the case $\lambda > m/2$, where λ is dimension of subspaces. More recently, F. Ivanov, E. Krouk and V. Zyablov proposed a new protocol [15] based on subfield images of GRS–codes, with the public code being neither subfield image of GRS–code naither its subcode. However, in this paper we show that Ivanov–Krouk–Zyablov (IKZ) cryptosystem is also insecure.

This paper is organized is follows. In Sect. 2 we give necessary preliminaries on m–block codes, subfield images of codes, generalized subspace subcodes and generalized projected codes. In Sect. 3, we consider a generalization of Ivanov–Krouk–Zyablov protocol and estimate the complexity of information–set decoding attack on it. In Sect. 4, we propose a key–recovery attack based on linear algebra. In Sect. 5, we propose a faster attack based on twisted squares attack of [9] which however requires larger degree field extensions.

2 Preliminaries

Let $\mathbb{F}_q$ be a finite field of size q. Given a vector $\mathbf{c} \in \mathbb{F}_q^n$, by $\mathrm{supp}(c) = \{i = 1, \ldots, n \mid c_i \neq 0\}$ we denote the support of $\mathbf{c}$ and by $\mathrm{wt}(\mathbf{c}) = |\mathrm{supp}(\mathbf{c})|$ we denote the Hamming weight of $\mathbf{c}$. The Hamming distance between $\mathbf{x}, \mathbf{y} \in \mathbb{F}^n$ is denoted by $d(\mathbf{x}, \mathbf{y}) = \mathrm{wt}(\mathbf{x} - \mathbf{y})$. A linear $[n, k, d]_q$–code is a linear subspace $C \subset \mathbb{F}_q^n$, such that $\dim(C) = k$ and $d = \min_{c \in C \setminus \{0\}} \mathrm{wt}(c)$. G_C denotes a generator matrix of C and H_C denotes a parity–check matrix of C. Given a code C, its dual code is denoted by $C^\perp$. By I_n we denote $n \times n$–identity matrix.

Shortened and punctured codes are well–known constructions for building new codes from existing ones. Let $\overline{1, n} = \{1, \ldots, n\}$ and let $I \subset \overline{1, n}$. Given $[n, k, d]_q$–code C, the *punctured code of C on positions I* is defined as follows

$$\mathrm{Pct}_I(C) = \left\{(c_i)_{i \notin I} \mid (c_1, c_2, \ldots, c_n) \in C\right\},$$

i.e. $\mathrm{Pct}_I(C)$ is obtained from C by deleting coordinates indexed by I. The *shortened code of C on I* is

$$\mathrm{Sh}_I(C) = \mathrm{Pct}_I\left(\{c \in C \mid \mathrm{supp}(c) \cap I = \varnothing\}\right).$$

Note that $\mathrm{Pct}_I(C)$ and $\mathrm{Sh}_I(C)$ are also linear codes and the following relations hold.

Proposition 1 ([14], Theorem 1.5.7). *Let C be a $[n, k, d]_q$–code. Then*

1. $\mathrm{Pct}_I(C)^\perp = \mathrm{Sh}_I(C^\perp)$ *and* $\mathrm{Sh}_I(C)^\perp = \mathrm{Pct}_I(C^\perp)$;
2. *if* $|I| < d$, *then* $\dim(\mathrm{Pct}_I(C)) = k$ *and* $\dim\left(\mathrm{Sh}(C^\perp)\right) = n - k - |I|$; *if* $|I| = d$ *and I is the set of coordinates where a minimum weight codeword is nonzero, then*

$$\dim(\mathrm{Pct}_I(C)) = k - 1, \quad \dim(\mathrm{Sh}_I(C^\perp)) = n - k - |I| + 1.$$

2.1 m–block Codes

In [4,5] T. Berger et. al. proposed the notion of m–block codes for which the ambient alphabet is the set of m–tuples of elements of $\mathbb{F}_q$. Namely, a *m–block code of length n* is an additive code over the alphabet $\mathbb{E}_m = \mathbb{F}_q^m$ (i.e. a subgroup of $(\mathbb{E}_m^n, +)$), which is stable by scalar multiplication by any $\lambda \in \mathbb{F}_q$. The integer m is called the *block size.* Given $\mathbf{c} = (\mathbf{c_1}, \dots, \mathbf{c_n}) \in \mathbb{E}_m^n \simeq \mathbb{F}_q^{mn}$, by $\mathrm{supp}_m(\mathbf{c}) = \{i \mid \mathbf{c_i} \neq 0\}$ we denote block support of c, by $\mathrm{wt}_m(\mathbf{c}) = |\mathrm{supp}_m(\mathbf{c})|$ and $d_m(\mathbf{x}, \mathbf{y}) = \mathrm{wt}_m(\mathbf{x} - \mathbf{y})$ we denote block Hamming weight and block Hamming distance respectively. Since $\mathbb{E}_m^n$ and $\mathbb{F}_q^{nm}$ can be identified, it follows that a m–block code is also a linear code over $\mathbb{F}_q$ of length mn, equipped with block Hamming metric. A m–block code C of block length n, $\mathbb{F}_q$–dimension k and minimum block distance $d_m = \min_{c \in C\setminus\{0\}} \mathrm{wt}_m(c)\}$ is said to be $[n, k, d_m]_q^m$–block code.

Block codes are of particular interest due to having ability to correct error bursts. Indeed, let $\mathcal{S}_{m,n,t} = \{e \in \mathbb{E}_m^n \mid \mathrm{wt}_m(e) \leq t\}$ be a set of *synchronous t* error burst of length m, then clearly a $[n, k, d_m]_q^m$–code can correct any error from $\mathcal{S}_{m,n,\lfloor (d_m - 1)/2 \rfloor}$.

Remark 1. Let $\mathcal{E}_{mn,l} \subset \mathbb{F}_q^{nm}$ denote a set of l error bursts of length up to m (non–ynchronous to m–block structure of a code). Note that if an m–block code can orrect any error from $\mathcal{S}_{m,n,t}$, then it can correct any error from $\mathcal{E}_{mn,\lfloor t/2 \rfloor}$ since ny non–synchronous error burst of length m covers at most two m–blocks.

Note that the notion of block codes can be easily generalized to multi-block odes. Namely, *a multi–block code* is an additive subgroup of $\mathbb{E}_{m_1} \times \dots \times \mathbb{E}_{m_n}$, hich is stable by scalar multiplication by any $\lambda \in \mathbb{F}_q$.

Two multi–block codes C_1 and C_2 of length are said to be *multiplier equiva-nt* if there exist $\Lambda_1, \dots, \Lambda_n \in \mathrm{GL}_{m_i}(\mathbb{F}_q)$ such that

$$C_2 = \{\mathbf{c} \cdot \Lambda \mid \mathbf{c} \in C_1\}, \quad \Lambda = \mathrm{diag}(\Lambda_1, \dots, \Lambda_n).$$

oposition 2. *Let $C_2 = \{\mathbf{c} \cdot \Lambda \mid c \in C_1\}$. Then $C_2^\perp = \{\mathbf{h} \cdot \left(\Lambda^{-1}\right)^\mathsf{T} \mid \mathbf{h} \in C_1^\perp\}$.*

oof. Let G_{C_1} be a generator matrix of C_1 and H_{C_1} be a parity check matrix C_1. Since $G_{C_1} \cdot \Lambda$ is a generator matrix of C_2 and

$$(G_{C_1} \cdot \Lambda) \cdot (\Lambda^{-1} \cdot H_{C_1}^\mathsf{T}) = 0,$$

ollows that $H_{C_1} \cdot \left(\Lambda^{-1}\right)^\mathsf{T}$ is a parity–check matrix of C_2.

Let $V_1, \ldots, V_n$ be a tuple of $\mathbb{F}_q$–linear subspaces of $\mathbb{E}_{m_1}, \ldots, \mathbb{E}_{m_n}$ of $\mathbb{F}_q$–dimensions $\mu_i \leq m_i$, $i = 1, \ldots, n$. The *generalized subspace subcode* of a multi–block code C relative to $V_1, \ldots, V_n$ is defined as

$$C_{|V_1,\ldots,V_n} = C \cap (V_1 \oplus \cdots \oplus V_n).$$

One can easily notice that this codes allow short representation. Let $T_1, \ldots, T_n \in \mathbb{F}_q^{\mu_i \times m_i}$ be generator matrices of $V_1, \ldots, V_n$ viewed as $[m_i, \mu_i]_q$–linear codes. Define the maps

$$\psi_i : V_i \to \mathbb{E}_{\mu_i} = \mathbb{F}_q^{\mu_i}, \quad v \mapsto m, \text{ s.t. } v = mT_i.$$

Then *the short representation of $C_{|V_1,\ldots,V_n}$ relative to $T_1, \ldots, T_n$* is

$$\mathrm{GSS}(C; T_1, \ldots, T_n) = \left\{ (\psi_1(\mathbf{c_1}), \ldots, \psi_n(\mathbf{c_n})) \mid (\mathbf{c_1}, \ldots, \mathbf{c_n}) \in C_{|V_1,\ldots,V_n}, \ \mathbf{c_i} \in \mathbb{E}_{m_i} \right\}.$$

Remark 2. We clearly have

$$C_{|V_1,\ldots,V_n} = \{ c \cdot \mathrm{diag}(T_1, \ldots, T_n) \mid c \in \mathrm{GSS}(C; T_1, \ldots, T_n) \}.$$

Let $P_1, \ldots, P_n \in \mathbb{F}_q^{m_i \times \mu_i}$ be full-rank matrices, which define projection maps $x \mapsto xP_i$. Given a multi–block code C, *the generalized projected code relative to* $P_1, \ldots, P_n$ is defined as follows

$$\mathrm{GPC}(C; P_1, \ldots, P_n) = \{ (\mathbf{c_1}P_1, \ldots, \mathbf{c_n}P_n) \mid (\mathbf{c_1}, \ldots, \mathbf{c_n}) \in C, \ \mathbf{c_i} \in \mathbb{E}_{m_i} \}.$$

Proposition 3. *Let C be a multi–block code, $1 \leq \mu_i \leq m_i$, and let $T_1, \ldots, T_n \in \mathbb{F}_q^{\mu_i \times m_i}$ be full-rank matrices. Then*

$$\mathrm{GSS}(C; T_1, \ldots, T_n)^{\perp} = \mathrm{GPC}(C^{\perp}; T_1^{\mathsf{T}}, \ldots, T_n^{\mathsf{T}}).$$

Proof. Let $\widetilde{T}_i \in \mathbb{F}_q^{m_i \times m_i}$ be a non–singular matrix derived from T_i by adding $m_i - \mu_i$ linearly independent rows. Let

$$\widetilde{C} = \left\{ c \cdot \mathrm{diag}\left(\widetilde{T_1}^{-1}, \ldots, \widetilde{T_n}^{-1} \right) \mid c \in C \right\}.$$

Since $\mathrm{GSS}(C; T_1, \ldots, T_n)$ is shortened subcode of $\widetilde{C}$ on last $m_i - \mu_i$ positions of each m_i–block, using Proposition 1 we obtain that $\mathrm{GSS}(C; T_1, \ldots, T_n)^{\perp}$ is punctured code of

$$\widetilde{C}^{\perp} = \left\{ h \cdot \mathrm{diag}\left(\widetilde{T_1}^{\mathsf{T}}, \ldots, \widetilde{T_n}^{\mathsf{T}} \right) \mid h \in C^{\perp} \right\}$$

(see Proposition 2) on the same positions, which is $\mathrm{GPC}(C^{\perp}; T_1^{\mathsf{T}}, \ldots, T_n^{\mathsf{T}})$.

For more details on m–block codes, generalized subspace and generalized projected codes we refer to [4,5,9].

2.2 Subfield Images of Codes

A possible way to construct m–block codes with known parameters is to consider subfield images of codes over some extension field $\mathbb{F}_{q^m}$. Let $\mathcal{B} = \{b_1, \ldots, b_m\}$ be a $\mathbb{F}_q$–basis of $\mathbb{F}_{q^m}$, by $\phi_{\mathcal{B}}$ we denote $\mathbb{F}_q$–linear isomorphism between $\mathbb{F}_{q^m}$ and $\mathbb{E}_m = \mathbb{F}_q^m$, i.e.

$$\phi_{\mathcal{B}}\left(\sum_{i=1}^{m} t_i b_i\right) = (t_1, \ldots, t_m).$$

Let

$$\Phi_{\mathcal{B}} : \mathbb{F}_{q^m}^n \to \mathbb{E}_m^n, \quad (c_1, \ldots, c_n) \mapsto (\phi_{\mathcal{B}}(c_1), \ldots, \phi_{\mathcal{B}}(c_n))$$

be an extension of $\phi_{\mathcal{B}}$ to $\mathbb{F}_{q^m}^n$. *The subfield image of a* $[n, k, d]_{q^m}$ *code* $C \subset \mathbb{F}_{q^m}^n$ *relative to the basis* $\mathcal{B}$ is defined as $\Phi_{\mathcal{B}}(C) = \{\Phi_{\mathcal{B}}(c) \mid c \in C\}$. Clearly, $\Phi_{\mathcal{B}}(C)$ is $[n, k, d]_q^m$ block code and if $\mathrm{Dec}_C : \mathbb{F}_{q^m}^n \to C$ is a decoder of C, then $\Phi_{\mathcal{B}} \circ \mathrm{Dec}_C \circ \Phi_{\mathcal{B}}^{-1}$ is a decoder of $\Phi_{\mathcal{B}}(C)$.

Remark 3. Let $\mathbb{F}_{q^m} = \mathbb{F}_q[\gamma]$, where γ is a root of a primitive polynomial. Note that the usual choice of a basis of $\mathbb{F}_{q^m}$ is $\Gamma = \{\gamma^0, \ldots, \gamma^{m-1}\}$.

Proposition 4 (Proposition 3 of [5]**).** *Suppose* $\mathcal{B}'$ *is another basis of* $\mathbb{F}_{q^m}$ *and* M *is basis change matrix, i.e.* $\phi_{\mathcal{B}'}(x) = \phi_{\mathcal{B}}(x)M$ *for any* $x \in \mathbb{F}_{q^m}$, *then* $\Phi_{\mathcal{B}}(C)$ *and* $\Phi_{\mathcal{B}'}(C)$ *are multiplier equivalent with* $\Lambda_1 = \cdots = \Lambda_n = M$, *i.e.*

$$\Phi_{\mathcal{B}'}(C) = \{(\mathbf{c_1}M, \ldots, \mathbf{c_n}M) \mid (\mathbf{c_1}, \ldots, \mathbf{c_n}) \in \Phi_{\mathcal{B}}(C)\}$$

Remark 4. Note that $\Phi_{\mathcal{B}}(C) = \Phi_{\lambda\mathcal{B}}(C)$ for any nonzero $\lambda \in \mathbb{F}_{q^m}$.

Given $\xi \in \mathbb{F}_{q^m}$, by $\mathbf{M}_{\mathcal{B}}(\xi)$ we denote the matrix of transformation $x \mapsto \xi x$ written in basis $\mathcal{B}$, i.e.

$$\mathbf{M}_{\mathcal{B}}(\xi) = \begin{pmatrix} \phi_{\mathcal{B}}(b_1\xi) \\ \vdots \\ \phi_{\mathcal{B}}(b_m\xi) \end{pmatrix}.$$

Note that for any $\lambda, \xi \in \mathbb{F}_{q^m}$, $\xi \neq 0$, the following equality holds

$$\phi_{\mathcal{B}}(\xi\lambda) = \phi_{\mathcal{B}}(\lambda) \cdot \mathbf{M}_{\mathcal{B}}(\xi) = \phi_{\xi^{-1}\mathcal{B}}(\lambda).$$

Proposition 5 (Proposition 4 of [5]**).** *If* $G_C = (g_{i,j}) \in \mathbb{F}_{q^m}^{k\times n}$ *is a generator matrix of* C, *then*

$$\mathrm{Exp}_{\mathcal{B}}(G_C) = \begin{pmatrix} \mathbf{M}_{\mathcal{B}}(g_{1,1}) & \cdots & \mathbf{M}_{\mathcal{B}}(g_{1,n}) \\ \vdots & \ddots & \vdots \\ \mathbf{M}_{\mathcal{B}}(g_{k,1}) & \cdots & \mathbf{M}_{\mathcal{B}}(g_{k,n}) \end{pmatrix} = \begin{pmatrix} \Phi_{\mathcal{B}}(- \, b_1 g_1 \, -) \\ \cdots \\ \Phi_{\mathcal{B}}(- \, b_m g_1 \, -) \\ \vdots \\ \Phi_{\mathcal{B}}(- \, b_m g_k \, -) \end{pmatrix}$$

is a generator matrix of $\Phi_{\mathcal{B}}(C)$.

Given a basis $\mathcal{B}$ of $\mathbb{F}_{q^m}$, the dual basis $\mathcal{B}^*$ is the unique basis of $\mathbb{F}_{q^m}$, such that $\mathbf{M}_{\mathcal{B}^*}(\xi) = (\mathbf{M}_{\mathcal{B}}(\xi))^\intercal$ for any $\xi \in \mathbb{F}_{q^m}$.

Proposition 6 (Proposition 5 of [5]). *Let $C \subset \mathbb{F}_{q^m}$ be a $[n,k]_{q^m}$-code with a parity-check matrix H_C, then*

$$(\Phi_{\mathcal{B}}(C))^\perp = \Phi_{\mathcal{B}^*}(C^\perp).$$

and the parity-check matrix of $\Phi_{\mathcal{B}}(C)$ is

$$\mathrm{Exp}^*_{\mathcal{B}}(H_C) = \mathrm{Exp}_{\mathcal{B}^*}(H_C) = \begin{pmatrix} \mathbf{M}_{\mathcal{B}}(h_{1,1})^\intercal & \dots & \mathbf{M}_{\mathcal{B}}(h_{1,n})^\intercal \\ \vdots & \ddots & \vdots \\ \mathbf{M}_{\mathcal{B}}(h_{n-k,1})^\intercal & \dots & \mathbf{M}_{\mathcal{B}}(h_{n-k,n})^\intercal \end{pmatrix}.$$

Corollary 1. *Let $C \subset \mathbb{F}_{q^m}$ be a $[n,k]_{q^m}$-code. Then Proposition 3 and Proposition 6 imply*

$$\mathrm{GSS}(\Phi_{\mathcal{B}}(C); T_1, \dots, T_n)^\perp = \mathrm{GPC}(\Phi_{\mathcal{B}^*}(C^\perp); T_1^\intercal, \dots, T_n^\intercal).$$

2.3 Generalized Reed–Solomon Codes

Let $\mathbf{x} = (x_1, \dots, x_n) \in \mathbb{F}_q^n$ be a vector of distinct non-zero values and let $\mathbf{y} = (y_1, \dots, y_n) \in \mathbb{F}_q^n$ be a vector, such that $y_i \neq 0$ for all i. The *generalized Reed–Solomon code* with support $\mathbf{x}$ and multiplier $\mathbf{y}$ of length n and dimension k is

$$\mathrm{GRS}_k(\mathbf{x}, \mathbf{y}) = \{(y_1 f(x_1), \dots, y_n f(x_n)) \mid f \in \mathbb{F}_q[x],\ \deg(f) \leq k-1\}.$$

When $\mathbf{y} = (1, 1, \dots, 1)$, the code is said to be a *Reed–Solomon code* and denoted as $\mathrm{RS}_k(\mathbf{x})$. As is well-known, $\mathrm{GRS}_k(\mathbf{x}, \mathbf{y})$ is a $[n, k, n-k+1]_q$-code, the generator matrix of $\mathrm{GRS}_k(\mathbf{x}, \mathbf{y})$ is

$$G_k(\mathbf{x}, \mathbf{y}) = \begin{pmatrix} x_1^0 & \cdots & x_n^0 \\ x_1^1 & \cdots & x_n^1 \\ \vdots & \ddots & \vdots \\ x_1^{k-1} & \dots & x_n^{k-1} \end{pmatrix} \mathrm{diag}(y_1, \dots, y_n),$$

the generator matrix of $\mathrm{RS}_k(\mathbf{x})$ is $G_k(\mathbf{x}) = G_k(\mathbf{x}, \mathbf{1})$, the dual of $\mathrm{GRS}_k(\mathbf{x}, \mathbf{y})$ i $\mathrm{GRS}_{n-k}(\mathbf{x}, \mathbf{z})$, where

$$z_i^{-1} = y_i \prod_{\substack{i,j \in \overline{1,n} \\ j \neq i}} (x_i - x_j). \qquad (3$$

Note that for a given GRS code multiplier and support are not unique. We ref [18, Chapter 12] and [14, §5.3] for more details on GRS codes.

Remark 5. Any subfield image of $\mathrm{GRS}_k(\mathbf{x}, \mathbf{y})$ is multiplier equivalent to a su field image of $\mathrm{RS}_k(\mathbf{x})$. Indeed,

$$\Phi_{\mathcal{B}}(\mathrm{GRS}_k(\mathbf{x}, \mathbf{y})) = \left\{ (\phi_{\mathcal{B}}(c_i) \cdot \mathbf{M}_{\mathcal{B}}(y_i))_{i=1,\dots,n} \mid (c_1, \dots, c_n) \in \mathrm{RS}_k(\mathbf{x}) \right\}.$$

3 Ivanov–Krouk–Zyablov Cryptosystem

In [15] F. Ivanov, E. Krouk and V. Zyablov proposed a new cryptosystem based on subfield images of generalized Reed–Solomon codes, with its key feature being that public code is not equivalent to a subfield image. In this section, we give a generalized version of it, consider some of its properties, and estimate the complexity of a key–recovery attack.

3.1 Protocol Description

- **Key generation.** Let $C = \mathrm{RS}_k(\mathbf{x})$ be a random $[n,k]_{q^m}$ RS–code of even length with support $\mathbf{x} = (x_1, \ldots, x_n)$. Choose a random non–singular matrix $S \in \mathrm{GL}_{km}(\mathbb{F}_q)$, and random non–singular matrices $Y_j \in \mathrm{GL}_m(\mathbb{F}_q)$, $M_j \in \mathrm{GL}_{m_j}(\mathbb{F}_q)$, $j = 1, \ldots, n$, where

  $$m_j = \begin{cases} m-1, & j \text{ is odd} \\ m+1, & j \text{ is even} \end{cases}.$$

  The public key is $G_{pub} = S \cdot \mathrm{Exp}_{\Gamma}(G_k(\mathbf{x})) \cdot \overline{Y} \cdot \overline{M}$, where

  $$\overline{Y} = \mathrm{diag}(Y_1, \ldots, Y_n), \quad \overline{M} = \mathrm{diag}(M_1, \ldots, M_n)$$

  and secret key is $(\mathbf{x}, S, Q = \overline{Y} \cdot \overline{M})$.
- **Encryption.** Let $t = (n-k)/2$ be a number of errors that can be corrected by C. Let $m \in \mathbb{F}_q^{km}$ be a plain text, then the ciphertext is

  $$z = mG_{pub} + e, \quad e \in \mathcal{E}_{mn,t/3}.$$

- **Decryption.** Let $\mathrm{Dec}_C : \mathbb{F}_{q^m} \to C$ be a decoder of C. Then mG_{pub} can be found as follows

  $$mG_{pub} = \Phi_{\mathcal{B}} \circ \mathrm{Dec}_C \circ \Phi_{\mathcal{B}}^{-1}\left(z \cdot Q^{-1}\right).$$

emark 6. Note that $eQ^{-1} \in \mathcal{S}_{m,n,t}$. Indeed, let j be a starting position of an rror burst of length m. Two cases are possible:

$(2s-1)m + 1 \leq j \leq 2sm$ for some s. It follows that after multiplying by Q^{-1} only two m–blocks get corrupted.
$2sm + 1 \leq j \leq (2s+1)m$ for some s. It follows that after multiplying by Q^{-1} three m–blocks can get corrupted. Namely, $2s$, $2s+1$, $2s+2$–th blocks.

te that in [15] case 2) hasn't been considered and due to this it was erroneously posed to sample e from $\mathcal{E}_{mn,t/2}$.

mark 7. The use of GRS–codes in this protocol is equivalent to the use of –codes due to the presence of $\overline{Y}$ (see Remark 5).

Remark 8. Without loss of generality, one can assume that $Y_{2i} = I_m$ and $M_{2i-1} = I_{m-1}$. Indeed,

$$\operatorname{diag}(Y_{2i-1}, Y_{2i}) \operatorname{diag}(M_{2i-1}, M_{2i}) = \operatorname{diag}\left(Y_{2i-1}\begin{pmatrix} M_{2i-1} & \\ & 1 \end{pmatrix}, I_m\right) \cdot \operatorname{diag}\left(I_{m-1}, \begin{pmatrix} 1 & \\ & Y_{2i} \end{pmatrix} M_{2i}\right)$$

Proposition 7. *Let* $G_{pub} = S \cdot \mathrm{Exp}_\Gamma(G_k(\mathbf{x}, \mathbf{y})) \cdot Q$ *be a public key of IKZ–cryptosystem based on* $\mathrm{GRS}_k(\mathbf{x}, \mathbf{y})$*–code. Then any parity–check matrix of* $C_{pub}^{\perp}$ *is of the form*

$$H = S' \cdot \mathrm{Exp}_{\Gamma *}(G_{n-k}(\mathbf{x}, \mathbf{z})) \cdot {Q^{-1}}^{\mathsf{T}}, \quad z_i^{-1} = y_i \prod_{\substack{i,j \in \overline{1,n} \\ j \neq i}} (x_i - x_j).$$

In addition, since

$${Q^{-1}}^{\mathsf{T}} = \operatorname{diag}({Y_1^{-1}}^{\mathsf{T}}, \ldots, {Y_n^{-1}}^{\mathsf{T}}) \cdot \operatorname{diag}({M_1^{-1}}^{\mathsf{T}}, \ldots, {M_n^{-1}}^{\mathsf{T}}),$$

it follows that H *is a public key of IKZ cryptosystem based on* $\mathrm{GRS}_{n-k}(\mathbf{x}, \mathbf{z})$*–code.*

Proof. Using Proposition 6 and (3), we obtain

$$G_{pub} H^{\mathsf{T}} = S \cdot \mathrm{Exp}_\Gamma(G_k(\mathbf{x}, \mathbf{y})) \cdot Q \cdot Q^{-1} \cdot \mathrm{Exp}_{\Gamma^*}(G_{n-k}(\mathbf{x}, \mathbf{z}))^{\mathsf{T}} \cdot S'^{\mathsf{T}} = 0.$$

3.2 Message–Recovery Attack

Since the error $\mathbf{e}$ is structured, it is possible to exploit it for reducing complexity of information–set decoding attack. Indeed, we can consider $C_{pub} = \mathrm{Span}_{\mathbb{F}_q}(G_{pub})$ as a m–block code, then any error from $\mathcal{E}_{mn,t/3}$ covers at most $2t/3$ m–blocks (see Fig. 1). It follows that remaining $n - 2t/3$ blocks are error–free and the probability of finding error–free information set of k blocks is

$$\mathrm{Prob}_{\mathrm{ISD}} = \frac{\binom{n-2t/3}{k}}{\binom{n}{k}},$$

which does not depend on m. Therefore, the workfactor of Ivanov–Krouk–Zyablov cryptosystem is significantly lower than estimates of [15]. We also note that due to using structured errors a significant reduction in complexity of ISD attacks also extends to several more IKZ–like cryptosystems recently proposed in [30].

Fig. 1. non–synchronous error burst of length 2 corrupts 4 blocks

So, due to simple message–recovery attack, Ivanov–Krouk–Zyablov cryptosystem [15] can only be considered as a way to avoid key–recovery attacks since it produces a public code which is not multiplier equivalent to a subfield image of a GRS–code. However, below we show that such application of Ivanov–Krouk–Zyablov protocol is also insecure.

4 Direct Key–Recovery Attack

In this section, we propose a key–recovery attack which is based on the uniqueness of systematic generator matrix of C_{pub} and distinguishability of matrices $\mathbf{M}_{\Gamma}(a)$, $a \in \mathbb{F}_{q^m}$, from random ones.

4.1 Case of Even k

Define $Q_i \in \mathbb{F}_q^{2m\times 2m}$ as

$$Q_i = \mathrm{diag}(Y_{2i-1}, Y_{2i}) \cdot \mathrm{diag}(M_{2i-1}, M_{2i}),$$

so $Q = \mathrm{diag}(Q_1, \dots, Q_{n/2})$. Let $G_C^{sys} = [I_k \mid L] = (l_{i,j}) \in \mathbb{F}_{q^m}^{k\times n}$ be the systematic generator matrix of C. One can easily notice that

$$\left(\begin{array}{ccc|ccc} Q_1 & & & K_{1,k/2+1}Q_{k/2+1} & \cdots & K_{1,(n-k)/2}Q_{n/2} \\ & \ddots & & \vdots & \ddots & \vdots \\ & & Q_{k/2} & K_{k/2,k/2+1}Q_{k/2+1} & \cdots & K_{k/2,(n-k)/2}Q_{n/2} \end{array}\right),$$

where

$$K_{i,j} = \begin{pmatrix} \mathbf{M}_{\Gamma}(l_{2i-1,2j-1}) & \mathbf{M}_{\Gamma}(l_{2i-1,2j}) \\ \mathbf{M}_{\Gamma}(l_{2i,2j-1}) & \mathbf{M}_{\Gamma}(l_{2i,2j}) \end{pmatrix},$$

is a generator matrix of C_{pub}. It follows that the unique systematic generator matrix G_{pub}^{sys} of C_{pub} is of the form

$$\left(\begin{array}{ccc|ccc} I_{2m} & & & Q_1^{-1}K_{1,k/2+1}Q_{k/2+1} & \cdots & Q_1^{-1}K_{1,(n-k)/2}Q_{n/2} \\ & \ddots & & \vdots & \ddots & \vdots \\ & & I_{2m} & Q_{k/2}^{-1}K_{k/2,k/2+1}Q_{k/2+1} & \cdots & Q_{k/2}^{-1}K_{k/2,(n-k)/2}Q_{n/2} \end{array}\right). \quad (4)$$

Let us denote $Q_i^{-1}K_{i,j}Q_j$ by $K'_{i,j}$. For $1 \le i, r \le k/2$ and $k/2+1 \le j, s \le n/2$ define

$$V_{i,j,r,s} = K'_{i,j}(K'_{r,j})^{-1}K'_{r,s}(K'_{i,s})^{-1} = Q_i^{-1}\left(K_{i,j}K_{r,j}^{-1}K_{r,s}K_{i,s}^{-1}\right)Q_i, \quad (5)$$

$$W_{i,j,r,s} = (K'_{i,j})^{-1}K'_{i,s}(K'_{r,s})^{-1}K'_{r,j} = Q_j^{-1}\left(K_{i,j}^{-1}K_{i,s}K_{r,s}^{-1}K_{r,j}\right)Q_j \quad (6)$$

corresponding inverse matrices exist (which is true in most cases). Since matrices $K_{i,j}$ have very special structure, namely, $K_{i,j}$ belong to the $\mathbb{F}_q$–algebra

$$\Delta = \left\{ \begin{pmatrix} \mathbf{M}_{\Gamma}(a) & \mathbf{M}_{\Gamma}(b) \\ \mathbf{M}_{\Gamma}(c) & \mathbf{M}_{\Gamma}(d) \end{pmatrix} \,\middle|\, a, b, c, d \in \mathbb{F}_{q^m} \right\},$$

can exploit it to recover the matrix Q *up to certain equivalences.*

Proposition 8. *Let a $\mathbb{F}_{q^m}$–code C' be semi–linear equivalent over $\mathbb{F}_q$ to C, i.e.*

$$C' = \{(\theta(\alpha_1 c_1), \theta(\alpha_2 c_2), \ldots, \theta(\alpha_n c_n)) \mid (c_1, \ldots, c_n) \in C\}$$

(see [14]), where $\alpha_i \in \mathbb{F}_{q^m} \setminus \{0\}$, and $\theta \in \mathsf{Gal}(\mathbb{F}_{q^m}/\mathbb{F}_q)$ is an automorphism of $\mathbb{F}_{q^m}$ that fixes $\mathbb{F}_q$ pointwise. Let A_θ be a matrix representation of θ written in the basis $\Gamma = \{\gamma^0, \ldots, \gamma^{m-1}\}$ of $\mathbb{F}_{q^m} = \mathbb{F}_q[\gamma]$, i.e.

$$A_\theta = \begin{pmatrix} - & \phi_\Gamma\left(\theta(\gamma^0)\right) & - \\ \vdots & \ddots & \vdots \\ - & \phi_\Gamma\left(\theta(\gamma^{m-1})\right) & - \end{pmatrix}.$$

Then the matrix $\mathrm{Exp}_\Gamma(G_{C'}) \cdot \mathrm{diag}(Q'_1, \ldots, Q'_{n/2})$, *where*

$$Q'_{i+1} = \mathrm{diag}\left(A_\theta^{-1} \cdot \mathbf{M}_\Gamma(\alpha_{2i+1}^{-1}), A_\theta^{-1} \cdot \mathbf{M}_\Gamma(\alpha_{2i+2}^{-1})\right) \cdot Q_{i+1}, \quad (7)$$

also spans C_{pub}.

Conjecture 1. Let $X, Y \in \mathsf{QMat}$, where

$$\mathsf{QMat} = \{\mathrm{diag}(Y, I_m) \cdot \mathrm{diag}(I_{m-1}, M) \mid Y \in \mathrm{GL}_m(\mathbb{F}_q), M \in \mathrm{GL}_{m+1}(\mathbb{F}_q)\}.$$

Let $\varXi$ be a sufficiently large subset of $\varDelta$ and $\zeta \in \varDelta$ be non–zero. Then

1. if $\left\{YX^{-1} \cdot \xi \cdot XY^{-1} \mid \xi \in \varXi\right\} \subset \varDelta$, then there exist $a, b \in \mathbb{F}_{q^m}^*$ and $\theta \in \mathsf{Gal}(\mathbb{F}_{q^m}/\mathbb{F}_q)$, such that
$$Y = \mathrm{diag}(A_\theta^{-1} \cdot \mathbf{M}_\Gamma(a), A_\theta^{-1} \cdot \mathbf{M}_\Gamma(b)) \cdot X,$$
2. if $\zeta \cdot XY^{-1} \in \varDelta$ or $YX^{-1} \cdot \zeta \in \varDelta$ and $\left\{YX^{-1} \cdot \xi \cdot XY^{-1} \mid \xi \in \varXi\right\} \subset \varDelta$, then there exist $a, b \in \mathbb{F}_{q^m}^*$, such that
$$Y = \mathrm{diag}(\mathbf{M}_\Gamma(a), \mathbf{M}_\Gamma(b)) \cdot X$$

with high probability.

Remark 9. Note that the set $\varXi$ has to contain at least one matrix which is no of the form

$$\xi = \mathrm{diag}(\mathbf{M}_\Gamma(\alpha), \mathbf{M}_\Gamma(\beta)).$$

Otherwise, the conjecture does not hold, i.e. $Y = \mathrm{diag}(A_{\theta_1} \cdot \mathbf{M}_\Gamma(a), A_{\theta_2} \cdot \mathbf{M}_\Gamma(b)$ X for some $a, b \in \mathbb{F}_{q^m}^*$, $\theta_1, \theta_2 \in \mathsf{Gal}(\mathbb{F}_{q^m}/\mathbb{F}_q)$. Indeed,

$$YX^{-1} \cdot \xi \cdot XY^{-1} = \mathrm{diag}\left(\mathbf{M}_\Gamma(\theta_1^{-1}(\alpha)), \mathbf{M}_\Gamma(\theta_2^{-1}(\beta))\right) \in \varDelta.$$

Our experiments performed in computer algebra system Sage evince th Conjecture 1 is most likely correct as soon as $|\varXi| \geq 3$. So, the resulting ke recovery algorithm can be summarized as follows.[1]

[1] The code for our implementation is available on https://github.com/kirill-vedene ikz-cryptanalysis.

Step 1. Compute the systematic generator matrix (4) of C_{pub}. Using a brute-force search, find a matrix $Q'_1 \in \mathsf{QMat}$ such that

$$\left\{ Q'_1 \cdot V_{1,j,r,s} \cdot {Q'_1}^{-1} \in \Delta \right.$$

(see (5)) for some set of indices $1 \leq r \leq k/2$ and $k/2+1 \leq j, s \leq n/2$ of size ≥ 5. Conjecture 1 implies that Q'_1 is of the form (7). Since Proposition 8 allows replacing C with any semi–linear equivalent code, it follows that without loss of generality, we may assume that $\theta \in \mathsf{Gal}(\mathbb{F}_{q^m}/\mathbb{F}_q)$ is the identity automorphism.

Step 2. For $j = k/2+1, \ldots, n/2$, find matrices $Q'_j \in \mathsf{QMat}$, such that

$$\begin{cases} (Q'_1 \cdot K'_{1,j}) \cdot {Q'_j}^{-1} \in \Delta, \\ Q'_j \cdot W_{i,j,r,s} \cdot {Q'_j}^{-1} \in \Delta, \end{cases}$$

(see (4), (6)) for some set of indices $1 \leq i, r \leq k/2$ and $k/2+1 \leq s \leq n/2$ of size ≥ 5.

Step 3. Finally, for $i = 2, \ldots, k$ find $Q'_i \in \mathsf{QMat}$ satisfying

$$\left\{ Q'_i \cdot \left(K_i \cdot {Q'_j}^{-1} \right) \in \Delta \quad \text{for all } j = k/2+1, \ldots, n/2. \right.$$

Step 4. Let $Q' = \mathrm{diag}(Q'_1, \ldots, Q'_{n/2})$, using Conjecture 1 we obtain

$$Q' = \mathrm{diag}(A_\theta^{-1}\mathbf{M}_\Gamma(\alpha_1), \ldots A_\theta^{-1}\mathbf{M}_\Gamma(\alpha_n)) \cdot Q$$

for some $\theta \in \mathsf{Gal}(\mathbb{F}_{q^m}/\mathbb{F}_q)$ and $(\alpha_1, \ldots, \alpha_n) \in \mathbb{F}^*_{q^m}$. Hence

$$C' = \Phi_\Gamma^{-1}\left(\mathrm{Span}_{\mathbb{F}_{q^m}}(G_{pub} \cdot Q'^{-1})\right)$$

is semi–linear equivalent to C and is therefore a GRS code. Indeed,

$$\begin{aligned} C' &= \{(\theta(\alpha_1 c_1), \ldots, \theta(\alpha_n c_n)) \mid (c_1, \ldots, c_n) \in \mathrm{RS}_k(\mathbf{x})\} = \\ &= \{(\theta(\alpha_1) f(\theta(x_1)), \ldots, \theta(\alpha_1) f(\theta(x_n))) \mid f \in \mathbb{F}_{q^m}[x], \deg(f) \leq k-1\}. \end{aligned}$$

So, after applying the Sidelnikov–Shestakov attack [27] to C', it is possible to decode C_{pub}.

.2 Case of Odd k

ıppose first that $Q_{(k+1)/2}$ is known. Let $G_C^{sys} = (l_{i,j}) \in \mathbb{F}_{q^m}^{k \times n}$ be the sys- matic generator matrix of C. It follows that the systematic form of $G_{pub} \cdot$ ag$(I_{(k-1)m}, Q_{(k+1)/2}^{-1}, I_{(n-k-1)m})$ is

$$\begin{pmatrix} I_{2m} & & & J_1 & K'_{1,(k+1)/2+1} & \cdots & K'_{1,n/2} \\ & \ddots & & \vdots & \vdots & \ddots & \vdots \\ & & I_{2m} & J_{(k-1)/2} & K'_{(k-1)/2,(k+1)/2+1} & \cdots & K'_{(k-1)/2,n/2} \\ & & I_m & C & D_{(k+1)/2+1} & \cdots & D_{n/2} \end{pmatrix}, \qquad (8)$$

where

$$J_i = Q_i^{-1} \cdot (\mathbf{M}_\Gamma(l_{2i-1,k+1})\ \mathbf{M}_\Gamma(l_{2i,k+1}))^\top \in \mathbb{F}_q^{2m\times m},$$

$$C = \mathbf{M}_\Gamma(l_{k,k+1}) \in \mathbb{F}_q^{m\times m},$$

$$D_j = (\mathbf{M}_\Gamma(l_{k,2j-1})\ \mathbf{M}_\Gamma(l_{k,2j})) \cdot Q_j \in \mathbb{F}_q^{m\times 2m},$$

$$K'_{i,j} = Q_i^{-1} \cdot \begin{pmatrix} \mathbf{M}_\Gamma(l_{2i-1,2j-1}) & \mathbf{M}_\Gamma(l_{2i-1,2j}) \\ \mathbf{M}_\Gamma(l_{2i,2j-1}) & \mathbf{M}_\Gamma(l_{2i,2j}) \end{pmatrix} \cdot Q_j \in \mathbb{F}_q^{2m\times 2m}.$$

Hence the above–described attack can be modified as follows.

Step 1. In this step, we try to guess $Q_{(k+1)/2}$ (up to equivalences described in Proposition 8). To do this, for each $Q'_{(k+1)/2} \in \mathsf{QMat}$ we compute the systematic form (8) of

$$G_{pub} \cdot \operatorname{diag}(I_{(k-1)m}, {Q'_{(k+1)/2}}^{-1}, I_{(n-k-1)m})$$

and then check

$$\begin{cases} C \in \{\mathbf{M}_\Gamma(a) \mid a \in \mathbb{F}_{q^m}\}, \\ D_j {K'_{i,j}}^{-1} J_i, \in \{\mathbf{M}_\Gamma(a) \mid a \in \mathbb{F}_{q^m}\} \\ \quad \text{for all } 1 \le i \le (k-1)/2, (k+1)/2+1 \le j \le n/2 \end{cases}$$

until proper $Q'_{(k+1)/2}$ is found.

Step 2. For $j = (k+1)/2+1, \ldots, n/2$, find matrices $Q'_j \in \mathsf{QMat}$, such that

$$\begin{cases} Q'_j \cdot W_{i,j,r,s} \cdot {Q'_j}^{-1} \in \Delta, \\ D_j \cdot {Q'_j}^{-1} \in \{(\mathbf{M}_\Gamma(a), \mathbf{M}_\Gamma(b)) \mid a, b \in \mathbb{F}_{q^m}\} \end{cases}$$

(see (4), (6)) for some set of indices $1 \le i, r \le (k-1)/2$ and $(k+1)/2+1 \le s \le n/2$ of size ≥ 5.

Step 3. For $i = 1, \ldots, (k-1)/2$ find $Q'_i \in \mathsf{QMat}$ satisfying

$$\left\{Q'_i \cdot \left(K_i \cdot {Q'_j}^{-1}\right) \in \Delta \quad \text{for all } j = (k+1)/2+1, \ldots, n/2.\right.$$

Compute $Q' = \operatorname{diag}(Q'_1, \ldots, Q_{n/2})$ and run Step 4 of Sect. 4.1.

Since the size of QMat is $O(q^{m^2+(m+1)^2})$, it follows that the complexity of the attack is $O(nq^{m^2+(m+1)^2}m^3)$ assuming brute–force search is used in each step. Note that for large m this attack is too complex. However, for $m \ge 3$ it is possible to implement another attack based on twisted squares.

5 Twisted Squares–Based Attack

Let $\mathbf{U}_i$ be an i–th m_i–block column of G_{pub}, i.e.

$$G_{pub} = \Big(\underbrace{\mathbf{U}_1}_{m-1}\ \underbrace{\mathbf{U}_2}_{m+1} \cdots \underbrace{\mathbf{U}_{n-1}}_{m-1}\ \underbrace{\mathbf{U}_n}_{m+1}\Big).$$

Attack we propose is consist of the following steps.

5.1 Recovering the Support x

By $\mathbf{x_{odd}}$ we denote $(x_1, x_3, \ldots, x_{n-1})$. Let $\Pi \in \mathbb{F}_q^{m\times(m-1)}$ be the projection matrix of the following form

$$\Pi = \begin{pmatrix} I_{m-1} \\ 0 \end{pmatrix},$$

Consider

$$G_{odd} = (\mathbf{U}_1 \mid \mathbf{U}_3 \mid \cdots \mid \mathbf{U}_{n-1}).$$

We have

$$G_{odd} = S \operatorname{Exp}_\Gamma (G_k(\mathbf{x_{odd}})) \operatorname{diag}(N_1, N_3, \ldots N_{n-1}), \tag{9}$$

where $N_i = Y_i \Pi M_i \in \mathbb{F}_q^{m\times m-1}$. It follows that G_{odd} is a generator matrix of

$$\operatorname{GPC}(\Phi_\Gamma(\operatorname{RS}_k(\mathbf{x_{odd}})); N_1, \ldots, N_{n-1}).$$

So, Proposition 3 and Corollary 1 imply that G_{odd} is a parity–check matrix of the code

$$\begin{aligned} D &= \operatorname{GSS}(\Phi_\Gamma(\operatorname{RS}_k(\mathbf{x_{odd}}))^\perp; N_1^T, N_3^T, \ldots, N_{n-1}^T) = \\ &= \operatorname{GSS}(\Phi_{\Gamma^*}(\operatorname{RS}_k(\mathbf{x_{odd}})^\perp); N_1^T, N_3^T, \ldots, N_{n-1}^T), \end{aligned} \tag{10}$$

Remark 10. Recall that, $\operatorname{RS}_k(\mathbf{x_{odd}})^\perp = \operatorname{GRS}_{n-k}(\mathbf{x_{odd}}, \mathbf{z_{odd}})$, where

$$\mathbf{z_{odd}} = (z_1, z_3, \ldots, z_{n-1}), \quad z_i^{-1} = \prod_{\substack{i,j\in\{1,3,\ldots,n-1\} \\ j\neq i}} (x_i - x_j) \tag{11}$$

Hence D is short representation of generalized subspace subcode of a GRS code.

It follows that it is possible to recover one of the supports $\mathbf{x_{odd}}'$ of $\operatorname{RS}_k(\mathbf{x_{odd}})^\perp$ from D by applying CL–attack [9, Alg. 1 and Alg. 2] to D. Indeed, given GSS–subcode of $\operatorname{GRS}_k(\mathbf{a}, \mathbf{b})$, such that the dimension of all subspaces is $\lambda > m/2$, CL–attack reconstructs a support of corresponding GRS–code by applying the algorithm of [5, §VI.B] to its twisted square.

Remark 11. Note that in order to apply CL–attack, G_{odd} has to be singular, which is true if

$$km < (m-1)n/2.$$

In addition, it is also possible to find $\mathbf{x_{odd}}$ in the case when

$$(n-k)m < (m-1)n/2$$

by attacking the dual of the public code (see Proposition 7).

Remark 12. Since the support of a GRS code is completely defined by fixing arbitrary three points, it follows that without loss of generality we may assume that $\mathbf{x_{odd}}' = \mathbf{x_{odd}}$.

It remains now to recover $x_2, x_4, \ldots, x_n$. For the sake of convenience, we describe the recovering procedure only for x_2. Consider the matrix

$$G_{odd+2} = (\mathbf{U}_1 \mid \mathbf{U}_2 \mid \mathbf{U}_3 \mid \mathbf{U}_5 \mid \cdots \mid \mathbf{U}_{n-1}).$$

One can easily notice that

$$G_{odd+2} = S \cdot \mathrm{Exp}^*_{\Gamma}\left(G_k\left(x_1, x_2, x_3, x_5, \ldots, x_{n-1}\right)\right) \cdot \mathrm{diag}(Q_1, N_3, N_5, \ldots, N_{n-1}),$$

where N_i are the same as in (9) and

$$Q_1 = \mathrm{diag}(Y_2, Y_2) \cdot \mathrm{diag}(M_1, M_2) \in \mathrm{GL}_{2m}(\mathbb{F}_q).$$

Using Proposition 3 and Corollary 1, we see that G_{odd+2} is a generator matrix of

$$\mathrm{GPC}\left(\Phi_{\Gamma}(\mathrm{RS}_k(x_1, x_2, x_3, x_5, \ldots, x_{n-1})); Q_1, N_3, \ldots, N_{n-1}\right).$$

and a parity–check matrix of

$$D_2 = \mathrm{GSS}\left(\Phi_{\Gamma}(\mathrm{RS}_k(x_1, x_2, x_3, x_5, \ldots, x_{n-1}))^{\perp}; Q_1^{\mathsf{T}}, N_3^{\mathsf{T}}, \ldots, N_{n-1}^{\mathsf{T}}\right).$$

Let G_{D_2} be a generator matrix of D_2. We have

$$\mathrm{Span}_{\mathbb{F}_q}\left(G_{D_2} \cdot \mathrm{diag}\left(Q_1^{\mathsf{T}}, N_3^{\mathsf{T}}, \ldots, N_{n-1}^{\mathsf{T}}\right)\right) \subset \left[\Phi_{\Gamma}\left(\mathrm{RS}_k\left(x_1, x_2, x_3, x_5, \ldots, x_{n-1}\right)\right)\right]^{\perp}$$

(see Sect. 2.1), it follows that

$$G_{D_2} \cdot \mathrm{diag}\left(Q_1^{\mathsf{T}}, N_3^{\mathsf{T}}, \ldots, N_{n-1}^{\mathsf{T}}\right) \cdot \mathrm{Exp}_{\Gamma}\left(G_k(x_1, x_2, x_3, x_5, \ldots, x_{n-1})\right)^{\mathsf{T}} = 0.$$

With $\mathbf{x_{odd}} = (x_1, x_3, \ldots, x_{n-1})$ being known, it is possible to find x_2 by iterating $w \in \mathbb{F}^*_{q^m} \setminus \{x_1, x_3, x_5, \ldots, x_{n-1}\}$ and checking whether the linear system

$$G_{D_2} \cdot \mathrm{diag}\left(X_1^{\mathsf{T}}, X_3^{\mathsf{T}}, \ldots, X_{n-1}^{\mathsf{T}}\right) \cdot \mathrm{Exp}_{\Gamma}\left(G_k(x_1, w, x_3, x_5, \ldots, x_{n-1})\right)^{\mathsf{T}} = 0, \quad (12)$$

where $X_3, \ldots, X_{n-1} \in \mathbb{F}_q^{m \times m-1}$ and

$$X_1 = \begin{pmatrix} X_1^{(1)} & X_1^{(2)} \\ 0 & X_1^{(3)} \end{pmatrix}, \quad X_1^{(1)} \in \mathbb{F}_q^{m \times m-1}, X_1^{(2)} \in \mathbb{F}_q^{m \times m+1}, X_1^{(3)} \in \mathbb{F}_q^{m \times m+1}$$

has a non–zero solution. Note that in most practical cases the number o unknowns $(n/2-1)(m-1)m + 3m^2 + m = O(nm^2/2)$ is much less than th number of equations $(n/2+1-k)km^2$ and the solution, if it exists, is most likel unique up to multiplication by

$$\mathrm{diag}(\mathbf{M}_{\Gamma}(a_1), \mathbf{M}_{\Gamma}(a_2), \mathbf{M}_{\Gamma}(a_3), \mathbf{M}_{\Gamma}(a_5), \ldots, \mathbf{M}_{\Gamma}(a_{n-1})), \quad a_i \in \mathbb{F}^*_{q^m}.$$

In our experiments, the above described method allowed successfully recoveri correct x_2 in all cases.[2]

[2] The code for our implementation of this and the next step is available on https github.com/kirill-vedenev/ikz-cryptanalysis.

Remark 13. It is also possible to reconstruct $\mathbf{x}$ when neither $km < (m-1)n/2$ and $(n-k)m < (m-1)n/2$ hold. Choose the smallest $s \in \overline{1, n/2}$ such that

$$(n'-k)m > (m-1)n'/2$$

where $n' = n - 2s$. Consider

$$G'_{pub} = \left(\mathbf{U}_1\, \mathbf{U}_2 \ldots \mathbf{U}_{n-2s-1}\, \mathbf{U}_{n-2s}\right) \in \mathbb{F}_q^{km \times n'm},$$

$$G''_{pub} = \left(\mathbf{U}_{2s+1}\, \mathbf{U}_{2s+2} \ldots \mathbf{U}_{n-1}\, \mathbf{U}_n\right) \in \mathbb{F}_q^{km \times n'm}.$$

One can easily notice that

$$G'_{pub} = S \cdot \mathrm{Exp}_{\mathcal{B}}\left(G_k\left((x_1, \ldots, x_{n-2s})\right)\right) \cdot \mathrm{diag}(Y_1, \ldots Y_{n-2s}) \cdot \mathrm{diag}(M_1, \ldots M_{n-2s}),$$

$$G''_{pub} = S \cdot \mathrm{Exp}_{\mathcal{B}}\left(G_k\left((x_{2s+1}, \ldots, x_n)\right)\right) \cdot \mathrm{diag}(Y_{2s+1}, \ldots Y_n) \cdot \mathrm{diag}(M_{2s+1}, \ldots M_n),$$

i.e. G'_{pub} and G''_{pub} are public keys of IKZ–cryptosystem. Therefore, it is possible to recover $x_1, \ldots, x_{n-2s}$ by attacking G'_{pub} as above first and then to recover $x_{n-2s+1}, \cdots x_n$ by attacking G''_{pub}.

5.2 Recovering the Matrix Q

Since $G_{pub} = S \cdot \mathrm{Exp}_{\Gamma}(G_k(\mathbf{x})) \cdot \mathrm{diag}(Q_1, \ldots, Q_{n/2})$, is follows that G_{pub} is a generator matrix of

$$\mathrm{GPC}(\Phi_{\Gamma}(G_k(\mathbf{x}); Q_1, \ldots, Q_{n/2}),$$

so, due to Proposition 3 G_{pub} a parity–check matrix of

$$\hat{D} = \mathrm{GSS}(\Phi_{\Gamma}(G_k(\mathbf{x})^{\perp}; Q_1^{\mathsf{T}}, \ldots, Q_{n/2}^{\mathsf{T}}).$$

Let $G_{\hat{D}}$ be a generator matrix of $\hat{D}$. Since

$$\mathrm{Span}_{\mathbb{F}_q}\left(G_{\hat{D}} \cdot \mathrm{diag}\left(Q_1^{\mathsf{T}}, \ldots, Q_{n/2}^{\mathsf{T}}\right)\right) \subset \Phi_{\Gamma}(G_k(\mathbf{x}))^{\perp},$$

t follows that

$$G_{\hat{D}} \cdot \mathrm{diag}\left(Q_1^{\mathsf{T}}, \ldots, Q_{n/2}^{\mathsf{T}}\right) \cdot \mathrm{Exp}_{\Gamma}(G_k(\mathbf{x}))^{\mathsf{T}} = 0.$$

Vith $\mathbf{x}$ being known after previous step, $Q_1, \cdots, Q_{n/2}$ can be found by solving he linear system

$$G_{\hat{D}} \cdot \mathrm{diag}\left(X_1^{\mathsf{T}}, \ldots, X_{n/2}^{\mathsf{T}}\right) \cdot \mathrm{Exp}_{\Gamma}(G_k(\mathbf{x}))^{\mathsf{T}} = 0,$$

here X_i are of the form

$$X_i = \begin{pmatrix} X_i^{(1)} & X_i^{(2)} \\ 0 & X_i^{(3)} \end{pmatrix}, \quad X_i^{(1)} \in \mathbb{F}_q^{m \times m-1}, X_1^{(2)} \in \mathbb{F}_q^{m \times m+1}, X_1^{(3)} \in \mathbb{F}_q^{m \times m+1}.$$

nce again the number of equations is larger than the number of unknowns the ution is most likely be unique up to multiplication by $\mathrm{diag}_n(\mathbf{M}_{\Gamma}(\beta))$ for some $\in \mathbb{F}_{q^m}$, which was experimentally validated. The complexity of CL-attack is nq^m) operations in $\mathbb{F}_q$, the complexity of support recovering is $O(q^m(mn)^3)$ l the complexity of recovering Q is $O((mn)^3)$. Hence the overall complexity he attack is $O((mn)^3 q^m)$.

6 Conclusion

In this paper, it was shown that Ivanov–Krouk–Zyablov cryptosystem is insecure and its secret key can be recovered in polynomial time due to proposed key-recovery attacks. Since the first one is based only on linear algebra, it can easily be generalized to recover the matrix Q even for other classes of codes. So, the masking transform used by Ivanov, Krouk and Zyablov is intrinsically flawed. It also seems that using hiding transforms that allow decoding error bursts cannot improve key sizes compared to classic approaches due to simple message–recovery attacks based on information–set decoding.

References

1. Aragon, N., et al.: BIKE - Bit-Flipping Key Encapsulation. https://bikesuite.org
2. Aragon, N., Blazy, O., Deneuville, J.C., Gaborit, P., Zémor, G.: Ouroboros: an efficient and provably secure KEM family. IEEE Trans. Inf. Theory **68**, 6233–6244 (2022)
3. Baldi, M., Bianchi, M., Chiaraluce, F., Rosenthal, J., Schipani, D.: Enhanced Public Key Security for the McEliece Cryptosystem. J. Cryptol. **29**(1), 1–27 (2014). https://doi.org/10.1007/s00145-014-9187-8
4. Berger, T.P., El Amrani, N.: Codes over $\mathcal{L}(GF(2)^m, GF(2)^m)$, MDS diffusion matrices and cryptographic applications. In: El Hajji, S., Nitaj, A., Carlet, C., Souidi, E.M. (eds.) C2SI 2015. LNCS, vol. 9084, pp. 197–214. Springer, Cham (2015). https://doi.org/10.1007/978-3-319-18681-8_16
5. Berger, T.P., Gueye, C.T., Klamti, J.B.: Generalized subspace subcodes with application in cryptology. IEEE Trans. Inf. Theory **65**, 4641–4657 (2019). https://doi.org/10.1109/TIT.2019.2909872
6. Berger, T.P., Loidreau, P.: How to mask the structure of codes for a cryptographic use. Des. Codes Crypt. **35**(1), 63–79 (2005). https://doi.org/10.1007/s10623-003-6151-2
7. Bernstein, D.J., et al.: Classic McEliece: conservative code-based cryptography NIST Submissions (2020)
8. Borodin, M.A., Chizhov, I.V.: Effective attack on the McEliece cryptosystem based on Reed-Muller codes. Discret. Math. Appl. **24**(5), 273–280 (2014)
9. Couvreur, A., Lequesne, M.: On the security of subspace subcodes of Reed-Solomon codes for public key encryption. IEEE Trans. Inf. Theory **68**, 632–648 (2022). https://doi.org/10.1109/TIT.2021.3120440
10. Couvreur, A., Lequesne, M., Tillich, J.-P.: Recovering short secret keys of RLCE in polynomial time. In: Ding, J., Steinwandt, R. (eds.) PQCrypto 2019. LNCS, vol. 11505, pp. 133–152. Springer, Cham (2019). https://doi.org/10.1007/978-3-030-25510-7_8
11. Couvreur, A., Márquez-Corbella, I., Pellikaan, R.: Cryptanalysis of public-key cryptosystems that use subcodes of algebraic geometry codes. In: Pinto, R., Malonek, P.R., Vettori, P. (eds.) Coding Theory and Applications. CSMS, vol. 3, pp. 133–140. Springer, Cham (2015). https://doi.org/10.1007/978-3-319-17296-5_13
12. Couvreur, A., Otmani, A., Tillich, J.-P., Gauthier–Umaña, V.: A Polynomial-Time Attack on the BBCRS Scheme. In: Katz, J. (ed.) PKC 2015. LNCS, vol. 9020, pp. 175–193. Springer, Heidelberg (2015). https://doi.org/10.1007/978-3-662-46447-2_8

13. Gabidulin, E.M., Paramonov, A.V., Tretjakov, O.V.: Ideals over a non-commutative ring and their application in cryptology. In: Davies, D.W. (ed.) EUROCRYPT 1991. LNCS, vol. 547, pp. 482–489. Springer, Heidelberg (1991). https://doi.org/10.1007/3-540-46416-6_41
14. Huffman, W.C., Pless, V.: Fundamentals of Error-Correcting Codes. Cambridge University Press, Cambridge (2010)
15. Ivanov, F., Krouk, E., Zyablov, V.: New code-based cryptosystem based on binary image of generalized Reed-Solomon code. In: 2021 XVII International Symposium "Problems of Redundancy in Information and Control Systems" (REDUNDANCY), pp. 66–69. IEEE (2021). https://doi.org/10.1109/REDUNDANCY52534.2021.9606467
16. Janwa, H., Moreno, O.: McEliece public key cryptosystems using algebraic-geometric codes. Des. Codes Crypt. **8**(3), 293–307 (1996). https://doi.org/10.1023/A:1027351723034
17. Khathuria, K., Rosenthal, J., Weger, V.: Encryption scheme based on expanded Reed-Solomon codes. Adv. Math. Commun. **15**, 207–218 (2021). https://doi.org/10.3934/amc.2020053
18. MacWilliams, F.J., Sloane, N.J.A.: The Theory of Error Correcting Codes, vol. 16. Elsevier, Amsterdam (1977)
19. McEliece, R.J.: A public-key cryptosystem based on algebraic coding theory. DSN Prog. Rep. **4244**, 114–116 (1978)
20. Melchor, C.A., et al.: Hamming Quasi-Cyclic (HQC). https://pqc-hqc.org
21. Minder, L., Shokrollahi, A.: Cryptanalysis of the sidelnikov cryptosystem. In: Naor, M. (ed.) EUROCRYPT 2007. LNCS, vol. 4515, pp. 347–360. Springer, Heidelberg (2007). https://doi.org/10.1007/978-3-540-72540-4_20
22. Niederreiter, H.: Knapsack-type cryptosystems and algebraic coding theory. Prob. Contr. Inf. Theory **15**, 159–166 (1986)
23. Otmani, A., Tillich, J.P., Dallot, L.: Cryptanalysis of two McEliece cryptosystems based on quasi-cyclic codes. Math. Comput. Sci. **3**(2), 129–140 (2010). https://doi.org/10.1007/s11786-009-0015-8
24. Overbeck, R.: Structural attacks for public key cryptosystems based on gabidulin codes. J. Cryptol. **21**(2), 280–301 (2008). https://doi.org/10.1007/s00145-007-9003-9
25. Sendrier, N.: On the structure of randomly permuted concatenated code. Ph.D. thesis, INRIA (1995)
26. Sidelnikov, V.M.: A public-key cryptosystem based on binary Reed-Muller codes. Discret. Math. Appl. **4**(3), 191–208 (1994)
27. Sidelnikov, V.M., Shestakov, S.O.: On insecurity of cryptosystems based on generalized Reed-Solomon codes. Discrete Math. Appl. **2**, 439–444 (1992)
28. Wang, Y.: Quantum resistant random linear code based public key encryption scheme RLCE. In: 2016 IEEE International Symposium on Information Theory (ISIT), pp. 2519–2523. IEEE (2016)
29. Wieschebrink, C.: Cryptanalysis of the niederreiter public key scheme based on GRS subcodes. In: Sendrier, N. (ed.) PQCrypto 2010. LNCS, vol. 6061, pp. 61–72. Springer, Heidelberg (2010). https://doi.org/10.1007/978-3-642-12929-2_5
30. Zyablov, V.V., Ivanov, F.I., Krouk, E.A., Sidorenko, V.R.: On new problems in asymmetric cryptography based on error-resistant coding. Probl. Inf. Transm. **58**, 184–201 (2022). https://doi.org/10.1134/S0032946022020077

Author Index

. Deneuville (Ed.): CBCrypto 2022, LNCS 13839, p. 155, 2023.
s://doi.org/10.1007/978-3-031-29689-5

Printed in the United States
by Baker & Taylor Publisher Services